RISK, SOCIETY AND POLICY SERIES
Edited by Ragnar E Löfstedt

Social Trust and the Management of Risk

Edited by
George Cvetkovich
and
Ragnar E Löfstedt

Earthscan Publications Ltd, London

This edition first published in the UK in 1999 by
Earthscan Publications Ltd

A catalogue record for this book is available from the British Library

ISBN: 1 85383 604 4 paperback

Typesetting by JS Typesetting, Wellingborough, Northants
Printed and bound by Bell & Bain Ltd, Glasgow
Cover design by Yvonne Booth

For a full list of publications please contact:

Earthscan Publications Ltd
120 Pentonville Road
London, N1 9JN, UK
Tel: +44 (0)171 278 0433
Fax: +44 (0)171 278 1142
Email: earthinfo@earthscan.co.uk
WWW: http://www.earthscan.co.uk

Earthscan is an editorially independent subsidiary of Kogan Page Limited and
publishes in association with WWF-UK and the International Institute for Environment
and Development.

This book is printed on elemental chlorine free paper.

Contents

List of Tables, Figures and Boxes   v
Acronyms and Abbreviations   vii
Foreword by Baruch Fischhoff   viii
Preface   xi

Introduction   1

1   Social Trust and Culture in Risk Management
     Timothy C Earle and George Cvetkovich   9

2   Risk, Trust and Democratic Theory
     Roger E Kasperson, Dominic Golding and Jeanne X Kasperson   22

3   Perceived Risk, Trust, and Democracy
     Paul Slovic   42

4   The Attribution of Social Trust
     George Cvetkovich   53

5   Trust Judgements in Complex Hazard Management
     Systems: The Potential Role of Concepts of the System
     Branden B Johnson   62

6   Environmental Regulation in the UK: Politics,
     Institutional Change and Public Trust
     Ragnar E Löfstedt and Tom Horlick-Jones   73

7   Perceived Competence and Motivation in Industry
     and Government as Factors in Risk Perception
     Lennart Sjoberg   89

8   Institutional Trust and Confidence: A Journey into
     a Conceptual Quagmire
     Daniel Metlay   100

9   Trust and Public Participation in Risk Policy Issues
     Judith A Bradbury, Kristi M Branch and Will Focht   117

10   **Social Trust, Risk Management, and Culture: Insights from Native America**
M V Rajeev Gowda   128

11   **Who Calls the Shots? Credible Vaccine Risk Communication**
Ann Bostrom   140

12   **Conclusion: Social Trust: Consolidation and Future Advances**
George Cvetkovich and *Ragnar E Löfstedt*   153

References   *168*
Index   *189*

List of Tables, Figures and Boxes

TABLES

1.1	Items used to measure culture of individuals: culture theory	12
1.2	Social trust and trust values by culture of respondents and culture of stories: culture theory	14
1.3	Items used to measure culture of individuals: Fiske's elementary forms	17
1.4	Social trust and trust values by culture of respondents and culture of stories: Fiske's elementary forms	19
3.1	Judged impact of a trust-increasing event and a similar trust-decreasing event	47
7.1	Intercorrelations among the trust scales	92
7.2	Correlations between trust scales and CT scales	92
7.3	Intercorrelations among the CT scales	92
7.4	Regression analyses of demand for risk mitigation	94
7.5	Means of trust and risk indices in a five cluster solution	96
7.6	Correlations between demand for risk mitigation and trust and risk indices in a five cluster solution	96
7.7	Regression analyses of nuclear waste ratings with trust dimensions added	97
7.8	Regression analyses of nuclear waste ratings with CT scales added	97
8.1	The components of trust and confidence	107
8.2	The impact of values in predicting DOEPTC	112
10.1	Native American (Indian) and modern Western approaches to health risk management	133
11.1	Reported cases of vaccine-preventable childhood diseases in the US	141
11.2	Vaccine licensure dates	145

FIGURES

2.1	Social trust, risk, and democracy: Contrasting approaches	24
2.2	Economic and cultural prerequisites of stable democracy	26
2.3	Actual effects among civic involvement, socioeconomic development, and institutional performance: Italy, 1900–1980	30

2.4   Average percentage of respondents expressing a 'great
       deal of confidence' in the leadership of ten institutions,
       1966–95   33
2.5   Average percentage of respondents expressing a 'great
       deal of confidence' in the leadership of seven institutions,
       1987–95   34
2.6   Percentage of respondents expressing a 'great deal' and
       'quite a lot' of confidence in the seven institutions, 1973–95   35
2.7   Mean percentage of respondents expressing confidence in
       seven institutions, Harris vs. Gallup, 1987–95   36
3.1   Differential impact of trust-increasing and trust-decreasing
       events   48
8.1   Relationship between the two components and DOEPTC   108

Boxes

3.1   Viewpoints on the risks from nuclear waste disposal   45
11.1   Disease description, vaccine policy development and
       recommendations   143

Acronyms and Abbreviations

ACIP	Advance Committee on Immunization Practices
BATNEEC	best available technology not entailing excessive cost
BIST	Bellingham International Social Trust Conference
BPEO	best practice environmental option
BSE	Bovine Spongiform Encephalitis
CBA	cost-benefit analysis
CBI	Confederation of British Industry
CDC	Centers for Disease Control and Prevention
CT	cultural theory
DOE	Department of Energy
DOEPTC	Department of Energy Public Trust and Confidence
EM	Office of Environmental Management
FDA	Food and Drug Administration
GSS	General Social Survey
HMIP	Her Majesty's Inspectorate of Pollution
IHS	Indian Health Service
IOM	Institute of Medicine
IPC	integrated pollution control
HMS	hazard management system
MRS	monitored retrievable storage
NGO	non-governmental organization
NRA	National Rivers Authority
NORC	National Opinion Research Center
NVAC	National Vaccine Advance Committee
NVICP	National Vaccine Injury Compensation Program
NVP	National Vaccine Program
NWMA	Nuclear Waste Management Agency
OCRWM	Office of Radioactive Waste Management
OPRA	operator and risk appraisal system
QGA	quasi government agency
QUANGO	quasi non-governmental organization
SSAB	Site Specific Advisory Board
SVS	Salient Values Similarity
VAERS	Vaccine Adverse Effect Reporting System
VIS	Vaccine Information Statement

Foreword: If Trust Is So Good, Why Isn't There More of It?

Things can go better with trust. People can enjoy their interpersonal relations more if there is no shadow of distrust hanging of them. They have a better chance of consummating mutually beneficial agreements if they don't have to decode proposals and positions, always guessing at 'what do they mean by that?' With trust, people can create the social capital that is only possible when people work together.

These are not novel observations. Many cultures have adages regarding the cultivation of trust. Psychologists and sociologists have long considered its role in interpersonal relations. Survey researchers have created extensive times series, eliciting respondents' confidence in various public institutions. Building on such work, the contributors to this volume have examined how issues of trust emerge when citizens confront powerful institutions, threatening their health, safety, and environment. Their research shows the theoretical and methodological issues that arise when extending the trust concept to these complex surroundings. As a result, the authors' efforts extend our scientific understanding, even if they fail to persuade practitioners who wish to create (or erode) trust. Conversely, the research presented here highlights a variety of factors that have been shown (or at least proposed) as affecting trust. As a result, reading about the research should enrich nonscientists' repertoire of potentially relevant variables, even when the research cannot (yet) support firm predictions or explanations. Having a larger set of hypotheses can help to sustain one's hope of eventually figuring things out.

INFORMATIVE INCONCLUSIVENESS

This volume's candid summaries of the limits to existing trust research not only provide valuable insight into these processes, but also practical guidance. If researchers can't sort things out, it seems ill-advised to make confident predictions about trust in real-world settings. Having realistic expectations can protect one against simplistic strategies and premature frustration ('I tried being open (once) and it didn't work; that's it for me').

The sheer diversity of the theoretical perspectives represented here shows just how many things can happen when individually simple processes interact in complex ways. For example, all other things being equal, both perceived openness and perceived competence can increase trust (as several authors postulate). However, it may be difficult to achieve one without undermining the other: the opportunity for close observation that openness provides may reveal previously unknown problems. Whereas continued close observation may show that those problems are less critical than they initially seemed, the short-term impact of greater openness may be a reduction in trust.

It would take many studies to sort out the relationships among the many variables considered in this volume. Even more studies will be needed if the relationships are not universals, but play themselves out differently in, say, different national and organizational cultures (as some authors here suggest). Data demands increase when measurement is poor, thereby reducing statistical power. In this light, progress in trust research has been hampered by the inconsistent definitions of 'trust' and other variables, which is lamented by many of the present authors. Where inconsistency reflects imprecision, it will slow the rate at which a signal emerges. Where inconsistency reflects clear but contradictory definitions, that signal may not come through at all. Inconsistent definitions also make it much easier to explain away awkward results, by challenging measurement procedures ('that's not what I meant by trust, competence . . .'), further impeding progress.

COMMUNITY STANDARDS

These data demands suggest that the community of social trust researchers faces a significant challenge, whose resolution may depend on the community's own level of social trust. A high level of trust would allow researchers to settle on a consensual definition of each key concept (trust, competence, openness, etc.). All investigators would then agree to use that definition in their own research and to accept it in one another's. Having reached consensus, the community could then invest in the development of suitable measures for each concept (which some authors have started on their own). That, in turn, would facilitate accumulating and sharing experience about each measure's strengths and weaknesses, so that researchers could get the most out of procedures that are, inevitably, imperfect.

If community members agreed on the definitions of key concepts, but not on the ways to measure them, then they could hold a run-off, seeing which measures work best. If community members disagreed on definitions as well (eg, what is 'trust?'), then they could still agree to incorporate one another's versions in their own studies. Including separate measures for $trust_1$, $trust_2$, . . . $trust_n$; $competence_1$, $competence_2$, . . . $competence_m$, and so on, would increase the measurement burden on each study. However, without some such standardization, the inconclusive state of current research, which is a recurrent theme throughout the volume, is likely to persist. Almost every author either laments the lack of closure or is attacked for being too easily satisfied (of course, response and rebuttal at the workshop may have revealed more or less convergence than is apparent from the written text).

Alternatively, the trust community could decide to separate, abandoning the search for universal behavioural truths – or it could decide to look for the truths that emerge in separate, smaller universes. That separation might be along domain lines, assuming, say, that people use different rules when judging the trustworthiness of potential lovers, friends, doctors, mentors, presidents, and industrial neighbours (or whatever partition seemed appropriate). Such separation would not preclude using similar measures, and testing similar hypotheses, in the different domains. It is conceivable that, in all domains, people look at similar factors and use similar integration rules for determining trust; however, they still have very different thresholds for acting in a trusting way, when the action is, say, signing a contract, leaving a picket line, or marking 'strongly trust' on a questionnaire.

An additional reason for separation into domain-specific subcommunities is that performing research in any domain requires considerable substantive expertise. Researchers need to know how to access people who are relatively involved with the topic, what constitutes competence, and how accurately such competence is appraised. Collectively, social-trust researchers have more expertise in some domains than others. As a result, pooling results across domains may mean affording equal credibility to all studies, however well their domain is understood. As a result, it may pay to separate, even if there are consensual definitions of key terms.

SIGNALS FROM THE RESEARCH ENTERPRISE

The situation faced by social trust researchers offers clues to the situation faced by individuals seeking social trust. If researchers cannot agree on the definition of terms, then lay people may also think and talk imprecisely. Anything that blurs the quality of the feedback that people receive regarding their trust strategies should slow the pace at which those strategies stabilize. Anything that blurs the signals that people send one another will keep them from learning how they are perceived. Each such miscommunication will reduce people's chances of learning and applying the rules of social trust. As a result, they may miss chances to create social trust, and become frustrated when their efforts are rewarded, undermining their faith in others and in confidence-building processes.

The present authors have devoted themselves to understanding social trust. Yet, there are still fundamental questions regarding which variables are worth considering, how they should be defined in general, and what their values are in specific circumstances. Would it be any wonder if ordinary people missed opportunities to achieve social trust, even in circumstances where it was there to be found? Conversely, would it be any wonder if they sometimes deluded themselves regarding their own trustworthiness? We would all like to be accepted as we are, with little change and full credibility. The interpretative fluency demonstrated by the present authors, in their detailed analyses of one another's work, suggests the latitude that each of us has, when we want to see the best or worst in others and in ourselves. Analyses like those in this volume can help us to answer the questions, 'what do they want from me?' and 'what do I want from me?' The answers could help us to determine whether social trust is within reach and worth the effort.

Baruch Fischhoff
Department of Social & Decision Sciences
Carnegie Mellon University
Pittsburgh, USA

Preface

Many of us who have contributed to this volume believe that there is a need for an additional venue for the social science of risk. True, the usual 'outlets' for our work exist. There are the peer-reviewed journals and the large meetings of professional organizations, for example. These, however, are geared mainly for the presentation of well developed, empirically defended ideas about risk. Our sense is that there is now a special need for a more flexible, yet intensive venue. What we desire is the opportunity to discuss our 'half baked,' developing ideas and to get colleagues' reactions on how to continue the cooking. We also want the opportunity to discuss issues at greater length and detail than is usually possible at professional meetings. What we want is to establish small working meetings where our complete attention is focused on presentations by each member and which include intensive discussion at length by all. One issue that seemed to especially require this treatment was social trust and environmental risk management. Social science research and conceptualization has taken a number of different and perhaps divergent steps on this topic. Contributions to practical questions seem imminent but core issues still require intensive consideration.

The plan for holding such a meeting was set in motion in the summer of 1995 with the efforts of the two of us and Tim Earle. Others soon joined into the organizing and in July of 1996 the first Bellingham International Social Trust Conference (BIST I) was held on the campus of Western Washington University in Bellingham, Washington, at which approximately 15 presentations were made by social scientists. This book contains papers based on these presentations which were extensively critiqued both at the meeting and in written form later. Our experience of spending a concentrated period of time (around 12 hours on our long days) in close proximity with colleagues discussing matters of intense mutual interest was rewarding enough that a second meeting, BIST II, was held the following year in 1997.

The two BIST meetings and this book would not have been possible without the effort and enthusiastic support of the participants, many travelling great distances at their own expense to attend. We are particularly grateful to Tim Earle for co-organizing the BIST meetings as well as to Roger Kasperson for providing useful guidance in the planning process. We would also like to thank Peter Elich, Dean of the College of Arts and Sciences, Western Washington University, for providing funding for some of the conferences' basic expenses. Thanks are also due to Roland Clift, Director of the Centre for Environmental Strategy, for allowing leave time to one of us (RL) to work on this book. Several individuals who commented on earlier versions of sections of the book, including Tom Horlick-Jones and Paul Slovic, as well as an anonymous reviewer of the entire book, should also be thanked.

Finally, we wish to thank our respective wives, Fran Cvetkovich and Laura Kelly, for their love and support throughout the editing process (and a special thanks to Fran for her hard work in organizing the BIST welcoming dinners and for her excellent cooking that made them a reality).

George Cvetkovich
Ragnar Löfstedt

Introduction: Social Trust in Risk Management

Why the great interest in social trust now? Many have concluded that there is a problem in modern societies regarding the communication of risk. To date the outcomes of the various risk communication programmes implemented in Europe and the US have been less effective than hoped by their planners. The public often is hostile to the local siting of waste incinerators and nuclear waste dumps, a reaction that has not been influenced by the implementation of risk communication programmes (Adler and Pittle 1984; Cvetkovich et al 1986; Slovic and MacGregor 1994). In part such responses might be attributable to the practical problems associated with the lack of funding of risk communication programmes and, from this, failure to conduct proper evaluations (Kasperson and Palmlund 1987; Chess et al 1995a and b). Due account must also be taken of the inability of practitioners to understand that they have to work together with the public rather than simply 'educate' them (Fischhoff 1995; Leiss 1996). Researchers, frustrated by the lack of both practical and academic success of the various risk communication initiatives, have tried to identify underlying conceptual reasons why these programmes have failed. Among the factors currently receiving the greatest attention is trust.

There is a prevailing view, particularly among harried risk managers, that there has been a crisis-proportioned decline in trust. It is easy to remember numerous cases where public trust has been threatened or lost. Among these in the UK are the Bovine Spongiform Encephalitis (BSE) contamination of beef and the initial (lack of) reactions of the Royal Family to the death of Princess Diana. In the US recent examples include discoveries of unanticipated health problems resulting from the use of the widely-used diet pill Fen-Phen, E.coli contamination of meat, and revelations of unethical, if not quite illegal, federal political campaign finances. In both countries and others there have been numerous local cases involving water quality, toxic wastes, and other risks that have threatened trust. Many seem to believe that there has been a decline in trust making it difficult, if not impossible, to manage environmental risks and carry out the other important functions required in complex modern societies. If distrust could be reduced, the view holds, social trust would increase and risk management could function more efficiently and effectively. Risk managers[1] who hold this view have a practical interest in social trust.

1. The term 'risk managers' will be used to include persons or agencies in government, business, science and other institutions having responsibilities for making decisions and taking actions concerning environmental hazards. These decisions and actions might include identifying and mitigating hazards and related functions such as communicating to the general public or particular groups information about environmental hazards.

These managers want to know what they can do to restore the supposed loss of trust so that they can do their job.

One of the most likely explanations for the failures of risk communication initiatives is that reactions to risk communication are not only influenced by message content, that is, what is communicated about risks (and benefits) of particular hazards. It is also influenced by trust in those responsible for providing the information (Earle and Cvetkovich 1995; Kasperson et al 1992; Leiss 1996; Renn and Levine 1991; Slovic 1993; Slovic and MacGregor 1994; Nye et al 1997). Failure to successfully implement risk communication programmes often results from the public distrust of policy-makers and industrial officials due to credibility problems, past history or social alienation (see Löfstedt and Horlick-Jones 1998). Due to the recent theoretical developments in the trust area, risk researchers are arguing that the entire field has entered a new dimension (Fischhoff 1995 and 1996; Leiss 1996).

Leiss points out that in the early stages of risk communication, between 1975 and 1984, the main concern of the technical experts was to provide accurate numerical information. It was believed that if correct risk estimates were made then the public would believe in what the experts had to say and in what they recommended solely on the basis of their expertise. However, significant public opposition to risk-based decision-making resulted in experts expressing an 'open contempt toward the public perception of risk', which was discounted as being irrational (Leiss 1996). This would result in further distrust in these experts by the public who would view their actions as arrogant, self serving, and reflecting a 'hidden agenda' of vested interests. Today, experts realize that public trust is extremely important if they are to achieve effective risk communication, and indeed the area has received much attention from both theoreticians and practitioners in the field.

Concern about the loss of public trust in risk regulators, risk communicators, and indeed science in general has resulted in increased interest in the role more generally of trust and distrust in society. Barber (1983) has identified some of the reasons that he thought contributed to a decline in trust in science (and the professions more generally), including the increased influence that professions have over people's welfare, a greater value placed on equality and a better educated public. The political issue of who makes important decisions for others is central to recent discussions of reactions to potential technological hazards (Beck 1992). There appears to be a belief within the policy-making community that a greater understanding of the trust causing/destroying phenomena could contribute to resolving social, environmental and political problems.

A lack of trust towards policy-makers and industrial officials is seen to cause difficulties in siting hazardous industrial plants and installations (for example, the siting of a nuclear waste dump in Nevada) (Rosa et al 1993), and in managing environmental crises (for example, chemical spills and the proposed decommissioning of Brent Spar). Research indicates that the public believe governments work closely with industry, and the latter may be seen as possessing a vested interest in putting forward a particular point of view. This in turn causes public distrust in regulation and legislative controls (Kunreuther et al 1993; Linnerooth-Bayer and Fitzgerald 1996; Macfarlane 1993). Inappropriate handling of crises may lead to further loss of trust in the risk regulators. Failure to develop the most effective risk-communication strategies clearly has profound financial implications, as well as a 'policy cost'. Researchers have shown that controversies such as Brent Spar decrease the public's trust and confidence in policy-makers (Löfstedt and Renn 1997), and the cumulative effect of the crises is an increasing inability of policy-makers to handle situations effectively (Freudenburg 1996).

These controversies have caused serious problems for the waste and chemical industries in North America and Europe. It is becoming increasingly difficult to site and build a wide array of installations including hazardous waste disposal facilities and ordinary waste incinerators (eg Löfstedt 1997; Petts 1995), sewage treatment plants and power stations. These difficulties, to some extent, may be explained by a decline in public trust. In the US, where around 300 million tons of hazardous waste is produced per year (Field et al 1996), no large free standing hazardous waste facility has been sited anywhere since 1980 (Piller 1991; Rabe 1994). It is even becoming difficult to site and build renewable energy plants in some nations due to public opposition (Hargreaves 1996).

Social scientists also have become interested in social trust and risk management. Part of their interest is a desire to provide answers to the hazard managers' questions about what can be done to increase trust. But social scientists are also interested in broader, related issues that go beyond practical suggestions. Included in these are questions about how social trust should be defined, the functions of trust, how trust judgements are made, whether trust is necessary for the management of risks, if it is not necessary how risks can be managed in the absence of trust or in the presence of mistrust, and the role of trust in the operations of democratic societies. Social scientists also would like to be assured that the suggested trends in decreasing trust have actually occurred. The answers to these questions, discussed in the articles in this book and reviewed in the final chapter, might well provide insights about the nature of practical approaches to increasing trust as well as, perhaps, about their realistic limits.

The increased social science interest in trust is well reflected in the research literature related to risk assessment and management. In this literature an evolution in thinking can be traced. The initial issue was the determination of the levels of acceptable risk. This led quickly to a curiosity and concern about differences between lay people and experts in the judgements of the risks of hazards, particularly nuclear power. Research efforts were directed at investigating risk perception. The next step was focused on questions about what might be done to address the existing conflicts. At this stage concepts about risk perception were applied to considerations of risk communication. The current stage focusing on trust broadens the concerns further and recognizes that judgements of risk are not limited to assessments of physical processes. They are also reflections of the understanding of social systems and the actors playing roles within them.

A reflection of the evolution in the risk assessment literature to the current interest in trust are the two Bellingham International Social Trust Conferences on Risk Management (BIST) held in June of 1996 and 1997. The papers in this book are based on presentations made at these BIST conferences. A basic assumption of the conferences was that one of the most important contributions that social sciences can make at this time to the understanding of trust in risk management is asking the right questions. Three core questions that occupied delegates at both BIST meetings and which are analysed in various ways by the contributions in this book are: What is social trust? What are the levels of trust in society? What influences levels of trust?

WHAT IS SOCIAL TRUST?

It may seem strange that there should remain questions about the definition of a topic of so much recent interest and conceptual/research activity. The social science of trust is still at a period of development where such questions do exist. We will not attempt to review here the many efforts to define trust (see Earle and Cvetkovich 1995; Renn and Levine 1991; Miztal 1996; Johnson this volume). Suffice it to note that definitions of social trust often include special uses of common words and attempt to distinguish social trust from other tendencies such as cooperation or reliance. These definitions serve their creators' particular purposes but the distinctions may not be useful if one has different purposes. Some authors also entwine basic definitions with assumptions about the reasons why trust occurs. These efforts too may not be acceptable to those who hold other views. Efforts to develop explicit definitions frequently occur. Even more frequent are social scientists who leave the concept undefined. There is a widely-held assumption that common, everyday understandings of the term make explicit definitions unnecessary. The complexities of social trust would seem to leave this approach vulnerable to producing misunderstandings. There is a core of understanding among social scientists of what social trust is. To avoid confusion, attempts to explicate this core of common understanding should be made. We try to navigate between the 'overly specific' and the 'insufficiently articulate' extremes by offering the following.

It seems to us that most social scientists would find acceptable as a core definition one close to that found in English dictionaries (in all of the language's standard varieties). For example, the Merriam-Webster Dictionary of American English has as its first definition of trust: 'assured reliance on the character, ability, strength, or truth of someone or something'.[2] To be useful to social science we believe several additional properties must be added to this core definition. First, trust implies a difference in power and control. The one who trusts assumes a position of subordination and relinquishes decision and behaviour control to the one who is trusted. It is important to note that while trust implies a relinquishing of power and control, the act of trusting does not necessarily produce a feeling of loss of control or power. The trusting person

---

2. This core (dictionary) definition of trust is very similar to that of 'confidence'. Luhmann (1979, 1988) and others (Seligman 1997; Earle 1998) argue that it may be useful for risk management and other purposes to articulate differences between trust and confidence. The difference between the two lies in additional properties including those presented in the text. As is expected on the basis of the similarity of their formal definitions, trust and confidence are often used interchangeably in everyday language and, not surprisingly, by some social scientists.

trades behavioural and decision control for cognitive control (thinking that hazards will be controlled) and secondary control (selecting who is to be trusted). A few commentators have begun to explore the implications of this dependency for the course of how trust and mistrust develop (Wynne 1996; Bradbury and Branch this volume). Second, because it involves a subordination of position through the relinquishing of control, trust also involves risk. One may trust someone because of a strong expectation that the trusted one will act in certain ways. But one can never be entirely certain that one's trust will not be violated. Trust then trades a primary physical risk (What should I do about this environmental hazard?) for a social risk (Is the trusted one trustworthy?) which is followed by a physical risk (If the trusted one is not trustworthy I may not be protected from physical harm). Third, trust is an expectation about a relationship. This may be an expectation about a relationship with a particular individual (Risk Manager A) or it may be an expectation about relationships with members of a particular group (officials of the Government Pollution Inspectorate or the Environmental Protection Agency). We commonly talk about trust as if it were a characteristic of individuals (see Cvetkovich this volume). But, it is more. The attribution of the characteristic of trustworthiness is based on an expectation of how an individual will conduct him- or herself relative to me and my interests. Fourth, the above implies that individuals have choice about when to trust and who to trust. Fifth, in the domain of risk management social trust relates to individuals who have responsibilities imposed by formal organizational roles and who may be personally unknown to the one making the trust judgement. Risk management trust has aspects of impersonality that distinguish it from forms of interpersonal trust in face-to-face relationships. For social scientists this implies a need to study risk management and social trust as a phenomenon in its own right.[3]

WHAT ARE THE LEVELS OF TRUST IN SOCIETY?

Lipset and Schneider (1983; 1987) conclude that public trust in policy-makers in the US has declined over time and that trust towards policy-makers in other nations has also fallen. Much of their research is based on Harris and NORC polling data which supposedly shows a decline in trust in US society since the Vietnam war. This conclusion has been widely accepted and much work in the risk field has been based on it (Peters, Covello and McCallum 1997; Flynn

3. The distinction of the trust of directly interacting persons and the trust of individuals personally unknown raises questions about the applicability of two major historical studies often used, as is done later in this chapter, in discussions of risk management trust. Is the social trust studied by Putnam and Fukuyama the same as the risk management social trust which is the focus of this book? The trust of Putnam and Fukuyama is the trust of others interacted with for the most part within face-to-face encounters. According to Fukuyama, the establishment in northern Italy of financial institutions insuring the safety of trusting potential business partners promoted economic growth. Negotiations of the business deals in those pre-telecommunications times were often face to face. The trust of Putnam occurs in small communities where there is an expectation of reciprocity of help given to other personally known community members. Are these different from trust of a distant, personally unknown agent of an industry, government agency or citizen group?

et al 1994; Sandman 1993; Slovic this volume) including Breyer's labelling of the present as the 'era of distrust' (Breyer 1993).

However, some researchers have begun to question this assertion. Kasperson et al (this volume), Golding and Krueger (1997) and Rosa (1997) have raised questions about the original data. If the period of the mid-1960s is discarded, trust in policy-makers and other organizations has remained fairly static since 1970. Kasperson et al and others have therefore suggested that this level is in fact the societal norm for the US and, pre-Vietnam, trust in policy-makers was unusually high. Etzioni, in his book *The New Golden Rule*, further argues that since 1990 public trust in policy-makers, and society as a whole, is actually increasing (Etzioni 1996). He points out, during the period between 1960 and 1990 in the US, the decline in the respect for authority, decreased voter turnout, increasing alienation, the lessening role of the family, and the declining levels of trust between members of the public as evidence of the reduced trust in policy-makers.However, since 1990, he argues, the moral dialogue has moved from that of individualism to that of communitarianism. Anti-social behaviour such as crime is decreasing, voter turnout is increasing and the family is becoming important once again.

If Etzioni's analysis is right and US society is not in a trust crisis, as many researchers have argued, and trust toward policy-makers is actually increasing, this adds further weight to counter the accepted view and raises the issue of whether the distrust evident should be considered 'normal'.

We are left then with the question of whether Lipset and Schneider are right that trust is on the decline in other western nations. Etzioni points out that compared to the US the levels of trust in Europe and Japan are considerably higher but that they have followed a similar trajectory (eg since the 1960s trust declined until 1990, although public apathy towards policy-makers in western nations is not as high as in US). However, it is unclear, firstly, whether these trends mirror those in the US. For example, trust towards policy-makers among the public in Sweden fell from 48 per cent in 1986 to 19 per cent in 1997 (Holmberg and Weibull 1997), at a time when it was stable in the US, and in the UK trends indicate that public trust toward both national and regional policy-makers is decreasing (Gallup 1993; Löfstedt and Horlick-Jones this volume; Macnaghten et al 1995). At the time of writing it is unclear whether this decline in trust toward policy-makers is an ongoing trend or whether it can be reversed. In the UK, for example, there are indications that the decline in trust could have been associated with public disaffection toward the governing Tory party, as the present Prime Minister (elected in May 1997), is at the time of writing enjoying the highest ever recorded public approval figures (a 92 per cent approval rate!).

Results of a recent 'People and the Press' survey conducted by the Pew Research Center (1998) at Princeton University, in comparison to earlier surveys, indicate that many Americans are still distrustful of government, but the hostility towards government has diminished. Distrust does seem to be related to views about the overall state of the nation, particularly people's perception of the moral climate. The People and the Press survey does not indicate a crisis in trust, contrary to Lipset and Schneider (1983; 1987). Distrust is related to disillusionment and frustration, not anger. Furthermore, much of the disillusionment is directed at political leaders. US political leaders may have misread the public. While there is a decrease in trust, the public still wants the government to provide services and attempt to solve social problems. Interestingly, there is an improved evaluation of federal workers and specific government departments and agencies.

In other western nations such as Sweden and the UK it is unclear whether an apparent decline in trust might be the result of a temporary anomaly (eg antipathy toward the Tory government in the UK) or a more significant historic change such as the onset of the consequences of the so-called late modernity (due to global market forces the public is disenchanted with the nation state, as national policy-makers are decreasingly able to resolve national economic crises or high levels of unemployment) (Ayers 1998; Giddens 1990; 1991). This could be an interesting area for further study including comparative studies of nations to determine trends in public trust toward policy-makers, and to identify the factors behind these trends (eg by the move toward greater globalization or to factors of recent political incompetence).

It may not be very important to risk managers to know about trends in trust and distrust. They are usually more concerned about a particular domain of risk management or even just a specific project. From this practical standpoint it is more important to know about the evidence indicating that social trust is related to acceptance of risk management in particular domains (Hine et al 1997; Cvetkovich and Bostrom this volume; Gable et al 1997). Future research is likely to be directed toward extending this evidence.

What Influences Levels of Trust?

As reflected by the substance of the chapters in this book, trust is influenced at a number of different levels. These include individual psychological processes, the structure of national and other governments and the particular operations of specific organizations. In this book, several contributions give consideration to one explanation that focuses heavily on psychological processes, the Salient Values Similarity (SVS) theory. Chapters 1 and 4 provide descriptions of the theory, which holds that we trust those who are judged to share with us the values we deem appropriate in a particular risk management domain. Evidence supportive of the theory indicating that policies based on salient cultural values are judged to be more acceptable than those based on non-salient values is presented in Chapter 1. SVS theory does not attempt to contradict the insights of alternative perspectives (Chapter 5). Rather SVS theory holds that factors such as 'competence' and 'fiduciary responsibility' will dominate trust judgements only to the extent that they represent salient values in a particular risk management domain. It is also important to note that some of these factors, like trust, may themselves be judgements. In particular cases, these other judgements may be the result of trust, not the cause of it. In Chapter 10, Gowda uses SVS theory as a framework for considering leadership issues in a Native American group.

In Chapter 8, Metlay presents results of a survey measuring affective responses to, and judgements of, competence of the US Department of Energy. An interesting result is that people's emotional affective responses are much more strongly related to public trust and confidence than are more analytic estimation of technical competency. Among other findings, Metlay also reports an effort to test SVS theory using survey data from the US Department of Energy. These findings do not support SVS theory, nor do they disconfirm it. The survey interview questions were not designed originally to reflect the constructs of SVS theory. Their applicability requires several second-order assumptions about value similarity.

Slovic (Chapter 3) also discusses how psychological processes may influence trust. He argues that it is easier to lose trust than to gain trust because of the operation of tendencies to believe trust-lowering information and because there is more trust-lowering information available. Hazard managers acting in a trustful way may not be considered newsworthy and may not be reported on by the media. Hazard managers acting in a distrustful way may be more likely to get media attention. Also possibly involved is that information leading to distrust may be usefully used to avoid risks. It may, therefore, have a greater impact than information leading to an increase in trust.

Slovic discusses the possible strong psychological impact of trust-decreasing information in the context of hazard management in democratic societies. In Chapter 2, Kasperson, Golding and Kasperson also examine questions about trust and hazard management in democratic societies. Their analysis raises fundamental questions about the relationship between trust and the values followed in the operation of democracies. One implication of the discussion is that perhaps not as much attention should be directed toward trust in specific individuals or confidence in particular organizations or agencies. Rather, perhaps what is important is confidence in democracy as a system for managing risks. Johnson also explores this idea in Chapter 5 by examining the possibility that people hold concepts about systems. This leads to questions about understandings of how systems work.

The four remaining chapters each explore particular factors within systems that influence trust. As already noted, in Chapter 10 Gowda examines leadership and trust. In particular, the related questions of what trust is needed to become a leader and how leadership behaviour affects trust are considered. In Chapter 6, Löfstedt and Horlick-Jones discuss the possibilities and limits set by trust in the use of regulations by the Environment Agency in the UK. The evaluation by Bradbury, Branch and Focht in Chapter 9 raises key questions about the use by the US Department of Energy of public participation as a strategy to increase trust, while in Chapter 11 Bostrom examines the issue of participation in medical vaccination programmes and raises questions concerning the responsiveness of risk managers to those citizens who hold minority points of view. It is unlikely in some cases that risk managers could educe trust sufficient to produce participation in a programme against which individuals hold strongly held beliefs. What risk management strategy is the best under these conditions?

1 Social Trust and Culture in Risk Management

Timothy C. Earle and *George Cvetkovich*[1]

We have argued in a variety of reports over the past few years (Cvetkovich and Earle, 1992; Earle and Cvetkovich, 1994a, b, c; Earle and Cvetkovich, 1994b; Earle and Cvetkovich, 1994c), and in a recent monograph (Earle and Cvetkovich, 1995), that the development of useful ways of understanding social trust has been retarded by an all-but-universal acceptance of a dominant traditional interpretation. According to that tradition, social trust is a rational process based on competence and responsibility. Further, social trust traditionally is empirically-based, requiring evidence of competence and responsibility. In our critique of traditional social trust (Earle and Cvetkovich, 1995) we maintain that a basic function of social trust is the reduction of cognitive complexity. Because it is empirically-based, the traditional account of social trust increases complexity instead of supplying simplicity. We also argue that social trust must accommodate cultural variation. But traditional social trust is itself culture-specific, recognizing only competence and responsibility as legitimate bases. We conclude that, due to these and other flaws, the traditional interpretation acts to undermine social trust and to generate its functional equivalent, social distrust.

In this chapter we describe two studies that test the validity of the traditional account of social trust relative to our proposed alternative. In our formulation (Earle and Cvetkovich, 1995), social trust is based on value similarity, with the value basis varying across people, contexts and time. This cultural-values interpretation of social trust is a 'groundless' social trust, requiring no justification for its use. Instead of being deduced from evidence, social trust is inferred from value-bearing narratives.[2] People tend to trust other people and institu-

---

1. This material is based on work supported by the National Science Foundation under Grants No. SES-9110297 and No. SBR-9312426. We gratefully acknowledge the contributions of David Genz to the conduct of the experimental studies.

2. 'Narrative' is the term we use for a general type of cognitive representation of a person's experience. A narrative works by reducing cognitive complexity through meaning-guided processes of selection and organization. For example, narratives serve to structure time, constitute individuals and communities, guide action, comprise values, express emotions and persuade. As part of their action-guiding function, narratives identify what we should think about and how we should think about it. And, when activated by cues in social trust contexts, narratives help us decide when and whom we should trust.

tions that 'tell stories' expressing currently salient values, stories that interpret the world in the same way they do. Within this general construction, then, traditional social trust is simply a special case.

SOCIAL TRUST AND CULTURAL VALUES

Thinking about social trust as a 'construction' – as a human product that has evolved as a tool for achieving human goals – enables us to move beyond the rationalist tradition.[3] Social trust is a social construction that is based on varying sets of cultural values – the values of specific persons and institutions living in certain times and places – as expressed in cultural narratives. This is the fundamental contrast. Between cultural singularity (rationalist, the presumed normative) and cultural pluralism. Between what it is claimed by authorities that people should do and what it is they actually wind up doing.

The simple contrast between cultural singularity and cultural pluralism provided the basis for the two studies we describe below. In both studies, respondents were asked to read texts that consisted of two parts, one that varied across respondents and one that stayed the same. In the texts, descriptions of individuals and institutions were the same for all participants. The variable part of the texts consisted of brief policy descriptions written to express different sets of cultural values. Some respondents, for example, may have read policies expressing value set A while others read policies expressing value set B (or C or D). After reading a text, each respondent was asked to produce a social trust judgement for the institution described in it. If respondents' social trust judgements were based on the competence and responsibility of individuals and institutions (qualities we attempted to hold constant across texts), we would expect little variation in social trust judgements. This would be interpreted as support for the traditional interpretation of social trust. But if participants' social trust judgements were based on expressed cultural values, we would expect wide variation in judgements – specifically as a function of the similarity between the values expressed in the text and the values favoured by respondents. This would be interpreted as support for the cultural values interpretation of social trust.

To demonstrate that individuals base their social trust judgements on varying sets of cultural values, we must devise ways to reliably describe cultural pluralism – among individuals, their judgements and expressions. We present two ways of doing this. In Study One, we draw upon the cultural theory developed, in the main, by Douglas and Wildavsky (Douglas and Wildavsky, 1982), Dake (Dake, 1992), Thompson (Thompson, Ellis and Wildavsky, 1990), and Rayner (Rayner, 1992). In Study Two, our approach is based on the four elementary forms of sociality described by Fiske (Fiske, 1991a; Fiske, 1991b; Fiske, 1992).

---

3. We discuss the evolution of social trust in a recent report (Earle, 1997).

Study One

Method

The Survey Experiment.   The fundamental claim of our cultural-values interpretation of social trust is that social trust is based on value similarity: people tend to trust other people and institutions that 'tell stories' expressing currently salient values, stories that interpret the world in the same way they do. One way to test this cultural-values hypothesis is through the use of what we call the 'survey experiment', a procedure in which survey-like methods and materials are used – but with a twist: The contents of the materials (questionnaires) are manipulated so that they create the structure of an experiment. Thus, different forms of a basic questionnaire are used to create cells in an experimental design.

One version of the survey experiment, employed successfully by several research groups, incorporates systematic variations in both questionnaires and respondents. Clary and colleagues (Clary, Snyder, Ridge, Miene and Haugen, 1994), for example, varied the motives expressed in messages and the motives that were personally relevant to respondents (eg knowledge, social adjustment, value expression, ego defence and utilitarian). These researchers demonstrated that matches between message and respondent motives were more persuasive than mismatches. Matches on motives also produced higher levels of trust. Similarly, Arad and Carnevale (1994) showed that partisan individuals judged the trustworthiness of a neutral third party on the basis of whether his proposal matched their position. By using a method that can accommodate variation in both experimental materials and respondents, studies like these can explore interactions between the two sets of variables. The basic assumption of these studies, and of ours, is that the effects of a message, for example, depend critically on how it is interpreted by the person reading it. In our studies, we examined the effects of the culture of individuals on their interpretations of risk messages that expressed varying sets of cultural values. Based on our cultural-values theory of social trust, we expected matches between the culture of individuals and the culture of messages to produce higher trust judgements than mismatches.

The Culture of Individuals.   Our first attempt to describe and measure the culture of individual respondents was based primarily on the work of Karl Dake, who has expressed the categories (or 'cultural biases') of cultural theory in the form of questionnaire items (Dake and Wildavsky, 1990; Dake, 1992). There are three primary categories in cultural theory: Egalitarian, Individualistic and Hierarchical. A fourth category, Fatalism, was not included in this study. The items we used, given in Table 1.1, consisted of a mixture of those described by Dake and Wildavsky (1990) and our own. Standard statistical analyses (Jessor and Hammond, 1957; Judd, Jessor and Donovan, 1986) were used to select the items, based on data from 449 respondents.

Individual respondents were assigned scores on each of the three scales based on the mean of their responses to the items contained in a scale. Thus, each respondent had an Egalitarian score, an Individualistic score and a Hierarchical score. Respondents were classified in this way: if a respondent's

Table 1.1 *Items Used to Measure Culture of Individuals: Culture Theory*[a]

Culture of Individuals	Measurement Items
Egalitarian	a. Much of the conflict in this world could be eliminated if we had more equal distribution of resources among nations. b. I support a tax shift so that the burden falls more heavily on corporations and persons with large incomes.
Individualistic	a. Environmental and other problems would be more readily solved if there were less government intervention. b. Most of what I value in life is achieved through my own efforts; my community and the place I live in contribute little.
Hierarchical	a. I'm for my country, right or wrong. b. The police should have the right to listen in on private telephone conversations when investigating a crime. c. Centralization is one of the things that makes a country great.

[a]Individuals responded by marking one of seven points on a scale that ranged from 'agree' (1) to 'disagree' (7).

Egalitarian score was greater than or equal to his/her Individualistic score and greater than or equal to his/her Hierarchical score and, in addition, was greater than or equal to 4 (the midpoint on the response scale), then that individual was classified as Egalitarian. Analogous procedures were used to classify respondents as Individualistic and Hierarchical. A total of 402 respondents were classified into the three cultural categories: 282 Egalitarian; 76 Individualistic; 44 Hierarchical. These individuals were unpaid volunteers recruited from both university student and general populations in western Washington State. Their average age was 28.3 years, ranging from 15 to 72. Gender distribution was even, with 50.4 per cent male, and there was no relation between gender and culture.

The Culture of Messages.   The messages used in this study were written in the form of brief, simulated newspaper stories.[4] Each story was composed of two parts. The first part was a core story that was read by all respondents. Since the data were collected late in 1992, a (fictional) story concerning the prospective high-level nuclear waste management policy of the incoming Clinton administration was selected as timely and moderately involving to a broad range of potential respondents. A key part of the core story stated that 'a new

4. Space limitations prevent the presentation of the stories here. They are available from the authors upon request.

decision-making procedure' will be used. The second part of each message provided a description of that procedure in one of three forms designed to succinctly express the relevant Egalitarian, Individualistic or Hierarchical values identified in cultural theory.

Social Trust and Trust Values.   Our cultural-values interpretation of social trust claims that social trust is based on value similarity: individuals tend to trust institutions that express currently salient values. A simple test of this notion would include: a) a measure of judged value similarity; b) a trust judgement; and c) a measure of the relation between a) and b). Our measure of judged value similarity consisted, first, of the following question referring to the nuclear waste management message the respondents had read:

> The proposed new federal organization described in the story is the Nuclear Waste Management Agency (NWMA). Based on what you have read here, how do you feel about the NWMA?

This question was followed by a six-item trust-values scale. Each of the six items consisted of a seven-point response scale anchored by bipolar descriptors of the relations between the story and the respondent:

shares my values	|	|	|	|	|	|	different values
in line with me	|	|	|	|	|	|	wrong direction
same goals as me	|	|	|	|	|	|	different goals
supports my views	|	|	|	|	|	|	opposes my views
acts as I would	|	|	|	|	|	|	acts against me
thinks like me	|	|	|	|	|	|	thinks unlike me

Standard procedures (Jessor and Hammond, 1957; Judd, Jessor and Donovan, 1986) were used to select these items from an initial large pool. A trust-values score, consisting of the mean of the six response scales, was computed for each respondent. Our measure of social trust was a single judgement made in response to this question:

Based on what you have read here, would you say you would trust the NWMA?'

Would trust the   Would not trust
NWMA completely   \| \| \| \| \| \| the NWMA at all

The correlation between respondents' social trust judgements and their trust-values scores gives us a measure of the relation between the two, a simple test of our hypothesis that social trust is based on shared cultural values. In addition, of course, the social trust judgements and the trust-values scores are the dependent variables in our experimental test of this hypothesis.

Procedure.   The newspaper-style stories on nuclear waste management and the questionnaire items measuring social trust, trust values and the culture of individuals were presented to respondents in the form of a booklet. The booklet contained an unrelated task in addition to the one described in this report. The nuclear waste management task appeared first in half the booklets. Order had no effects on respondents' judgments, and it is ignored here. In the booklet, a general set of instructions dealing with the mechanics of responding to items was followed by the first task and the questionnaire items related to it; then came the second task and its items. The social trust items described in this report are a subset of the nuclear-waste-management-task items. The items used to measure respondent culture followed the two tasks, and the booklet ended with a set of questions about the respondents' backgrounds. The booklets were randomly assigned to respondents, and the respondents worked on the booklets individually, self-paced.

Results

The mean social trust and trust values judgements for the nine experimental groups (three respondent cultures crossed with three story cultures) are given in Table 1.2. The striking thing about this table of means is the dominance of the main diagonal: cultural matches between respondents and stories produced the highest judgements of social trust and trust values for all groups of respondents. This very strong result is reflected in significant analyses of variance for the respondent-culture-by-story-culture interactions ($F(4, 393) = 8.39$, $p < .001$ for social trust; $F(4, 393) = 5.61$, $p < .001$ for trust values).

Table 1.2 *Social Trust and Trust Values by Culture of Respondents and Culture of Stories: Culture Theory*

Culture of Stories	Culture of Respondents			
	Egalitarian	*Individualistic*	*Hierarchical*	*Totals*
Egalitarian				
Social Trust	4.733	3.833	3.182	4.449
Trust Values	4.804	3.993	3.364	4.544
N	101	24	11	136
Individualistic				
Social Trust	3.612	4.143	4.063	3.783
Trust Values	3.951	4.363	3.906	4.035
N	85	28	16	129
Hierarchical				
Social Trust	3.688	3.375	4.824	3.774
Trust Values	4.309	3.840	4.794	4.287
N	96	24	17	137
Totals				
Social Trust	4.039	3.802	4.137	4.005
Trust Values	4.378	4.081	4.113	4.287
N	282	76	44	402

These experimental results provide strong support for the cultural-values social trust hypothesis: the respondents in this experiment did tend to give higher levels of social trust to institutions that shared their cultural values. In addition, there was a high level of correlation between social trust and trust values across all respondents ($r = .66$, $p < .001$). This result indicates that individuals have some means of comparing the values expressed in a story with the values expressed in their favoured cultural narratives. And it suggests that they may use that information in making judgements of social trust.

Study Two

Method

The main purpose of our second study was the same as that of the first – to test the cultural-values hypothesis that social trust is based on value similarity. The method of the second study, including the use of the survey-experiment procedure, closely followed that of the first. The two studies differed greatly, however, in one fundamental respect – the method used to describe the cultures of individuals and the cultures of the stories they read.

In Study One, the descriptions of cultures were drawn from cultural theory (Douglas and Wildavsky, 1982; Thompson, Ellis and Wildavsky, 1990; Rayner, 1992). The questionnaire items and the stories based on cultural-theory categories produced strong results in support of the cultural-values hypothesis of social trust. Although we were grateful, of course, for the support of our theory, the results seemed too strong, too straightforward and pat. Could our results be due to, and limited by, some quirks in the specific items we used? They were general items, aimed at worldviews and not at the specific context described in our stories. Perhaps items designed for specific contexts would be more appropriate? Or perhaps the cultural-theory items were the best for our purpose: any introduction of contextual specificity might introduce noise and weaken our results.

This at least was clear: an attempt should be made to replicate Study One using cultural categories and measurement items drawn from a different theory. The theory we selected was Alan Paige Fiske's theory of the four elementary forms of sociality (Fiske, 1991a, 1992). Fiske's theory is independent from (but similar in some ways to) cultural theory; it is very well developed conceptually and strongly supported by a wide variety of empirical data. Using Fiske's cultural categories in Study Two, our expectations were the same as for the cultural-theory categories we used in Study One: matches between the culture of individuals and the culture of messages should produce higher judgements of social trust than mismatches.

Culture of Individuals.   The four elementary forms of sociality identified by Fiske are Communal Sharing, Authority Ranking, Equality Matching and Market Pricing. Fiske has described and discussed in detail the operations of these forms in specific social contexts. One of our goals in this study was to use items that referred more directly to environmental-risk-management contexts than did the items we used in Study One. Thus, drawing on Fiske's work, we first identified eight domains of social interaction that might be central to environmental risk management:

1. How environmental decisions are made;
2. Organization of environmental work;
3. Distribution of resources;
4. Orientation to the land;
5. Group membership;
6. Defining your self and social identity;
7. Moral judgement;
8. Moral interpretation of misfortune.

We then used Fiske's descriptions to construct items for each of the four forms of sociality within the eight domains.

Starting with the preliminary set of 32 items, we followed standard scale-construction procedures to produce four cultural-orientation scales for the classification of respondents. The items included in the final scales, along with the domain of social interaction each represents, are given in Table 1.3. Although we developed a scale for measuring the Authority Ranking form of sociality, too few of our respondents fell into this category for inclusion in the study. Note also that the three remaining cultural categories are measured by items representing different subsets of the eight original domains of social interaction.

As in Study One, individuals were assigned scores on each of the three scales based on the mean of their responses to the items contained in a scale. If a respondent's Communal-Sharing score was greater than or equal to his/her Equality-Matching score and greater than or equal to his/her Market-Pricing score and, in addition, was greater than or equal to 5 (one point above the midpoint on the response scale), then that individual was classified as Communal Sharing. Analogous procedures were used to classify respondents as Equality Matching and Market Pricing. A total of 137 respondents were classified into the three categories: 43 Communal Sharing; 62 Equality Matching; 32 Market Pricing. These respondents were unpaid volunteers recruited from a university student population in Bellingham, Washington. Their average age was 21.5 years, ranging from 18 to 54. Gender distribution was uneven, with 72 per cent female. There was no relation between gender and culture.

Culture of Messages.   The messages used in this study, as in Study One, were written in the form of brief, simulated newspaper stories.[5] The stories were composed of two parts, the first of which was a core story that was read by all respondents. The fictional story announced the release of the final report of the 'National Hazardous Waste Advisory Commission . . . established by Congress in 1992.' The data were collected in late 1994. The core story stated that a national plan for the management of non-radioactive hazardous wastes had been developed and that it may have profound effects on Washington State. The second part of each message described the reaction to the national

---

5. Copies of these stories are available on request from the authors.

Table 1.3 *Items Used to Measure Culture of Individuals: Fiske's Elementary Forms*[a]

Culture of Individuals	Measurement Items
Communal Sharing	a. *Environmental Decision Making:* Group members seek consensus, unity, the sense of the group. b. *Organization of Environmental Work:* Tasks are treated as the collective responsibility of the group. Everyone in the group pitches in and does what he or she can, without anyone keeping track of who does what. c. *Orientation to the Land:* Land is thought of as the motherland or homeland, defining a collective ethnic identity. Land is used by the group as a commons. d. *Group Membership:* Group membership is based on a sense of unity, solidarity and shared substance (e.g., 'blood', kinship). One-for-all, all-for-one.
Equality Matching	a. *Group Membership:* All members are of equal status – as in peer groups and cooperative associations. b. *Moral Interpretation of Misfortune:* Feeling that misfortune should be equally distributed – 'Things will even out in the long run.' Idea that misfortune balances a corresponding transgression—getting what one deserves.
Market Pricing	a. *Orientation to the Land:* Land is an investment, treated like any other form of capital. Land is purchased for expected increase in value, for lease or rent, or as a means of production. b. *Moral Interpretation of Misfortune:* Risk analysis: was this a reasonably expectable risk or calculable cost to pay for the benefits sought? Is this too high a price to pay?

[a]Individuals responded by marking one of seven points on a scale that ranged from 'I strongly *disagree* with this ideal' (1) to 'I strongly *agree* with this ideal' (7).

plan by a fictional spokesperson for Washington State. The reaction was written in four forms designed to very briefly express key values in the Communal Sharing, Authority Ranking, Equality Matching and Market Pricing forms of sociality described by Fiske. In addition, a fifth, 'No Culture' form of the message was included in the study; it contained only the core story.

Social Trust and Trust Values.   The measures of social trust and trust values used in this study were very similar to those used in Study One. The only differences between the two sets of measures were those required by differences in the contents of the two core stories. Thus, in this study, the trust values items were introduced by the following question:

> The Washington State organization described in the story is the Department of Ecology. Based on what you have read here, how do you feel about the Washington State Department of Ecology?

And the social trust measure was this:

> Based on what you have read here, would you say you would trust the Washington State Department of Ecology (WDOE)?

Would not trust   Would trust the
the WDOE at all | | | | | | WDOE completely

As in Study One, these two measures provide simple, direct tests of our hypothesis that social trust is based on shared cultural values.

Procedure.   The procedure for this study followed that of Study One with the exception of the order of tasks. As in Study One, respondents' booklets contained two tasks. Unlike Study One, however, the tasks in Study Two were related and were presented in a single order. The first task for all respondents was based on a newspaper-style story describing a national hazardous waste management plan.[6] The second task for all respondents was the task described here, dealing with reaction in Washington State to the announcement of a national plan. As in Study One, the items used to measure respondent culture followed the two tasks, and the booklet ended with background questions. The booklets were randomly assigned to respondents, and their work was self-paced.

Results

The mean social trust and trust values judgements for the 15 experimental groups (three respondent cultures crossed with five story cultures) are given in Table 1.4. Analyses of variance show that the results for this study produced significant respondent-culture-by-story-culture interactions ($F(8, 122) = 2.38$, $p = .021$ for social trust; $F(8, 122) = 2.67$, $p = .010$ for trust values). A high level of correlation between social trust and trust values was also produced across all respondents ($r = .68$, $p = .000$). Nonetheless, these results are clearly less straightforward in their support of the cultural-values social trust hypothesis than were those of Study One. The simplest results are those for the Equality Matching respondents (45.2 per cent of the total). For these individuals, judgements of social trust and trust values were highest for the story that

---

6. This task and its relations to the task described in Study Two are discussed in a separate article (Earle and Cvetkovich, 1997).

Table 1.4 *Social Trust and Trust Values by Culture of Respondents and Culture of Stories: Fiske's Elementary Forms*

Culture of Stories	Culture of Respondents			
	Communal Sharing	Equality Matching	Market Pricing	Totals
Communal Sharing				
Social Trust	3.400	4.474	5.400	4.448
Trust Values	4.033	4.842	4.467	4.707
N	5	19	5	29
Authority Ranking				
Social Trust	5.222	4.455	4.625	4.750
Trust Values	5.111	4.152	4.875	4.667
N	9	11	8	28
Equality Matching				
Social Trust	5.125	5.333	4.625	5.040
Trust Values	4.771	5.648	4.875	5.120
N	8	9	8	25
Market Pricing				
Social Trust	5.667	4.909	4.200	4.954
Trust Values	5.500	4.818	3.533	4.712
N	6	11	5	22
No Culture				
Social Trust	5.200	4.167	4.667	4.727
Trust Values	5.289	4.333	4.917	4.874
N	15	12	6	33
Totals				
Social Trust	5.046	4.613	4.688	4.766
Trust Values	5.039	4.734	4.672	4.815
N	43	62	32	137

matched their culture. This was not true for either the Communal Sharing respondents (31.4 per cent) or the Market Pricing respondents (23.4 per cent). The Communal Sharing respondents gave their highest judgements to the Market Pricing story, while the Market Pricing respondents gave their highest judgements (for social trust) to the Communal Sharing story.

Given the strength of the results of Study One, the most plausible explanation for the results of this study is that the stories written to express the Communal Sharing and Market Pricing cultures were not interpreted as intended. That is, the Communal Sharing story was interpreted by respondents as a Market Pricing story, and the Market Pricing story was interpreted as a Communal Sharing story: in these cases, our interpretations differed from respondents' interpretations. It may be useful to examine how this could happen. First, in the Communal Sharing story, we included elements referring to the ties of Washingtonians to their homeland and to their working together to solve their own problems. For us (and for the individuals with whom we pre-tested the stories), these elements evoked the Communal Sharing narrative. For our respondents, however, these elements, interpreted perhaps as expressions of individual property rights, evoked the Market Pricing narrative. Similarly, in the Market Pricing story, we included elements referring to the comparison of costs and benefits. Due simply to unfamiliarity, perhaps, these elements failed to evoke the intended Market Pricing narrative. Instead, they apparently were interpreted by our respondents as expressions favouring local government institutions over national, thereby evoking the Communal Sharing narrative.

Of course, the argument sketched above assumes the correctness of the cultural-values hypothesis: respondents gave higher social trust judgements to stories that expressed their values; we simply had two of the stories mis-labelled. One counter to this is the claim that our respondents' judgements were simply random. But, even with very few respondents in some of the cells, the regularity among the means is too great to accept randomness. For example, for all of the stories except the Authority Ranking story (where we would expect no differences), the means for the three cultural groups differed significantly ($p < .05$) for either the social trust measure (Communal Sharing story), the trust values measure (Equality Matching and Market Pricing stories) or both (No Culture story). The differences on the culture-identified stories are in line with our explanation above. The differences on the No Culture story reflect a general relation between the Communal Sharing culture and social trust: both are focused on shared values within groups. This is not true of the other two cultures included in this study. Only Communal Sharing is correlated with social trust across all respondents ($r = .22$, $p < .01$).

If our respondents' social trust judgements were not random, what alternatives do we have to the cultural-values hypothesis? The dominant alternative, of course, is the traditional rationalist hypothesis that social trust judgements are based on competence and responsibility. But application of the rationalist hypothesis in this case is blocked in two ways, one specific and one general. The specific problem is due to our experimental design. In that design, we limited the common cues for competence and responsibility (eg, the identities of persons and institutions) to those that were shared by all stories. To the extent that we could, then, we forced social trust judgements to be based on expressions of cultural values, not on cues for or evidence of competence and responsibility. One indication of the success of this manipulation is the lack of differences among the mean judgements for the five stories ($F(4, 122) = 0.94$, $p = .445$ for social trust; $F(4, 122) = 0.85$, $p = .498$ for trust values). The general problem with the rationalist hypothesis is its implicit assumption that competence and responsibility can be judged in some culture-free way. Do we all agree on the indicators of competence and responsibility? In certain, narrowly constrained contexts we may, perhaps; but in general we don't. Criteria are within narrative phenomena: what counts positively for one cultural group may mean nothing or be negative to another.

The best explanation for the results of this study is that respondents made their judgements of social trust based on the similarity between their own cultural values and those they took to be expressed in the stories they read. The use of new cultural materials and measurement scales, along with the small number of respondents in some of the cells of the design, created conditions that weakened our results somewhat. Nonetheless, the results of Study Two can be taken as a solid, independent replication of the results of Study One. In Study Two, as in Study One, the simplest indicator that respondents tended to give higher levels of social trust to institutions that shared their cultural values is the high level of correlation between social trust and trust values across all respondents ($r = .68$, $p < .001$). Unlike the experimental results, this correlation is unaffected by the expectations of the experimenters: it's all in the respondents' minds. This result indicates that individuals can compare the values they extract from a story with the values in their currently-favoured cultural narratives. And it suggests that they may use that information in making judgements of social trust.

DISCUSSION

In a previous monograph (Earle and Cvetkovich, 1995) we proposed a cultural-values theory of social trust as an alternative to the traditional, rationalist interpretation. Here, we have described two experimental studies designed as simple tests of the cultural-values theory, the second an independent replication of the first, using totally different cultural materials and measurement scales. Neither of these studies was designed to definitively pin down the measurement of particular cultural orientations. Their purpose was limited to the demonstration of the critical importance of cultural variation to social trust, a source of complexity that is ignored in the rationalist tradition. The results of both studies supported the cultural-values hypothesis that social trust is based on value similarity: people tend to trust other people and institutions that 'tell stories' expressing currently salient values, stories that interpret the world in the same way they do.

And this perhaps is the most important implication of the cultural-values hypothesis – that social trust tends to be a within-group phenomenon. Individuals are inclined to trust within group boundaries and to distrust outside them. If this is true, social trust may not be the risk management cure-all that many have hoped it to be. As we have argued elsewhere (Earle and Cvetkovich, 1995, 1997; Earle, 1997), however, the benefits of social trust can be redeemed by distinguishing two forms, pluralistic and cosmopolitan. Pluralistic social trust is singular, rooted in the pasts of existing groups; because of this, it is not useful in the management of complex societal problems. Cosmopolitan social trust is multiple, created in the emergence of new combinations of persons and groups. These new combinations are based on new sets of values that are constructed for the solution of specific problems. Successful risk management thus can be based in part on encouraging people to move toward more cosmopolitan forms of social trust.

2 Risk, Trust, and Democratic Theory

Roger E Kasperson, Dominic Golding and
Jeanne X Kasperson

Recent practice in managing environmental risks in the US demonstrates how firmly the principles of democratic values and procedures have intruded on the previously sheltered world of scientifically defined risk. Recurrent failures in risk management, it is now widely argued, stem from a failure to recognize the more general requirements of democratic society, and especially the need for social trust. Accordingly, risk-control strategies have gone awry due alternatively to a lack of openness and 'transparency', the failure to consult or involve so-called 'stakeholders' (usually a poorly defined misnomer), a loss of social trust in managers, inadequacies in due process, a lack of responsiveness to public concerns, or an insensitivity to questions of environmental justice.

Such interpretations abound across a wide spectrum of environmental debates: global warming, biodiversity, genetic engineering, clean-up of defence and other hazardous wastes, lead in the environment, the siting of hazardous waste facilities, and the protection of wetlands. Ruckelshaus has recently warned that:

> Mistrust engenders a vicious descending spiral. The more mistrust by the public, the less effective government becomes at delivering what people want and need; the more government bureaucrats in turn respond with enmity towards the citizens they serve, the more ineffective government becomes, the more people mistrust it, and so on, down and down (Ruckelshaus, 1996, p2).

Ruckelshaus's dread spiral is reminiscent of Supreme Court Justice Stephen Breyer's tripartite 'vicious circle – public perception, Congressional reaction, and the uncertainties of the regulatory process' (Breyer 1993, p50) that thwarts effective regulation of risk. Clearly, obligations to democratic procedures and attention to issues of trust have become essential elements of any successful regime's addressing environmental risks that command public concerns and place claims on limited societal resources.

A noteworthy marker of this recognition of democratic requirements is the US National Research Council (NRC) report *Understanding Risk* (Stern and

Fineberg, 1996). This report is the most recent in a series of NRC efforts to define and rationalize the risk-assessment function in government and, by inference, the relationship between the nation's assessment and management of environmental threats and the functioning of democratic society. Indeed, a striking change of social ethics and democratic expectations has attended the handling of environmental and health threats in American society. The progression of ethics is what Kates (1985, p53) would characterize as 'third generation ethics' bursting on American society in the twilight of the 20th century, ethics bearing on how risks will be allocated and managed with strong attention to the 'fairness of the process as well as the outcome'. (The two earlier generations of ethics involved, respectively, a time of nonmaleficence that called for avoiding unnecessary harm and informing those at risk, and a period of maximizing the aggregate societal utility of balancing risks and benefits.) Similarly, it is clear, as we approach the millennium, that those affected by risk must be informed and provided ample opportunity to participate in decisions and that managers must be publicly accountable for their actions.

These social reanchorings have found their way progressively, but often painfully slowly, into recognitions by government and corporations that the game has changed. The so-called 'Red Book', *Risk Assessment in the Federal Government* (NRC 1983), was predicated on the need to distinguish, and clarify, the technically based assessment process from the value-laden decision process. The first was, it was argued, the domain of science; the second that of politics. Beyond that, the book allotted little attention to the complications of reconciling the scientific process of risk assessment with the needs of democratic procedure; rather, noting the potential tensions and ambiguities, that volume, as well as subsequent NRC reports, concentrated on ways to improve the scientific bases of risk assessment. *Understanding Risk*, therefore, is a striking departure: the book explores in depth the bases of public response, enumerates contributions of public assessment to risk characterization, demarcates the myriad entrances of value questions into *both* assessment and policy, and investigates means for integrating expert assessment and democratic process. In short, the report symbolizes, and recognizes, that the new requirements of third-generation risk ethics and democratic procedure have invaded the main corridors of policy discourse.

Salutary as this is, the discussion of how to reconcile risk assessment, trust, and democratic procedure has thus far proceeded largely from the insights gained from the experience of those charged with the responsibility of managing risk or from those social scientists who analyse societal encounters with environmental and health threats. Meanwhile, a literature of democratic theorizing has emerged addressing the social conditions necessary for democracy and the relationships between democratic institutions and economic and social well-being. As yet, these discussions have remained quite separate.

We seek to join these disparate inquiries, but we do so by reversing the perspective that has thus far guided much of the discussion among risk analysts, whom we would characterize as seeking to answer a difficult question: what does our experience concerning the interaction of risk management and social trust suggest about how better to bring democratic procedures into risk manage-

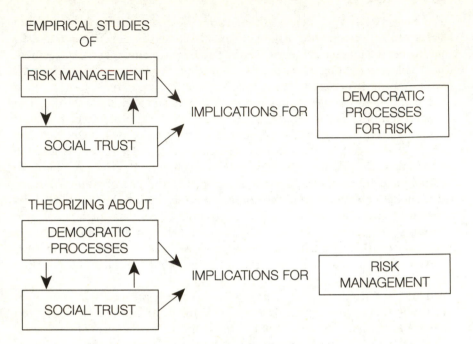

Figure 2.1 *Social trust, risk, and democracy: Contrasting approaches*

ment to improve the process? Rather, our approach is to examine recent theorizing about democracy and its relation to social trust for insights on how to bring risk assessment and management into greater conformity with democratic regimes (Figure 2.1). This exploration is heuristic in the best sense: we are uncertain whether this shift in perspective will afford new insights and leave it to the reader to judge.

APPROACHES TO DEMOCRATIC THEORY

After considering several examples of democratic theorizing, we turn to what various public surveys and opinion polls may suggest about trust in American democracy. We also inquire into how trust is lost and regained, the levels of social trust that enter into democratic processes, how we may think about social distrust, and finally we note some promising avenues of future inquiry. Discussions of democratic theory, and the role that trust plays in democratic society, are as rich and diverse as the examples of democracy found in different corners of the globe. Not only is there little consensus as to what democratic values are once one moves beyond the veneer of rhetoric but, more significantly, the underlying notions of democracy itself are so fundamentally different as to be frequently in direct conflict. Some approaches begin with the societal conditions or basic values necessary for the emergence of democratic institutions and processes; others stress the normative goals or outcomes that democracy should achieve. Pennock (1979, p161) distinguishes between *justificatory democratic theory*, treating how power ought to be distributed and exercised in democratic government, and *operational democratic theory*, focused on how people actually organize for the conduct of democratic institutions. Opting for the latter, Pennock classifies approaches to democratic theory according to their conceptualization of power relationships and whether they are descriptive theory, prescriptive theory, or models.

Here, in centring upon what appear to be the principal approaches in the literature over the past several decades, our intent is to distinguish among types of theorizing that are empirically based. Accordingly, we recognize five major approaches: institutional (or constitutional) designs, socioeconomic development, cultural perspectives, dialogic models, and civil society/civic engagement. Since the last, as represented particularly by the influential work of Robert Putnam (1993, 1995a, 1995b, 1996) has attracted much discussion and builds upon several of the other approaches, we examine it at greater length. For each approach, we characterize essentials of the theory and then explore what role, if any, social trust plays in the construct of democracy.

Institutional (Constitutional) Designs

This approach centres upon the design of institutions that maximize democratic values and processes. Implicit is the distribution of power over branches of government and institutions as well as means for limiting the exercise of power. Often this is coupled with notions of the rational political actor who, operating through rational choice, maximizes individual utility, as suggested by the work of Buchanan and Tullock (1962). Thus, Elinor Ostrom in *Governing the Commons* (1990) emphasizes the constitutional arrangement of rules and institutions that underlie the operation of successful common property systems. Given the strong role of rational individualism in such approaches, social trust is seen as implicit in that institutions function akin to markets, delivering outcomes associated with rational political choices according to requirements of the political regime.

Economic Development

Economic development, or 'modernization', sees the emergence of democracy as an outcome of economic growth and progress. Development promotes democracy by contributing to higher levels of legitimacy of political authority, decreased propensity for political radicalism, and increased stability of the political system. It is not economic development or growth per se, however, that is important to the emergence of democratic institutions and procedures, but a dense cluster of social changes and improvements that are broadly distributed over the population, such as the minimization of environmental risks (air pollution, groundwater depletion, etc.), improved health care, lowered infant mortality, and increased literacy and education of the population. Such outcomes encourage, and provide enabling conditions for, political participation while also serving to increase social trust and to reduce class tension and political radicalism. Broad support for this theory is available in a wide array of empirical studies; Figure 2.2 suggests a general relationship between economic development and the emergence of high levels of social trust across a spectrum of developed societies.

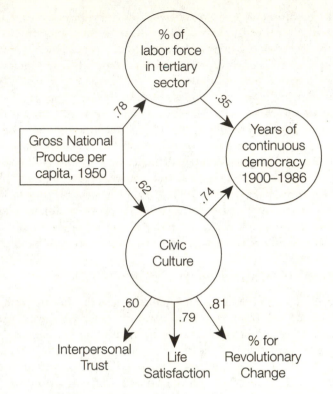

Note: Adjusted goodness of fit index = .88.

Figure 2.2 *Economic and cultural prerequisites of stable democracy*
Source: Inglehart (1988), 1218.

The structure of causality between economic development and democracy remains opaque in much of this theorizing. The argument generally claims that economic development facilitates the emergence of democratic values and institutions through key intervening variables, such as more democratic political culture, less polarized class structure, broadening of civil society, and more integrated state–society relations. But the exact causal mechanisms by which these linkages come into being are not precisely defined nor do they enjoy the support of incontrovertible empirical evidence.

Cultural Approaches

Analysts who take cultural approaches argue that a consistent syndrome of interrelated attitudes toward life satisfaction, political satisfaction, interpersonal trust, and support for the existing social order is apparent across a wide variety of societies (Inglehart 1988, 1997). This syndrome is the essential mediating link between economic and social development and the persistence of democratic institutions. Indeed, broad empirical evidence suggests that more than half the variance in such persistence can be attributed to this syndrome (Inglehart 1988).

In revisiting their classic 1963 work on political culture, Almond and Verba (1980) tapped the work of David Easton (1965) on the political system to distinguish among three attributes or components of political culture. *System culture* involves the distribution of public attitudes toward national community, regime, and political authorities, including different levels of political trust. *Process culture* includes attitudes towards oneself and toward other political actors, and, thus, levels of interpersonal trust. Such attitudes are cognitive, affective, and evaluative. *Policy culture* reflects the relatedness or internal consistency of the various components or attributes of the political system. Below, we also pick up this notion of multiple levels in the political system.

Figure 2.2 suggests the critical role of political culture in the persistence of democracy across a wide variety of societies. Using Linear Structural Relationships (LISREL) to help delineate the causal links among conditions leading to democracy, the analysis shows the importance of the syndrome of attitudes in the evolution of 'civic culture', a type of political culture conceptualized by Almond and Verba (1963) as particularly amenable to democratic regimes. The importance of the syndrome for this culture is quite apparent, as is the correlation between civic culture and years of continuous democracy.

From Almond and Verba's cross-national study of five political cultures, it is possible to glean a number of propositions concerning how social trust may contribute to democratic institutions and processes. In summary, social trust:

- increases individual propensity to join with others in political activity;
- tends to translate into politically relevant trust;
- leads to a closer fusion between the primary group structures of society and the secondary structures of politics;
- mediates, and ameliorates, the extent to which commitments to political subgroups lead to political fragmentations;
- makes citizens more willing to turn power over to political elites, who tend also to be viewed as part of the political community rather than as an alien force; and
- leads to a more integrated and stable political system.

(see Almond and Verba, 1963, pp284–288, 494–495).

Through such propositions, cultural studies elevate social trust to a key role in democratic theory.

Dialogic Models

Dialogic models of democracy proceed from several critical assumptions. First, democracy, in this view, depends upon the presence or creation of an enlightened citizenry that has broad-based opportunities for participating in public decisions and that is part of an ongoing, meaningful public dialogue. But such dialogue is greatly impeded by the fact that the various contending parties operate within the logic of alternative discourses. Such dialogue, according to Williams and Matheny (1995, pp3–10), includes such markedly different discourses as *managerial*, *pluralist*, and *communitarian languages*. Overcoming these impediments is essential to fulfilling the requisites for democracy: namely, the clarification of competing assumptions, the identification and narrowing of grounds of disagreement, and the capability of citizens to determine for themselves the adequacy of competing conceptions of public policy and the public interest (Williams and Matheny 1995, p61).

Barber (1984, p261) also maintains that a 'strong' democracy requires institutions that involve individuals at both the neighbourhood and national level in common 'talk', common decision-making and political judgement, and common action:

> To talk where one votes and to vote where one debates, to debate where one learns. . . . and to learn in a civic fashion where one talks is to integrate the several civic functions in a way that nurtures public seeing and strengthens political judgment (Barber 1984, p271).

An enlightened citizenry emerges only in a context of broad-based opportunities for participation, policy-making institutions capable of accommodating ambiguity and tentativeness, and a political community capable of transforming partial and private interests into public goods.

Democratic talk, then, is a powerful mechanism for building social trust and democratic institutions, what Inglehart (1997, p163) refers to as a 'culture of trust'. But several societal conditions must be met. Individual disputes need to be placed in the context of the full range of decisions that affect public life and not be viewed as idiosyncratic. Similarly public discourse needs to be continuous and ongoing and not, as often happens, occur only sporadically or episodically. For discourse to be continuous, citizens require not only the opportunities but the means and resources to acquire and evaluate information. Finally, people must be empowered to enter into decisions and to see the results actually implemented.

Some see in dialogue and narrative the potential for a new democratic order and a new basis for social trust. Earle and Cvetkovich (1995, p10), who observe that 'social trust [is] based on cultural values that are communicated in narrative form within society by elites', favour a movement away from divisive pluralism and toward what they term *cosmopolitanism*. Cosmopolitans pursue to free themselves of the past and to seek new community-based futures. All local narratives become open to 'continuing reconstruction based on unconstrained persuasion' by cosmopolitan leaders (Earle and Cvetkovich 1995, p152). As these authors reiterate in Chapter 1, cosmopolitan social trust bridges the gap between the past and the unknown future, and people enlist imagination and dialogue to fashion their own, and a new, future.

Across these different approaches to democratic theory, social trust is a central ingredient, viewed as providing important bases for democratic society. High levels of social trust ease the functioning of institutions and governance by facilitating greater cooperation in society. Indeed, as Etzioni (1990, p8) affirms, 'It is hard to conceive a modern economy without a strong element of trust running through it'. Trust creates and sustains solidarity in social relationships and systems. It also, as Luhmann (1979, 1993) maintains, functions 'to comprehend and reduce' social complexity and enlarges individual and societal benefits through the taking of risks. This enlargement of benefits accrues in no small part to the greater efficiency of economic and political transactions. And many theorists also see trust as indispensable to political stability – in values that underlie the political community, in the functioning of the regime and institutions, and in vesting requisite authority in those who govern. It is not surprising in this context that many risk-management analysts proceed from an underlying assumption that social trust is indispensable to institutional effectiveness and thus the more the better.

Civil Society/Civic Engagement

The fifth approach to democratic theory builds on all four discussed above. Over the past several decades, few works in the social sciences have evoked more attention and debate than Robert Putnam's publications on civic engagement and civil society (Putnam 1993; 1995a; 1995b; 1996). Although portrayal of Americans' 'bowling alone' (Putnam 1995a) has garnered much public attention, the major theoretical structure for his ideas is presented in his book *Making Democracy Work* (Putnam 1993).

Putnam identifies the conditions necessary for the creation and maintenance of strong and responsive democratic institutions. He characterizes the regionalization of government in Italy during the 1970s as a 'natural experiment' to explore the impact of civic engagement on economic development and institutional performance in particular. Tapping three of the four approaches outlined above, especially sociocultural explanations, he invokes Alexis de Tocqueville's (1969) *Democracy in America*:

> As depicted in Tocqueville's classic interpretation of American democracy and other accounts of civic virtue, the civic community is marked by an active, public-spirited citizenry, by egalitarian political relations, by a social fabric of trust and cooperation. Some regions of Italy, we discover, are cursed with vertically structured politics, a social life of fragmentation and isolation, and a culture of distrust. These differences in civic life turn out to play a key role in explaining institutional success (Putnam 1993, p15).

Putnam develops an elaborate set of indicators of institutional performance (eg cabinet stability, budget promptness, legislative innovation, expenditures), socioeconomic development (eg infant mortality, agricultural work-force, industrial work-force), and civic involvement (eg membership in cooperatives and mutual-aid associations) based on extensive interviews and historical data. Multiple-regression analyses of these data reveal some startling associations. Most notably, as Figure 2.3 shows, civic involvement is the prime driver of development and the major factor shaping institutional performance. Civic traditions between 1860 and 1920 are the most powerful predictor of contemporary civic community (arrow a), whereas historical socioeconomic development has little independent impact on contemporary socioeconomic conditions (d) and absolutely no impact on the contemporary civic community (b). Thus, the 'uncivic' south of Italy is socioeconomically blighted, whereas the civic north, with its dense network of civic engagement, experiences an economic prosperity comparable with the most developed regions and nations of the world.

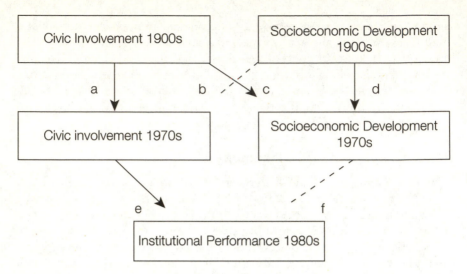

Figure 2.3 *Actual effects among civic involvement, socioeconomic development, and institutional performance: Italy, 1900–1980*
Source: Putnam (1993), p157.

Putnam elaborates an elegant theory to explain how civic involvement, such as membership in mutual-aid associations, creates this phenomenal difference in socioeconomic development. He begins by noting that all societies face 'dilemmas of collective action' where short-term individual interests, such as overgrazing of common lands and pollution of drinking water and other common-property resources, may result in collective harm (Putnam 1993, p162). Putnam asserts that third-party enforcement by government agencies has failed to overcome these kinds of dilemmas in the past, and that mutual trust and cooperation offer the only solution. Indeed, the many rotating-credit associations, mutual-aid societies, and farming cooperatives that exist in the world attest to the ability of communities to overcome such predicaments, but that entails the generation, through civic engagement, of a significant reservoir of social capital.

Social capital comprises stocks of trust, norms, or reciprocity and networks of civic engagement that make voluntary cooperation easier to attain. These stocks are 'moral resources' that may be created or destroyed through 'virtuous' and 'vicious' circles. Successful cooperation breeds economic prosperity by promoting civic ends that would otherwise be impossible. For example, a group of farmers may get together to help each other harvest crops or to raise barns, activities that they would not be able to do alone – in effect, putting the social capital of the community to work. Such successful cooperation not only leads to greater economic prosperity but also tends to be mutually reinforcing, so that the stock of social capital increases with each rewarding application.

Networks of civic engagement generate social capital by encouraging robust norms of reciprocity, reducing incentives to cheat, fostering communication (and thus reducing uncertainty about the trustworthiness of others), and building models of cooperation for use in the future. Norms of reciprocity evolve because they lower transaction costs, and cooperating individuals soon learn to trade off between long-term altruism and short-term self-interest. Horizontal networks typical of community associations, where individuals have equivalent status and power, facilitate communication among members. This reduces the uncertainty about the trustworthiness of new members and allows for rapid and effective application of sanctions should any member act opportunistically. By contrast, vertical networks involve hierarchies with asymmetric power relations that tend to discourage the flow of information and cannot sustain social trust and cooperation (Putnam 1993, p172).

Trust is an essential component of social capital generated by civic engagement. Trust lubricates cooperation and cooperation breeds trust (Putnam 1993, p171). Trust entails an expectation about the behaviour of individuals:

> You do not trust a person to do something merely because he says he will do it. You trust him because, knowing what you know of his disposition, his information, his ability, his available options and their consequences, you expect that he will *choose* to do it. (Dasgupta 1988, pp55–56).

Such predictions are based on the intimate, interpersonal, 'thick trust' (Williams 1988, p8) generated in small, closely-knit communities. The more indirect, impersonal, and 'thin trust' is typical of large, complex societies. With thin trust, the structure of the situation is more important than personal character.

Putnam (1993, p162) concludes that all societies face the 'dilemma of collective action' and evolve toward one of two social equilibria to avoid a Hobbesian war of all against all. The 'uncivic' south of Italy, with its patron-client relationships and extra-legal enforcers, epitomizes a social equilibrium of dependency and exploitation that harbours high social distrust and little cooperation beyond the limits of the family. This is the same lack of civic virtue that Banfield (1958) found in Montegrano, which he described as 'amoral familism'. The second equilibrium, characteristic of the north of Italy with its dense network of civic engagement and high levels of social trust, Putnam (1993) calls 'brave reciprocity'. Each of these equilibria is self-reinforcing and represents a polar extreme of what is possible.

Turning to the US, Putnam (1995b) is troubled by the declining levels of social trust and group membership observed in the 'general social survey' (GSS) conducted by the National Opinion Research Center (NORC). In *Tuning in, tuning out*, Putnam (1995b) explores several plausible but ultimately inadequate explanations, including levels of education, longer working hours, and the increasing participation of women in the workplace. Rising levels of education and increasing leisure time should have resulted in an increase in group membership, and although the increased number of women in the workplace might be expected to reduce civic engagement, working women tend to participate in group activities more than other women. But Putnam (1995b) concludes that generational effects best explain the downturn in social trust and group membership. Those people born in the earlier part of this century were always and remain more trusting and engaged than those born more recently. As the population ages and dies, overall levels of trust and engagement decline. But what accounts for this generational change?

Putnam believes television is the prime culprit. Those individuals born in the 1940s and 1950s came of age at about the time television became a major influence in day-to-day life. Several possible mechanisms explain the association between television viewing and declining trust and group membership. Watching television is invariably a solitary activity that takes up time and displaces group activities. Television also changes the outlook of viewers, especially children, so that they are less trusting of institutions and individuals around them. In sum, watching television destroys the social capital generated by civic engagement.

Some researchers have proposed that variations in trust and confidence are related to structural factors, such as the state of the economy (Lipset and Schneider 1983) whereas others see specific events, such as the Vietnam War and Watergate, as the culprits (Inglehart, Nevitte and Basañez 1997; Lipset and Schneider 1987; Zimmer 1979). In the next section we examine some of these arguments and take a closer look at some of the empirical evidence, especially that available in public surveys and opinion polls.

SURVEYS/OPINION POLLS

Given the recent litany of political scandals in the US, it is scarcely surprising that the public appears to have little trust or confidence in Congress. It may surprise some, however, that numerous opinion polls appear to show that public confidence in many of the other major social institutions in the US is also quite low and has declined precipitously from levels apparent three decades ago. For example, Lipset and Schneider (1983) found a rapid decline in confidence in ten major institutions during the late 1960s and early 1970s. In 'this era of political distrust' (Breyer 1993) since that time, public confidence has oscillated in response to important events but has remained at relatively low levels. Several factors have been proposed to explain this decline. Some see events such as the Vietnam War, the Watergate scandal, social protests, and the energy crisis as particularly important. Others point to structural changes in society and economy, such as unemployment and inflation, as altering the levels of social trust and explaining why business and government bear the brunt of public disaffection.

In their revised edition of *The Confidence Gap*, Lipset and Schneider (1987) offer a glint of optimism in noting that the average percentage of the public expressing 'a great deal of confidence' in the leadership of ten institutions rose from a low of 23 per cent in 1982 to an average of 31 per cent in 1984. Observing this trend back in 1985, it would have been difficult to say whether it would continue upwards or very soon collapse. Using poll data from Louis Harris and NORC, we have extended the graphs of Lipset and Schneider (Figure 2.4). Clearly the upswing evident in the most recent edition of *The Confidence Gap* (Lipset and Schneider 1987) was only short-lived and ended with the revelations emerging from the Iran-Contra affair. More important, however, the graph in Figure 2.4 illustrates two major points. On the one hand, public confidence in institutions appears to be quite sensitive (at least in the shortrun) to events, and rises and falls rather steeply over relatively short

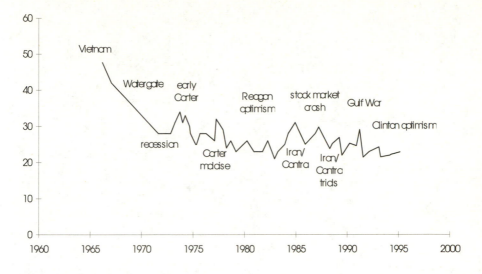

Figure 2.4 *Average percentage of respondents expressing a 'great deal of confidence' in the leadership of ten institutions, 1966–95*
Source: modified and updated from Lipset and Schneider (1983).

periods. On the other, although public confidence varies noticeably from month to month according to events, the overall trend has remained relatively stable since the mid-1970s and betrays no dramatic decline comparable with that during the 1960s and early 1970s. Hibbing and Theiss-Morse (1995, pp35–36), noting that 'data are the sparsest right where we need them to be the most dense', suggest that high levels of support may be 'fleeting' and 'atypical'. One might be tempted, therefore, to conclude that the high levels of confidence during the 1950s and 1960s were aberrations, and that the lower levels of confidence since 1970 are more 'normal' for American society (see Rosa and Clark 1999 for support for this view). Below, we take up the question of whether social distrust has positive social functions.

In Figure 2.4, the use of an average value of confidence in ten major institutions masks much of the interinstitutional variation in public confidence. Figure 2.5 breaks out levels of confidence for seven of the ten institutions and demonstrates how particular events may affect the confidence levels in particular institutions (three others are excluded for clarity and for comparability with the Gallup data), and how these are then reflected in the overall average confidence levels. Most notably, Figure 2.5 illustrates that the Gulf War boosted public confidence in the military beginning in late 1990 and that this accounts for the peak observed in Figure 2.4. Coincident with this peak in public confidence in the military, the apparent declining levels of confidence in the other institutions may reflect the worsening economic situation at the end of George Bush's presidency. The decline in confidence in the Supreme Court may also reflect public concern over the nomination of Judge Clarence Thomas in the summer of 1991. Without trying to explain every peak and valley, we note that Figure 2.5 gives credence to two important points made by Lipset

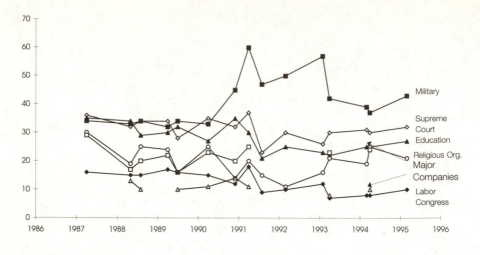

Figure 2.5 *Average percentage of respondents expressing a 'great deal of confidence' in the leadership of seven institutions, 1987–95*
Source: Harris/NORC.

and Schneider (1987, p8): confidence *trends* tend to be parallel for different institutions and may well, therefore, have the same general causes, whereas *patterns* of trust in different institutions tend to be more specific and may well have disparate causes (see also Hibbing and Theiss-Morse 1995).

When we compare the results from different polling organizations, we see that the general trends and patterns are similar (compare Figure 2.5 showing the Harris/NORC data with Figure 2.6 showing the Gallup data). Generally, the public appears to have relatively high levels of confidence in the military and organized religion and relatively low levels of confidence in Congress, big business, and organized labour. At the same time, however, a surprising 15-point difference separates the levels of confidence expressed to the different pollsters (Figure 2.7), with much higher levels of confidence being reported by Gallup than by Harris/NORC.

Subtle differences in wording and response categories may account for this discrepancy. The Harris/NORC survey asks:

> I am going to name some institutions in this country. As far as the *people* running these institutions are concerned, would you say you have a great deal of confidence, only some confidence, or hardly any confidence at all in them?

The Gallup organization asks:

> I am going to read you a list of institutions in American society. Would you tell me how much confidence you, yourself, have in each one – a great deal, quite a lot, some, or very little?

In 1980, Civic Service Inc. conducted a national survey to examine the impact of the different wording and response categories (Lipset and Schneider 1983,

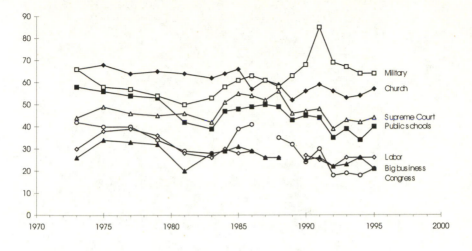

Figure 2.6 *Percentage of respondents expressing a 'great deal' and 'quite a lot' of confidence in the seven institutions, 1973–95*
Source: Gallup polls.

pp91–96). Surprisingly, perhaps, they found that the emphasis on *leaders* in the Harris/NORC polls had little impact on the expressed levels of confidence. The major influence is the choice of response categories. Whereas the Harris/NORC polls allow only one positive response ('a great deal' of confidence) and two negative ones ('only some' and 'hardly any'), the Gallup polls allow two positive responses ('a great deal' and 'quite a lot'), one neutral response ('some'), and one negative response ('very little').

The point here is not that survey results must be viewed with great caution, but rather that the purported decline in public trust and confidence over the past two decades may not be so severe as some analysts have claimed. Whereas the Harris/NORC polls are more commonly cited to demonstrate declining levels of public trust and confidence, the Gallup polls are the preferred evidence base for those more optimistic about US politics. Indeed, we do not know, as we shall argue later, what is an 'appropriate' level of confidence. So although the survey and poll evidence is persuasive, at least for the period between the 1950s and 1970s, as to the relative decline of social trust, it has little to say concerning different types of trust or the roots of apparent variations in levels of trust and confidence.

Types of Trust: Emergence and Erosion

For all the work on social trust, our understanding of it remains limited and incomplete. Our examination of the various approaches to democratic theory has yielded only partial explanations for the creation and loss of trust. Drawing on recent experience in radioactive waste management, Slovic (Chapter 3, this volume) has observed that trust is asymmetrical – it is easy to lose and

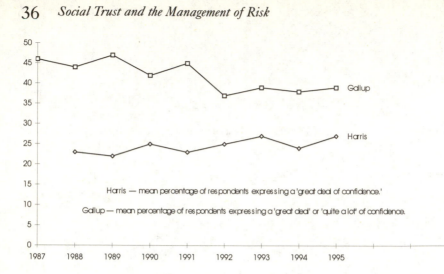

Figure 2.7 *Mean percentage of respondents expressing confidence in seven institutions, Harris vs Gallup, 1987–95*
Source: Harris/NORC and Gallup.

difficult to regain. As another author puts it: 'Trust takes a painfully long time to build. It can be destroyed in a heartbeat' (Carnevale 1995, p199). Unfortunately, social and political scientists can only speculate about the steps necessary to regain social trust, and little firm empirical evidence exists to support these views.

Elsewhere we define social trust as a person's expectation that other persons and institutions in a social relationship can be relied upon to act in ways that are competent, predictable, and caring (Kasperson, Golding and Tuler 1992). Social trust presumably is built slowly and incrementally in our socialization processes, especially when we are young, and in our day-to-day interactions with each other and the institutions around us. Since social trust is probably never completely or permanently attained or attainable, and, we will argue, probably should not be, it must be continuously maintained and reinforced through networks of civic engagement and norms of reciprocity (to use Putnam's terminology). Such networks and norms encourage the development of and bolster different types of trust, among them: *cognitive, emotional,* and *behavioural* (Kasperson, Golding and Tuler 1992; Koller 1988; Lewis and Weigert 1985).

Cognitive trust is based on the degree of knowledge one has about others in a relationship. We are better able to judge the trustworthiness of those we know than those we do not. Close social networks promote familiarity, either directly or vicariously, and thereby increase cognitive trust. Trusting someone we do not know requires a cognitive leap of faith. *Emotional trust* may provide a basis for this cognitive leap of faith. *Behavioural trust* is to act as if the uncertain future actions of others were certain and predictable. For example, an Amish farmer may choose to cooperate in raising a neighbour's barn with the expectation that the neighbour may one day reciprocate. This is what Putnam calls 'brave' reciprocity because it implies some level of risk (the neighbour may never reciprocate). Behavioural acts such as this within a social network tend to bolster both cognitive and emotional trust, reduce uncertainty about individuals, and provide positive models for future cooperation.

The mix of cognitive, emotional, and behavioural trust may well vary according to the nature of the social relationship in question. In primary-group relationships, such as between family and friends, emotional trust may be high and relatively resistant to contrary behaviour, especially since strong incentives or sanctions may effectively limit such behaviour (Lewis and Weigert 1985, p972). By contrast, behavioural and cognitive trust may be most important in secondary-group relationships (eg between community members and a government agency) where emotional trust is limited. Thus, Luhmann (1979) distinguishes between the *interpersonal trust* that prevails in small, relatively undifferentiated societies and the *systemic trust* that prevails in the bureaucratic institutions of modern, complex societies, a distinction relevant to the 'thick' and 'thin' trust discussed above. This differentiation is also consistent with Putnam's distinction between personal and social trust. Both authors view the shift from personal to social trust as one of the important transformations of modern times.

But perhaps the most important feature of social trust for democratic society is its multi-layered structure. Trust in the political system is onion-like, with the deepest level, the core of the onion, being trust in the basic *political community* that underlies the constitutional structure of politics and democratic institutions. Next is a layer of trust in the *political regime*, the norms and rules of the game that provide the context for democratic processes. Then comes trust in governmental and other *political institutions*. And finally there is the most superficial level of trust – that in the *particular representatives* of the institutions.

Among these layers, trust at the core is most essential for the continued functioning and effectiveness of democratic society. As long as high levels of trust prevail at the political-community and regime levels, distrust at the institutional and representative levels, particularly if strongly anchored in the rational assessment of institutional performance, may stimulate the reforms and changes that protect more basic levels of trust. This is where much writing on the 'trust crisis' in the US and elsewhere misses the mark. As we have seen above, the survey data that are invariably cited are those depicting trust at the most superficial levels of the political system. It is informative that surveys and opinion polls soliciting attitudes toward whether there are better societies or democracies than the US, or whether the economic system should undergo major changes, invariably return very high levels of regard and support. Particularly problematic is that erroneous inferences concerning trust in the core of democratic society are made from data that pertain to the most variable and transitory levels of the political system. Thus, it is the arrangement or layering of trust and the interrelationships among these layers that deserve close attention in assessing the 'system dynamics' of trust.

Whereas Putnam attributes much of the erosion of social trust to the decline in social networks, including the influence of television on the postwar generations, major social events that shape the general social climate may also play a significant role. The high levels of social trust evident during the 1950s and

1960s may have reflected the general social optimism associated with the end of World War II and the phenomenal economic growth of the post-war period. In such a positive social and economic climate, the public may have been more inclined to invest more trust in social institutions and to have been more forgiving when this trust was abused. Such extreme optimism, on the other hand, may be the exception rather than the rule.

The debacle of the Vietnam War, the protracted period of social unrest in the 1960s and 1970s, revelations about environmental problems, and scandals such as Watergate, have likely sown seeds of scepticism among the American public. In this more negative social climate, people may well have been more cautious about investing trust in any social institution, and indeed this scepticism may have been self-reinforcing since new scandals always came along to stoke the fires. In spite of the apparent lack of confidence in the major institutions in the US, Lipset and Schneider (1987, p8) argue:

> A striking characteristic of the decline of confidence is that it is almost entirely related to events beyond people's own personal experience: conflicts, scandals, protests, and failures that affect their own lives indirectly, if at all. Americans repeatedly express optimism and confidence about their own lives and their personal futures, even while decrying the terrible mess the country is in.

Hence *The Confidence Gap* is an apt title.

THE POSITIVE FUNCTIONS OF RATIONAL DISTRUST

In light of this mixture of personal and social trust, the widespread view that high levels of social trust are indispensable to democratic societies and that such trust should be maximized so that institutions work smoothly, public mandates are available to authorities, and social conflict is minimized, is somewhat surprising. Many apparently agree with Ruckelshaus (1996, p2) that we 'must generate a renaissance of trust, so that government, at all levels, is no longer *them* but *us*, as it ought to be in a democracy'.

There is another view. Social distrust may well arise from rational and realistic public assessments of government failures or breaches in fiduciary responsibility. As Breyer repeatedly emphasizes, public respect hinges on government's 'successful accomplishment of a mission that satisfies an important societal need' (Breyer 1993, p65). Public trust in government during the conduct of the Vietnam War or confidence in the government's management of environmental protection at the nation's nuclear weapons facilities was undoubtedly misplaced, and the decline in trust over these issues helped to stimulate policy changes.

The changing structural conditions that underlie conditions of American democracy may carry even more far-reaching implications. The 20th century has witnessed a dramatic growth of power and its increasing concentration in American society. Yankelovich (1991) argues persuasively that 'culture and technical control' are undermining the ability for agreement between publics and experts on the serious problems that beset US society. He echoes noted political scholar VO Key in arguing that when the 'proper balance' exists between the public and the nation's elites, US democracy works beautifully. When that balance becomes badly skewed, however, the system malfunctions. And a chief symptom of imbalance is a lack of national consensus on how to cope with the most urgent problems (Yankelovich 1991, p8). The growing dependence of policy decisions on highly specialized knowledge and technical expertise presents a major challenge to this balance.

In such a context, social distrust holds in check the growing power of economic elites and technical expertise. Distrust also generates alternative control mechanisms that enable democratic institutions to maintain social order as well as fragile political balances. In particular, social distrust encourages realistic appraisal of the operation of elites and the imperfections of democratic institutions without fostering the withdrawal of social mandates or the development of radical political movements aimed at regime-level change. Indeed, the absence of full trust in governmental institutions and representatives and the presence of distrust seem entirely consistent with the Madisonian conception of democracy in which any one economic interest is prevented from achieving dominance through the emergence of coalitions of other interests to hold it in check and to prescribe and limit the power of centralized authority.

So the pressing need is not to maximize trust but to concoct the appropriate mixtures of trust and distrust that should prevail within the political system. Different societies and political cultures presumably will function best with different mixture systems. And the appropriateness of the social-control mechanisms that arise out of distrust and how they function in the democratic system warrant greater attention. At the same time, levels of distrust cannot grow so high as to dissipate the reservoirs of social trust imperative for effective governance, thereby producing undue political transaction costs or threatening the stability of the political system, particularly at the regime or political-community levels.

INSIGHTS AND PROMISING AVENUES FOR EXPLORATION

The foregoing examination of recent writings on democratic theory, supplemented by our review of survey and poll data, suggests several insights about how social trust and risk issues may interact in a setting of democratic institutions and processes. It is clear, on the other hand, that a wide gap separates formal democratic theorizing and empirical studies of the role of social trust in risk controversies. The conjunction of empirical contributions in the rest of this volume and this tentative foray into democratic theory undoubtedly underscores this disjuncture. Nonetheless, the insights and hypotheses from this review may complement modestly some of the observations emanating from empirical studies.

Trust comes in different types, relates to different levels of the political system, and characterizes different relationships between people and aspects of democratic systems. These are often muddled in empirical research. In particular, social trust may relate to different levels of the political system – to institutions, the political regime, or, more basically, the political community itself. Survey results reveal that trust or confidence in the representatives of institutions is more transitory and superficial than trust in the institutions themselves. It is also apparent from studies of political culture that trust exists in some graduated or hierarchical form, with the deepest and most resilient forms associated with the more basic levels of the political system (ie, the regime and the political community). This suggests that losses of trust in institutional representatives or even institutions may be less dire than analysts often surmise, *provided* that trust in the more foundational levels of the political system remains strong. But what are the relationships among these different trust relationships? How do losses or gains in trust at one level affect trust patterns at other levels? Obviously we need a better understanding of those linkages and interlevel effects and the dynamics that shape change and stability. But in the meantime, making inferences from particular trust patterns to the functioning of democratic societies needs to proceed with utmost caution and restraint.

Although our understanding of how social trust emerges and is lost in different societies is incomplete, it seems clear that trust is the result of cumulative processes and protracted political socialization, attachment to culture, and continuing encounters with social institutions and political authority. Some democratic theorists would also point to structural characteristics of society and economy as well as the flow of major events shaping and anchoring public perceptions and assessments. These interpretations are at odds with the oft-proclaimed objective of building trust around a particular risk management effort or a particular sector of society. Risk decisions and management processes sit in a fabric of social trust that has emerged historically and that is stitched to other parts of the social system and political culture. How changes in trust occur in the context of this 'embedding' in social and cultural fabric, how durable such changes are, and what causal factors produce the greatest departures are clearly important to understand. In the meantime, expectations of the degree to which trust 'leverage' will contribute to virtue and good decisions, such as suggested in the 'cardinal rules of risk communication' (Covello and Allen 1988), may need tempering if not outright revision.

At least one conception of democracy regards social trust as one of the more important ingredients of social capital. Social capital refers to features of societies – such as social networks, norms, and trust – that increase their productive potentials. The presence of social capital is a major asset for effective and efficient governance, for widely based civic engagement and public participation, for conflict resolution, for political stability, and ultimately for enhanced economic growth and social well-being. How trust functions as social capital and how large stocks of such social capital may enhance the functioning of democratic institutions, including how matters of risk are addressed and negotiated, rather than contribute to elitism and more authoritarian systems, needs more careful empirical investigation.

Finally, conceptual and empirical studies have yet to grapple fully with social distrust, let alone prepare frameworks that open up new questions concerning its role in social and political processes. Discussions of the need for more trust generally proceed from a set of assumptions concerning the disutility and dysfunctional effects of distrust and, not uncommonly, reflect where the author sits. Yet it seems apparent that complete trust in political institutions and authority would be highly dangerous to democratic processes. Why, then, should we assume that greater levels of trust are necessarily advantageous to democratic societies? Indeed, the architecture of US constitutional authority reflects a high degree of distrust of any concentrations of elite power and political dominance. Greater attention, in our view, should centre on the positive functions of distrust rooted in rational assessments and on the mix of trust and distrust that serves different political systems and cultures.

3 Perceived Risk, Trust, and Democracy[1]

Paul Slovic

My objective in this paper is to examine the interplay between several remarkable trends within our society pertaining to the perception and management of risk.

The first of these trends is the fact that during a 20-year period during which our society has grown healthier and safer on average and spent billions of dollars and immense effort to become so, the American public has become more – rather than less – concerned about risk. We have come to perceive ourselves as increasingly vulnerable to life's hazards and to believe that our land, air, and water are more contaminated by toxic substances than ever before.

A second dramatic trend that I believe is closely related to the first is the fact that risk assessment and risk management – like many other facets of our society – have become much more contentious. Polarized views, controversy and overt conflict have become pervasive. Frustrated scientists and industrialists castigate the public for behaviour they judge to be based on irrationality or ignorance. Members of the public feel similarly antagonistic toward industry and government. A desperate search for salvation through risk communication efforts began in the mid-1980s yet, despite some localized successes, this effort has not stemmed the major conflicts or reduced much of the dissatisfaction with risk management.

Early studies of risk perception demonstrated that the public's concerns could not simply be blamed on ignorance or irrationality. Instead, research showed that many of the public's reactions to risk could be attributed to a sensitivity to technical, social and psychological qualities of hazards that were not well-modelled in technical risk assessments (eg, qualities such as

1. This is a revised version of the address given upon receipt of the Distinguished Contribution Award of the Society for Risk Analysis in Baltimore in December, 1991. Preparation of this paper was supported by the Alfred P. Sloan Foundation, the Electric Power Research Institute, and the National Science Foundation under Grant No. SES-91-10592. I wish to thank my colleagues at Decision Research for their contributions to the ideas and work underlying this paper. Jim Flynn, C.K. Mertz, and Leisha Mullican deserve special thanks in this regard. Marc Poumadere and Claire Mays assisted in the collection of the French data reported here. Howard Kunreuther provided valuable comments on the manuscript.

uncertainty in risk assessments, perceived inequity in the distribution of risks and benefits, and aversion to being exposed to risks that were involuntary, not under one's control, or dreaded). The important role of social values in risk perception and risk acceptance thus became apparent (Slovic 1987).

More recently, another important aspect of the risk-perception problem has come to be recognized. This is the role of trust. In recent years there have been numerous articles and surveys pointing out the importance of trust in risk management and documenting the extreme distrust we now have in many of the individuals, industries, and institutions responsible for risk management. This pervasive distrust has also been shown to be strongly linked to risk perception and to political activism to reduce risk (Bord and O'Connor 1990; Flynn et al 1992; Jenkins-Smith 1992; Mushkatel and Pijawka 1992; Slovic et al 1991).

In this paper I shall look beyond current perceptions of risk and distrust and attempt to explain how they came to be this way. My explanation begins with the idiosyncrasies of individual human minds, befitting my background as a psychologist. However, individual psychology is not fully adequate to account for risk perception and conflict. A broader perspective is necessary, one that includes the complex mix of scientific, social, political, legal, institutional, and psychological factors operating within our society's risk-management system.

THE IMPORTANCE OF TRUST

Everyone knows intuitively that trust is important for all forms of human social interaction. Perhaps because it is such a familiar concept, its importance in risk management has not been adequately appreciated. However, numerous recent studies clearly point to lack of trust as a critical factor underlying the divisive controversies that surround the management of technological hazards (Bella 1987; Bella et al 1988a,b; Cvetkovich and Earle 1992; English 1992; Flynn and Slovic 1993; Freudenburg 1991; Johnson 1992; Kasperson et al 1992; Laird 1989; Mitchell 1992; Pijawka and Mushkatel 1991/1992; Rayner and Cantor 1987; Renn and Levine 1991; US Dept of Energy 1992).

To appreciate the importance of trust, it is instructive to compare those risks that we fear and avoid with those we casually accept. Starr (1985) has pointed to the public's lack of concern about the risks from tigers in urban zoos as evidence that acceptance of risks is strongly dependent upon confidence in risk management. Similarly, risk perception research (Slovic 1990) documents that people view medical technologies based upon use of radiation and chemicals (ie, x-rays and prescription drugs) as high in benefit, low in risk, and clearly acceptable. However, they view industrial technologies involving radiation and chemicals (ie, nuclear power, pesticides, industrial chemicals) as high in risk, low in benefit, and unacceptable. Although x-rays and medicines pose significant risks, our relatively high degree of trust in the physicians who manage these devices makes them acceptable. Numerous polls have shown that the government and industry officials who oversee the management of nuclear power and nonmedical chemicals are not highly trusted (Flynn et al 1992; McCallum et al 1990; Pijawka and Mushkatel 1991/92; Slovic et al 1991).

During the past several decades, the field of risk assessment has developed to impart rationality to the management of technological hazards. Risk assessment has its roots in epidemiology, toxicology, systems analysis, reliability theory, and many other disciplines. Probably more than one billion dollars has been spent to conduct innumerable animal bioassays and epidemiological studies to assess the human health consequences of exposure to radiation and chemicals and to develop probabilistic risk analyses for nuclear reactors, dams, hazardous waste treatment, and other engineered facilities. The Environmental Protection Agency, the Nuclear Regulatory Commission, and numerous other government agencies have made risk assessment the centrepiece of their regulatory efforts (Levine 1984; Ruckelshaus 1983; USNRC 1983).

It is now evident that public perceptions and acceptance of risk from nuclear and chemical technologies are not much influenced by technical risk assessments. Nowhere is this phenomenon more dramatically illustrated than in the unsuccessful struggle, across many years, to dispose of the accumulating volume of spent fuel from the nation's commercial nuclear reactors. The Department of Energy's programme to establish a national repository has been stymied by overwhelming public opposition, fuelled by public perceptions that the risks are immense and unacceptable (Slovic et al 1991). These perceptions stand in stark contrast to the prevailing view of the technical community, whose risk assessments assert that nuclear wastes can be disposed of safely in an underground repository (see Box 3.1).

Public fears and opposition to nuclear waste disposal plans can be seen as a 'crisis in confidence', a profound breakdown of trust in the scientific, governmental, and industrial managers of nuclear technologies. It is clear that the Department of Energy and the US Congress have not adequately appreciated the importance of (dis)trust in the failure of the nuclear waste programme, nor have they recognized the implications of this situation (Slovic et al 1991; US Dept of Energy 1992). Analogous crises of confidence can be demonstrated in numerous controversies surrounding exposures to chemicals. Again, risk assessment, in these situations based primarily upon toxicology, is often impotent when it comes to resolving conflict about chemical risks (Graham et al 1988).

Because it is impossible to exclude the public in our uniquely participatory democracy, the response of industry and government to this crisis of confidence has been to turn to the young and still primitive field of risk communication in search of methods to bring experts and lay people into alignment and make conflicts over technological decisions easier to resolve – see, eg, William Ruckelshaus' stirring speeches on this topic (Ruckelshaus 1983, 1984), the National Academy of Sciences' report on risk communication (NRC 1989), and the Chemical Manufacturers' Association communication manual for plant managers (Covello et al 1988). Although attention to communication can prevent blunders that exacerbate conflict, there is rather little evidence that risk communication has made any significant contribution to reducing the gap between technical risk assessments and public perceptions or to facilitating decisions about nuclear waste or other major sources of risk conflict. The

Box 3.1 *Viewpoints on the risks from nuclear waste disposal*

The following comments reflect expert viewpoints on the risks from nuclear waste disposal and the public's perceptions of these risks.

'Several years ago... I talked with Sir John Hill, ... chairman of the United Kingdom's Atomic Energy Authority. 'I've never come across any industry where the public perception of the problem is so totally different from the problems as seen by those of us in the industry ...,' Hill told me. In Hill's view, the problem of radioactive waste disposal was, in a technical sense, comparatively easy.' (L J Carter, Nuclear Imperatives and Public Trust. Resources for the Future, Inc, Washington, DC, 1987)

'Nuclear wastes can be sequestered with essentially no chance of any member of the public receiving a non-stochastic dose of radiation. ... Why is the public's perception of the nuclear waste issue at such odds with the experts' perception?' (AM Weinberg, Public Perceptions of Hazardous Technologies and Democratic Political Institutions. Paper presented at Waste Management 1989, Tucson, Arizona, 1989,)

'The fourth major reason for public misunderstanding of nuclear power is a grossly unjustified fear of the hazards from radioactive waste ... there is general agreement among those scientists involved with waste management that *radioactive waste disposal is a rather trivial technical problem*.' (BL Cohen, *Before It's Too Late: A Scientist's Case for Nuclear Energy.* Plenum, New York, 1983)

'The risk is as negligible as it is possible to imagine ... It is embarrassingly easy to solve the technical problems, yet impossible to solve the political ones.' (HW Lewis, *Technological Risk.* WW. Norton, New York, 1990).

limited effectiveness of risk communication efforts can be attributed to the lack of trust. If you trust the risk manager, communication is relatively easy. If trust is lacking, no form or process of communication will be satisfactory (Fessendon-Raden et al 1987). Thus trust is more fundamental to conflict resolution than is risk communication.

CREATION AND DESTRUCTION OF TRUST

One of the most fundamental qualities of trust has been known for ages. Trust is fragile. It is typically created rather slowly, but it can be destroyed in an instant – by a single mishap or mistake. Thus, once trust is lost, it may take a long time to rebuild it to its former state. In some instances, lost trust may never be regained. Abraham Lincoln understood this quality. In a letter to Alexander McClure he observed: 'If you *once* forfeit the confidence of your fellow citizens, you can *never* regain their respect and esteem' [italics added].

The asymmetry between the difficulty of creating trust and the ease of destroying it has been studied by social psychologists within the domain of interpersonal perception. For example, Rothbart and Park (1986) had people rate 150 descriptive traits (adventurous, gentle, lazy, trustworthy, etc.) in terms of the number of relevant behavioural instances necessary to establish or disconfirm the trait. Favourable traits (like trustworthiness) were judged to be hard to acquire (many behavioural instances needed) and easy to lose. Unfavourable traits were judged to be easier to acquire and harder to lose. The number of behavioural instances required to disconfirm a negative quality (eg, dishonesty) was greater than the number required to disconfirm a positive trait. As Abraham Lincoln might have predicted, trustworthiness stood out among the 150 traits as requiring a relatively large number of confirming instances to establish the trait and a relatively small number of relevant instances to disconfirm it. (Note that data here were *judgements* of the number of instances that would be required as opposed to data documenting the number of instances that actually confirmed or disconfirmed a trait.)

The fact that trust is easier to destroy than to create reflects certain fundamental mechanisms of human psychology that I shall call 'the asymmetry principle'. When it comes to winning trust, the playing field is not level. It is tilted toward distrust for each of the following four reasons.

First, negative (trust-destroying) events are more visible or noticeable than positive (trust-building) events. Negative events often take the form of specific, well-defined incidents such as accidents, lies, discoveries of errors or other mismanagement. Positive events, while sometimes visible, more often are fuzzy or indistinct. For example, how many positive events are represented by the safe operation of a nuclear power plant for one day? Is this one event? Dozens of events? Hundreds? There is no precise answer. When events are invisible or poorly-defined, they carry little or no weight in shaping our attitudes and opinions.

Second, when events do come to our attention, negative (trust-destroying) events carry much greater weight than positive events. This important psychological tendency is illustrated by a study in which my colleagues and I asked 103 college students to rate the impact on trust of 45 hypothetical news events pertaining to the management of a large nuclear power plant in their community (Slovic et al 1993). Some of these events were designed to be trust increasing, such as:

- There have been no reported safety problems at the plant during the past year.
- There is careful selection and training of employees at the plant.
- Plant managers live nearby the plant.
- The county medical examiner reports that the health of people living near the plant is *better* than the average for the region.

Other events were designed to be trust decreasing, such as:

- A potential safety problem was found to have been covered up by plant officials.

- Plant safety inspections are delayed in order to meet the electricity production quota for the month.
- A nuclear power plant in another state has a serious accident.
- The county medical examiner reports that the health of people living near the plant is *worse* than the average for the region.

The respondents were asked to indicate, for each event, whether their trust in the management of the plant would be increased or decreased upon learning of that event. After doing this, they rated how strongly their trust would be affected by the event on a scale ranging from 1 (very small impact on trust) to 7 (very powerful impact on trust). The percentages of Category 7 ratings, shown in Figure 3.1, dramatically demonstrate that negative events are seen as far more likely to have a powerful effect on trust than are positive events.

The data shown in Table 3.1 are typical. The negative event, reporting plant neighbours' health as *worse* than average, was rated 6 or 7 on the impact scale by 50 per cent of the respondents. A matched event, reporting neighbours' health to be *better* than average, was rated 6 or 7 by only 18.3 per cent of the respondents.

There was only one event perceived to have any substantial impact on increasing trust. This event stated: 'An advisory board of local citizens and environmentalists is established to monitor the plant and is given legal authority to shut the plant down if they believe it to be unsafe.' This strong delegation of authority to the local public was rated 6 or 7 on the impact scale by 38.4 per cent of the respondents. Although this was a far stronger showing than for any other positive event, it would have been a rather average performance in the distribution of impacts for negative events.

Table 3.1 *Judged Impact of a Trust-Increasing Event and a Similar Trust-Decreasing Event*

| | Impact on Trust | | | | | | |
| | very small | | | | | very powerful | |
	1	2	3	4	5	6	7
Trust-Increasing Event The county medical examiner reports that the health of people living near the plant is *better* than average.	21.5	14.0	10.8	18.3	17.2	16.1	2.2
Trust-Decreasing Event The county medical examiner reports that the health of people living near the plant is *worse* than average.	3.0	8.0	2.0	16.0	21.0	26.0	24.0

Note: Cell entries indicate the percentage of respondents in each impact rating category.

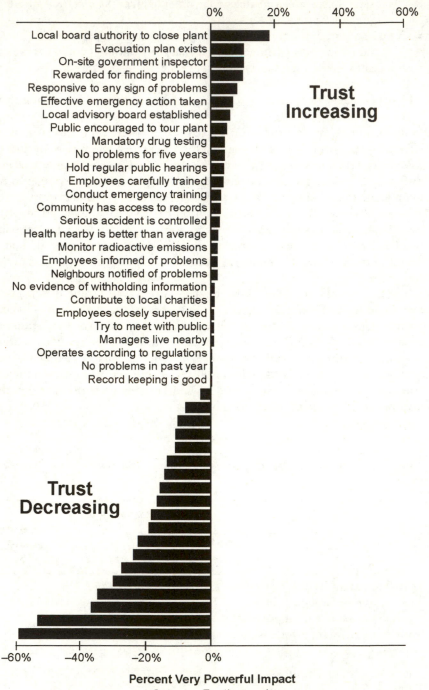

Figure 3.1 *Differential impact of trust-increasing and trust-decreasing events*

The reasons for the greater impact of trust-destroying incidents are complex and I shall not discuss them here except to note that the importance of an event is at least in part related to its frequency (or rarity). An accident in a nuclear plant is more informative with regard to risk than is a day (or even a large number of days) without an accident. Thus, in systems where we are concerned about low-probability/high consequence events, problematic events will increase our perceptions of risk to a much greater degree than favourable events will decrease them.

Third, adding fuel to the fire of asymmetry is yet another idiosyncracy of human psychology – sources of bad (trust-destroying) news tend to be seen as more credible than sources of good news. For example, in several studies of what we call 'intuitive toxicology'(Kraus et al 1992), we have examined people's confidence in the ability of animal studies to predict human health effects from chemicals. In general, confidence in the validity of animal studies is not particularly high. However, when told that a study has found that a chemical is carcinogenic in animals, people express considerable confidence in the validity of this study for predicting health effects in humans. Regulators respond like the public. Positive (bad news) evidence from animal bioassays is presumptive evidence of risk to humans; negative evidence (eg, the chemical was not found to be harmful) carries little weight (Efron 1984).)

Fourth, another important psychological tendency is that distrust, once initiated, tends to reinforce and perpetuate distrust. This occurs in two ways. First, distrust tends to inhibit the kinds of personal contacts and experiences that are necessary to overcome distrust. By avoiding others whose motives or actions we distrust, we never get to see that these people are competent, well-meaning, and trustworthy. Second, initial trust or distrust colours our interpretation of events, thus reinforcing our prior beliefs. Persons who trusted the nuclear power industry saw the events at Three Mile Island as demonstrating the soundness of the 'defence in depth' principle, noting that the multiple safety systems shut the plant down and contained most of its radiation. Persons who distrusted nuclear power prior to the accident took an entirely different message from the same events, perceiving that those in charge did not understand what was wrong or how to fix it and that catastrophe was averted only by sheer luck.

'THE SYSTEM DESTROYS TRUST'

Thus far I have been discussing the psychological tendencies that create and reinforce distrust in situations of risk. Appreciation of those psychological principles leads us toward a new perspective on risk perception, trust, and conflict. Conflicts and controversies surrounding risk management are not due to public irrationality or ignorance but, instead, can be seen as expected side effects of these psychological tendencies, interacting with our remarkable form of participatory democratic government, and amplified by certain powerful technological and social changes in our society. The technological change has given the electronic and print media the capability (effectively utilized) of informing us of news from all over the world – often right as it happens.

Moreover, just as individuals give greater weight and attention to negative events, so do the news media. Much of what the media reports is bad (trust-destroying) news (Lichtenberg and MacLean 1992). This is convincingly demonstrated by Koren and Klein (1991), who compared the rates of newspaper reporting of two studies, one providing bad news and one good news, published back to back in the March 20, 1991 issue of the *Journal of the American Medical Association*. Both studies examined the link between radiation exposure and cancer. The bad news study showed an increased risk to leukaemia in white men working at the Oak Risk National Laboratory. The good news study failed to show an increased risk of cancer in people residing near nuclear facilities. Koren and Klein found that subsequent newspaper coverage was far greater for the study showing increased risk.

The second important change, a social phenomenon, is the rise of powerful special interest groups – well funded (by a fearful public) and sophisticated in using their own experts and the media to communicate their concerns and their distrust to the public in order to influence risk policy debates and decisions (*Wall Street Journal* 1989). The social problem is compounded by the fact that we tend to manage our risks within an adversarial legal system that pits expert vs expert, contradicting each other's risk assessments and further destroying the public trust.

The young science of risk assessment is too fragile, too indirect to prevail in such a hostile atmosphere. Scientific analysis of risks cannot allay our fears of low-probability catastrophes or delayed cancers unless we trust the system. In the absence of trust, science (and risk assessment) can only feed distrust, by uncovering more bad news. A single study demonstrating an association between exposure to chemicals or radiation and some adverse health effect cannot easily be offset by numerous studies failing to find such an association. Thus, for example, the more studies that are conducted looking for effects of electric and magnetic fields or other difficult to evaluate hazards, the more likely it is that these studies will increase public concerns, even if the majority of these studies fail to find any association with ill health (MacGregor et al 1992; Morgan et al 1985). In short, risk assessment studies tend to increase perceived risk.

WHERE NEXT? RISK AND DEMOCRACY

Although the study of risk perception and trust has not yet led to a solution to our risk-management problems, it appears to be leading to a more adequate diagnosis of the root causes of risk concerns and risk conflicts. As we begin to understand the complexity of risk conflicts, we recognize the need for new approaches to risk management. The road branches in two very different directions (Fiorino 1989). One direction leads towards less public participation and more centralized control. One might call this the French model. France leads the world in the percentage of electricity generated by nuclear power (73 per cent in 1991, compared to 21 per cent for the US). France, like the US, was rocked by strong anti-nuclear protests during the late 1970s but the state acted forcefully to repress these protests and the anti-nuclear movement never gained favour with the political parties in power. Today, surprisingly, the perception of risk from nuclear power remains extremely high in France – as high as in the US, according to national surveys my colleagues and I recently conducted in both countries. However, French citizens, while recognizing that they have little control over risks to their health and safety, have a high degree of trust in their government and in the experts who design and operate nuclear power plants. Americans, in contrast, combine their similarly high degree of perceived risk with a distrust of government, science and industry, and a belief that they do have some ability to control risks. In fact, the US system does provide individual citizens and citizen groups considerable freedom to intervene in administrative proceedings, to question expert judgements of government agencies, and to force changes in policy through litigation (Jasanoff 1986).

Political scientists have recognized that, in a climate of strong distrust, the French approach, in which policy formation and implementation is not accessible to public intervention, is expedient (Moore and Woodhouse 1989). Campbell (1988), for example, argues that formal democratic institutions providing political access to nuclear critics may be fundamentally incompatible with commercial success of nuclear power.

What works in France, however, is unlikely to be achievable in the US. The French nuclear power programme is run by the state, not private industry. Electricité de France has long had a strong reputation for being competent and putting service above profits. The French have a tradition of looking to a scientific elite for guidance in policy matters. Jasper (1990), noting that the word as well as the image of a 'technocrat' arose in France, observed that 'Perhaps no other political system provides as large a role for people to exercise power on the basis of technical training and certification.'

The US, since Thomas Jefferson, has had a different approach to democracy and it is not surprising that attempts to restrict citizens' rights to intervene directly in national risk management policies have been vigorously opposed. A recent example is the unsuccessful attempt in Congress to strip the state of Nevada of its rights to issue environmental and safety permits for nuclear waste studies at Yucca Mountain (Batt 1992).

Given that the French approach is not likely to be acceptable in the US, restoration of trust may require a degree of openness and involvement with the public that goes far beyond public relations, and 'two-way communication' to encompass levels of power sharing and public participation in decision-making and that have rarely been attempted (Flynn et al 1992; Kunreuther et al 1993; Leroy and Nadler 1993). Even this, however, is no guarantee of success (Bord 1988; Nelkin and Pollak 1979). In many situations, we may have to recognize that relationships are so poisoned that trust and conflict resolution cannot realistically be achieved in the short-run. The bitter conflict over the proposed nuclear waste repository in Nevada is a prime example of such a situation. To preserve the form of democracy we value so highly, we will need to develop ways to work constructively in situations where we cannot assume that trust is attainable (Kasperson et al 1992).

We have a long way to go in improving our risk-management processes. Although we have expended massive amounts of time, money, and resources on scientific studies designed to identify and quantify risks, we have failed to expend the effort needed to learn how to manage the hazards that science is so good at identifying. Gerald Jacob (1990) frames the challenge well in the context of nuclear waste disposal, and his words are also relevant to many other risk problems:

> While everyone can appreciate that a complex, highly sophisticated engineering is required to safely store nuclear materials for thousands of years, few have appreciated the political requirements necessary to design and implement such a solution. While vast resources have been expended on developing complex and sophisticated technologies, the equally sophisticated political processes and institutions required to develop a credible and legitimate strategy for nuclear waste management have not been developed. The history of high-level radioactive waste management describes repeated failure to recognize the need for institutional reform and reconstruction.

Some may view the analysis in this paper as a depressing one. I do not. Understanding the root causes of social conflict and recognizing the need to create better risk-management processes are essential first steps toward improving the situation. It is far more depressing, in my view, to fail to understand the complex psychological, social, cultural, and political forces that dictate the successes and failures of risk management.

4 The Attribution of Social Trust

George Cvetkovich

Trust and distrust are expectations about the kind of relationship that one will likely have with another person or an organization.[1] This chapter discusses the psychological processes involved in arriving at these expectations. Consider that you have just learned from the newspaper that the officials of a local hazardous industrial facility previously unknown to you have been discovered concealing poor safety records. You also learn that the city government is currently negotiating evacuation plans with managers of the facility to be used should a major industrial accident occur. Certain options for the emergency preparations could be very costly to the company owning the facility. To what extent do you think the facility managers can be trusted to negotiate in the interests of the community? Even though there is very little information available, I venture most of us are able to make such an attribution about trust. Moreover, we do it rapidly and with little hesitation. From a phenomenological point of view the making of such attributions of trust seems so automatic and natural we might ask 'What is there to explain?' This chapter is one analytic effort to answer this question. The chapter is based on the assumption that the effort to systematically understand social trust attributions not only advances our general understanding of social trust but can provide insights useful to risk managers concerned about social trust.

THE SOCIAL PSYCHOLOGY OF TRUST ATTRIBUTIONS

The following seem to me to be reasonable conjectures about how attributions of trust occur. We can begin by assuming that attributions of trust include information available to us about the other person's behaviour. Behaviour such as verbal statements, regulatory and other actions (such as the above example of concealing safety information), and formulations of policy, are the 'raw' materials of social trust attributions. But any attribution is probably impossible

1. To simplify the presentation, I'll only refer to individuals. Most points made also apply to institutions.

to make based only on available information (Read 1987). Understanding of episodes of human behaviour requires knowing four things:

1. how the actions form a plan;
2. what the goals of the sequence are;
3. how this particular plan achieves the goals;
4. what conditions initiated the goals (Read 1987).

Rarely, if ever, do we have all of this information directly available to us. We are able to give meaning and make sense of our observations of others by adding to our observations the social knowledge stored in memory. It is through the interaction of the information available and our social knowledge, information that goes beyond the data given, that we arrive at attributions of trust (Bruner 1958). Tim Earle and I (1995) have argued that central to this sense making are conclusions (feelings, in most cases) that the one performing the behaviour shares the values that are salient to us at the time of the attribution. Values are preferences, most times unarticulated, about general goals and ways of doing things.

Implicit in the above characterization of social trust attribution is that there is a parallel typing of the observed behaviour and the individual committing the behaviour. Individuals who engage in behaviour judged to reflect salient shared values (that is, trustworthy behaviour) are typed as having the personal characteristic of trustworthiness. This leads to an expectation that the future relationship with this individual will be characterized by a continued application of shared values and, therefore, continued trustworthy behaviour. In the social psychology literature on attribution this inferential sequence from behaviour to disposition is known as a *correspondent inference* (Jones and Davis 1965). Inferences about the actor, as a person, and inferences about the actions correspond to each other. The sequence operates because we seek meaningful explanations that are stable and that allow understanding across situations. Dispositional characteristics of a person are stable tendencies to act in certain ways even though the circumstances may change.

So far we have considered the initial categorization of an individual as trustworthy or not. Once formed, attributions of trust tend to influence interpretations of subsequent behaviours. The same act committed by a trusted person may be differently interpreted if committed by one who is distrusted. The attributions about the sending of the US military to the Persian Gulf area by US Presidents George Bush and Bill Clinton might have differed depending on previous attributions of trustworthiness. Those who believed that President Bush was trustworthy because he was a war veteran and a supporter of the military, might conclude that his was a necessary, honourable act (a trustworthy act). Those who believed President Clinton was a draft dodger and opposed to the military, might conclude that he demonstrated disregard for the life and safety of US military personnel and acted for political reasons (an untrustworthy act).

The causal inferences leading to attributions of trust might involve either explicit or implicit reasoning. Explicit (conscious, analytic) reasoning is more likely to occur when it is not possible to easily make sense of an observed episode of behaviour. One must then resort to an active, conscious effort to create an explanation in which logic, explicit comparison, information seeking, and other analytic strategies might be applied. In social life this is apparently a relatively rare occurrence. Greenwald and Banaji (1995) have reviewed extensive evidence showing that social behaviour often operates in an implicit or unconscious fashion. Research on attitudes, self-esteem, and stereotypes illustrates this by showing that 'past experience influences judgement in a fashion not introspectively known to the actor'. Studies on the judgement of credibility also indicate the operation of implicit processes.

It has been argued that implicit forms of inference are preferred because they operate rapidly and reduce cognitive complexity (Earle and Cvetkovich 1995). Attributions of trust are most often implicitly formed. This suggests that implicit attributions of trust will be strongly influenced by past experiences and the context in which the attribution is made and that the person making the attribution will be unaware of these influences. To summarize, the above sketch indicates:

1. Trust attributions when first formed or when revised begin with inferences about value similarity based on a combination of observed behaviour and existing social knowledge.
2. There is a tendency to make corresponding attributions about observed behaviour and the personal characteristics of the person committing the behaviour.
3. Once established, attributions of trust influence, up to a point, interpretations of actions. Actions are inferred to have the same character as the dispositional category of the person committing them. (Of course, if a trusted individual begins committing what are considered to be untrustworthy acts, our characterization of her may change.)
4. Attributions of social trust are more frequently the result of implicit reasoning than explicit reasoning.

STUDIES OF THE ATTRIBUTION OF SOCIAL TRUST

This chapter focuses on the initial formation of trust attributions. Reported here are the results of three studies demonstrating some of the characteristics of implicit social cognition, social knowledge, and cognitive processes involved in the attribution of trust as well as the importance of salient values similarity.

Study 1. Salient Values Similarity and Trust

As already noted, Timothy Earle and I have argued that inferences about shared salient values are central to the making of attributions of trust (Earle and Cvetkovich 1995). Persons who are judged to share values which the individual believes are important to the making of decisions and the taking of actions in a particular domain (ie, salient values) will be trusted. This study investigated some implications of salient values similarity theory. As part of a public participation effort in forest management, meetings were held regarding planned research on US national forest lands in the Hayfork Adaptive Management Area of northern California (Cvetkovich, Winter and Earle 1995). Citizen participants had been mailed descriptions of the planned research. At the meetings a more detailed description of the plans, including their scientific and practical justification, was presented by a National Forest Service staff member, followed by the opportunity to ask questions. Responses to a questionnaire completed at the end of the meetings indicated four significant predictors of trust judgements. These predictors in the order that they were identified by a sequential multiple regression analysis are as follows. Those who rated their trust in the National Forest Service researchers as high were likely to judge that: a) the researchers shared the rater's values ($ß = .46$; Adjusted $R^2 = .79$); b) the rater understood the research design ($ß = .30$; Adjusted $R^2 = .85$); c) the research plan was taking forest management in the right direction ($ß = .31$; Adjusted $R^2 = .90$); and were more likely to be d) males ($ß = .18$; Adjusted $R^2 = .93$). It is noteworthy that ratings having to do with whether the citizen understood the specific reasons and goals of the research project, approved of the project, or assessed the technical competency of the researchers as high, were not significant predictors of the trust judgements.

This field study supports the conclusion of several earlier experimental studies (Earle and Cvetkovich 1995; 1997; Chapter 1, this volume) which also show that judged communality of values is related to attributions of social trust. Our previous research, like this study, also indicates that competency is only one value that may be salient in a given context. Results of the present study are also compatible with those of other recent work showing that judgements of credibility can precede assessments of technical competency (Jungermann, Pfister and Fischer 1996). It has often been argued that technical competency and other characteristics directly related to responsibility are fundamental to trust attributions (see Earle and Cvetkovich 1995 and Johnson, Chapter 5, this volume, for reviews). These formulations overlook the possibility that the direction of inference may be reversed. Those who are trusted may be positively evaluated in a number of ways, including being judged as technically competent. Taken together, this research suggests that efforts to understand social trust should focus on social knowledge relating to the judgement of common values, rather than only to those having to do with the direct assessment of competency.

Study 2. Context Effects, Social Cognition and Trust

As noted earlier, implicit social cognition can be significantly influenced by context. This study investigated the effects of context in cueing implicit comparisons between the social perceiver and the person being judged. People were cued to either think of how they were the same or different from those who have the responsibility for managing risks. Thinking about how risk managers are different from oneself should activate thoughts leading to conclusions that the managers share few values. Thinking about how risk managers are the same as oneself should activate thoughts leading to conclusions that the managers share values. The basic Salient Values Similarity model then leads to the expectation that those who are thinking that risk managers are different from themselves will have less trust than those who are thinking that risk managers are similar to themselves. Forty-six college students were asked to 'consider how your views are different than (or the same as) those responsible for managing hazards' and to 'list five things that make you different (or the same).' Participants were then asked to rate, using five-point scales, the risks of ten health hazards including bacterial contamination of food, climate change, chemical pollution, earthquakes, storms, and floods and to rate on a 7-point scale how much they trusted those who have been given the responsibility to manage each risk.

Those who had activated thoughts about how they were different from risk managers made higher ratings of risk and lower ratings of trust than did those who had activated thoughts about how they were the same (mean risk judgements for 'Similar' and 'Different' Conditions, respectively, equal 2.6 and 2.9; $F = 10.19$; $p = .004$). Males made lower risk ratings than did females (means = 2.46 and 2.91; $F = 9.13$, $p = .004$). There was a significant negative correlation between ratings of risk and judgements of trust ($r = -.40$, $p < .05$). These results replicate those of Flynn, Slovic and Mertz (1994) who also identified a connection between judgements of risk and trust with persons who rated risks as high being less trusting. In a comparison of gender and racial groups the national survey by Flynn et al also showed that white males were more likely to judge risks as lower than were white females and non-whites of both genders. Flynn et al explained their findings on the basis of differences in power, status, alienation, and trust. The Salient Values Similarity theory adds another dimension to these explanations. It suggests that judgements of power, status, alienation, and trust might be the result of attributions about those who make decisions affecting one's life chances. Inferences that those with decision-making power share one's values lead to a sense of having power, high status, of not being alienated, and of greater trust.

Interestingly, differences between means for males and females in the present study were 0.7 in the Similar Condition versus 0.2 in Different Condition. This suggests that it may be more difficult for females to think of ways that they are similar to (mostly male) hazard managers than it is for males to think of ways that they might be different from risk managers.

Study 3. Order of Events, Social Cognition and Trust

Read (1987) cites evidence demonstrating the effects of order of events on scenario construction and resulting attribution inferences. Study participants who learned about the same events, but in reverse order, arrived at quite different conclusions about the individual depicted. For example, learning that an individual had expressed regret that an owner had failed to renew his store's insurance policy the day before a fire tended to produced the impression that the person was a gangster who had threatened the store owner. Learning that the person had expressed regret after the fire tended to produced the impression that the person was a friend of the owner. First heard events activate particular memories that establish a context for the interpretation of subsequent events.

Another example of sequence effects is given by the order of books in the Jewish Bible (the *Tanakh*) and the Old Testament of the Christian Bible. Miles

(1996) relates that the technology of book binding required that the books of the Bible be placed in a single sequence, a requirement not imposed when the books were kept on individual scrolls. Both Bibles contain the same content. But, Miles concludes, because of their different sequences, they are not quite the same work. 'The distinctive, broad movement of the Hebrew Bible from (God's) action to speech to silence is not matched in the Old Testament, whose movement is from action to silence to speech.' He argues that the Christian editor consciously placed the prophecies (God speaking) at the end of the Old Testament presumably because '. . . in this position the prophets would better announce their relationship to the now immediately following Gospels. Christianity believes that the life of Christ is the fulfilment of prophecy. The Gospels that open the New Testament make this point repeatedly. The Christian editor edited the Hebrew Bible to reflect this Christian Belief'.

The importance of the order in which information is learned and its effects on establishing context are supported by Slovic's (1995) review of two decades of research on preferences. Preferences are often constructed in the process of elicitation. Methods that are normatively equivalent yield 'preference reversals' resulting from the different ordering of options.

The 73 college students who participated in this study learned about two events that supposedly had occurred at each of six toxic chemical plants. The events were paraphrases of those used by Slovic (Chapter 3, this volume). One of each pair of events had been identified by Slovic as potentially having a strong effect on increasing trust and the other as potentially having a strong effect on decreasing trust. Examples of 'trust-increasing' events are 'an evacuation plan is developed with local authorities' and 'local board has authority to close plant'. Examples of 'trust-decreasing' events are 'records were falsified' and 'employees were found drunk on the job'. The order of the events describing each plant was reversed for half of the participants. Individuals who first leaned of the 'trust-increasing' event were less trusting of the plant officials (M = 5.06; S.D. = .77) than individuals learning of the events in the reverse order (M = 5.56; S.D. = .78; F = 6.62; p = .013) (see Figure 3.1).

Trust ratings of the two-event descriptions were also compared to the trust ratings by 48 additional college students who were provided with each of the 'trust-increasing' and 'trust-decreasing' events alone. For example, with the two-event descriptions, participants were asked to rate the trustworthiness of managers of a single plant where both 'It was discovered that records about the safety of the plant operations had been falsified (trust-decreasing event)' and 'through negotiations between plant administration and local government officials a local board of citizens was established that reviewed the plant operations and had authority to close plant if the plant seems unsafe'. With the one-event descriptors participants were asked to rate the trustworthiness of managers of one plant where 'it was discovered that records about the safety of the plant operations had been falsified (trust-decreasing event)'. They also were asked to rate the trustworthiness of managers of another plant where 'through negotiations between plant administration and local government officials a local board of citizens was established that reviewed the plant operations and had authority to close plant if the plant seems unsafe'. The one event descriptor task is equivalent to that used by Slovic (Chapter 3).[2] The mean trust ratings for both single 'trust-increasing' events and for two-event descriptions, regardless of order of events, are high. Mean trust ratings for single 'trust-increasing' events and two-event descriptions with the 'trust-increasing' event first were almost identical. Two-event descriptions and the single event 'trust-increasing' descriptions produced significantly higher mean trust ratings than did the one-event 'trust-decreasing' descriptions (F = 81.4; p = .0001).

Two points are applicable to these findings. First, the results demonstrate that order affects context and that context does make a difference to trust ratings. Second, they raise questions about the asymmetry principle of trust. Slovic argues that it is easier to lose trust than to regain it. The basis for the argument are judgements of single event descriptions – 'trust-decreasing' events had a larger effect than did 'trust-increasing' events. When this study compares single-event descriptions and the richer-context two-event descriptions, it is found that 'trust-decreasing' events have little if any effect when they are paired with a 'trust-increasing' event'. 'Trust-increasing' events have a large effect when they follow a 'trust-decreasing' event. In this position they significantly increase trust judgements compared to single-event 'trust-decreasing' descriptions. The asymmetry principle leads to the expectation, not confirmed in this study, that two-event descriptions, since they contain a 'trust-decreasing' event, should produce lower trust judgements than do single 'trust-increasing' events.

CONCLUSION

This chapter considers the process used in the making of attributions of social trust. The three reported studies provide further evidence that an inference of salient-value similarity parallels an attribution of trustworthiness (Study 1) and that trust attributions are affected by the operational characteristics of implicit social cognition such as accessibility (Study 2) and the sequence (context) of learning the information on which inferences are based (Study 3). Together the studies demonstrate the profitability of continuing work on social knowledge and the implicit cognitive processing involved in social trust attributions.

Efforts to understand trust attributions should continue to investigate how inferences of salient value similarity are constructed. In doing this, efforts should be made to explore questions concerning values in addition to those about judgements of expertise and competency. Talcott Parson (1970), some time ago, described the basic paradox of trust judgements based on an evaluation of technical expertise. A person without expertise in an area can not rationally evaluate the technical competence of an expert. On logical grounds, assuming Parson's premise, trust can not be based on an assessment of competence in

2. The response scales used by Slovic and those used in this study differ. This study requested direct ratings of trust. Slovic asked for ratings of the 'how big of an effect would learning this have on your trust?'

the limited sense of technical expertise. Empirical evidence that people do not make trust judgements based largely on technical expertise is growing. In line with the research reported earlier, Frewer, Howard, Hedderley and Shepherd (1996), in discussing their recent research on the credibility of sources of information about the risk and safety of food, state: 'freedom (to provide information) and expertise do not, in themselves, lead to trust in information, but must be associated with other factors'. 'Competence' as used in common attributions seems to have a broader meaning than technical expertise. An additional point that can be made is that efforts by risk managers at emphasizing their technical competence may actually reduce trust. To the extent that this emphasis gives the message that the risk managers are different from the public, it may induce thoughts of value dissimilarity, rather than similarity.

Attributions are not only the product of individual thinking, but are reflections of social knowledge. Elsewhere we have argued that trust and distrust are cultural tendencies which, once adopted, operate to reduce complexity and facilitate the implicit processing of judgements of others (Earle and Cvetkovich 1995). Thus, in their effort to make sense and give meaning to their experiences with risk managers, citizens in 'trust' cultures have a tendency to use cultural narratives that generate an attribution of trust. The converse is true of citizens of 'mistrust' cultures like the US. This suggests that understanding of how these cultural influences operate will come through the understanding of citizens' models of how the 'system' works and how common, available models of shared categories of social groups such as 'bureaucrat' or 'politician' are accepted and used (Read and Miller 1993). Such research, for example, might provide answers to questions about the connection between the attributions about individuals who represent institutions and attributions about the institutions being represented (see Kasperson, Golding and Kasperson, Chapter 2, this volume).

Commonly, trust attributions are characterized by the use of implicit cognitive processes. It is not that we can not or do not ever use more explicit, conscious, analytic means for reaching conclusions about others. Under normal conditions we usually do not because of the functional advantages of implicit cognition. It is quicker and less energy intensive than more explicit cognitive processes (Earle and Cvetkovich 1995). One consequence of this is that attributions are highly affected by context effects, as illustrated by Studies 2 and 3. Another consequence is that people are not aware that their judgement *is* being affected by context.

It also seems the case that the context in which the environmental manager operates may not influence the attribution of trustworthiness of the manager. Frewer et al's (1996) study of the credibility of sources of information about food safety indicates a tendency for attributions not to consider extenuating circumstances. For example, a source tended to be mistrusted regardless of the reasons for withholding information. Attributions of mistrust occurred even if the withholding of information was for reasons of confidentiality, rather than potential vested interest.

In attempting to explain the general tendency of attributions to overlook constraints and other situational characteristics that might be accounting for the behaviour observed, Thorpe and Higgins (1993) argue that situational inducements are commonly assumed to have different effects on different behaviour. Commonly, they argue, it is assumed that a situation can make anyone act immorally or not do well – good people can go bad, under appropriate conditions. But, it is argued, people believe that a situation can not make someone act morally or do well. A person must be already inclined in this direction to act so. Therefore, attributions commonly concluded that immoral or otherwise unsatisfactory behaviour is a reflection of personal characteristics, not extenuating situational conditions.

Taken together, these considerations suggest the possibility that: a) acts judged untrustworthy lead to attributions that the actor has the characteristic of untrustworthiness, despite situational conditions constraining behaviour (as illustrated by the Frewer et al (1996) results), but also, b) trustworthy acts committed because of situational conditions lead to characterizations of the actor as trustworthy, nevertheless. Whether both are true or not must await further investigation. Such investigation is certainly justified given the vexing issues posed by either. With regard to 'a', managers at many levels face legal, resource, historical, and other limits on what they can say and do. Attributions uninfluenced by considerations of these limits increase the likelihood that managers will be mistrusted, regardless of their intentions. With regard to 'b', attributions uninfluenced by considerations of situational requirements would not seem to be good predictors of behaviour in situations lacking those requirements. The salient values similarity construction suggests that managers faced with 'a' might do well to indicate explicitly how their adherence to constraints on their behaviour reflects common values, such as respect for confidentiality. It may not be likely that managers in situations characterized by 'b' will conclude that they have much of a problem. They are essentially getting a free ride. It is, however, in the general interest that considerations be given to how frequently this happens and whether it should be of concern.

5 Trust Judgements in Complex Hazard Management Systems: The Potential Role of Concepts of the System

Brand B Johnson

Trust has attracted great interest for its potential role in both general social interaction and the specific activities involved with managing (preventing, reducing, avoiding, etc.) hazards of various kinds. Much research on the latter topic has focused on how much particular actors (eg, government, industry, environmentalists, Environmental Protection Agency, Department of Energy) are trusted, the origins of such trust, and how trust judgements affect estimates and evaluations of risk, among other outcomes. My focus here is on whether our understanding of the role and nature of trust would benefit from exploring how the trust judge conceives of the system of hazard managers. I shall attempt to show that this neglected issue raises some useful questions about the motivations and processes of trust judgements.

HAZARD MANAGEMENT SYSTEMS

It does not take much imagination to recognize that various institutions, groups and individuals can be thought of as forming a hazard management system (HMS) for a given issue. Take the example of drinking water safety. In a state like New Jersey, drinking water can come to the consumer through three channels: utility-provided tapwater, private residential wells (serving about 11 per cent of the population), and bottled water. Utility and private wellwater can be substitutes, most often when local pollution or suburban expansion into rural areas leads people to abandon their private wells to hook up to utility water lines. Bottled water can be a substitute for (as a temporary replacement for contaminated water, or a long-term replacement on grounds of taste or safety, for example) or a complement to the other channels.

Each channel is governed by a complex of entities whose joint efforts tend to provide safe drinking water; in New Jersey, these HMSs overlap (without being identical) for the three channels. The utility system includes federal regulators, state regulators, private and public water utilities, purveyors of in-home water treatment systems, and consumers, among others. The wellwater system includes state regulators (but largely a different set than those overseeing utilities), local health officials, private well drillers, septic tank installers, purveyors of in-home water treatment systems, and consumers, among others. The bottled-water system includes federal officials (a different agency from those regulating utility waters), state regulators (largely a separate set from those regulating the other two drinking-water channels), private bottled water firms, owners (if not the bottled-water firms) of sources of drinking water, retailers of bottled water, and consumers, among others. Environmentalists, politicians and journalists may perform an episodic role, particularly to provide information and to oversee others' performance in managing the safety of drinking water. Knowingly or not, whether as a primary goal or as a means to other ends, each of these actors affects the level of risk from drinking water, either directly or through its impact on such factors as judgements of trust or risk (Johnson 1999). Although the systemic nature of most hazard management is obvious to all but the most casual observer, research to date has asked for – and its methods are only capable of analysing – judgements on trustworthiness of individual managers considered one at a time (see Methods, below). Although this approach is valuable, a more direct assessment of the HMS role in trust judgements would be a useful complement.

TRUST AND THE HAZARD MANAGEMENT SYSTEM

I suggest that for many people the question of trust in a particular actor is pertinent only in certain situations (see Constraints, below), and that in general trust tends to be a far more global entity. For example, the implicit (that is, tending to habit) trust judgement about drinking water for most people day to day is likely to be 'Do I trust that the hazard management system is acting to ensure that my water is safe to drink?' Of course, if they ever made this question explicit to themselves, they would tend to ask only whether they trusted that their utility-supplied or private well or bottled water was safe; the HMS is likely to be implied rather than directly acknowledged. I would argue that this global or systemic judgement of trust applies in many other cases most of the time, whether those cases involve something as familiar as automobile driving or electricity use, or as new as bungee jumping or biotechnology.

This argument is based on an understanding of trust judgements as being both purposive and cognitively constrained (for the latter, see Earle and Cvetkovich 1995). Trust is not an end in itself, but only one among many means to other ends, including gaining a tolerable or acceptable level of safety from hazards within whatever constraints are salient to the trust judge. If trust is a better way to achieve that goal than distrust (eg, because of relative effectiveness or costs), one will trust; if not, one will choose another strategy. It is not necessary (although sometimes it might be helpful) to decide the trustworthiness of individual managers of drinking water safety before deciding how well the perceived HMS as a whole achieves safe drinking water. The cognitive demand is less for judging trust in the HMS than it is for summing judgements of trust for each of several hazard managers. And, I will argue (see Constraints, below), specific managers for most threats are likely to come to mind only on special occasions.

There is at least one potential drawback to assuming that people judge the trustworthiness of the system more often than they do that of individual hazard managers. The systemic trust judgement, as people are likely to think of it to themselves (see above), comes perilously close to being an evaluation of the safety of the drinking water: an evaluation of which trust might be presumed to be a cause, or predictor, or correlative. Only if people spontaneously (that is, in the presence of a researcher without directive prompting) phrase their trust in terms of unspecified actions by the HMS as a whole could researchers be confident that they are not inadvertently forcing people to conflate trust judgement and hazard evaluation. However, it is not obvious that most people keep these two judgements distinct in their minds most of the time for most hazards. In the absence of researchers asking questions, cognitive efficiency would encourage such conflation, whether by a judgement of trust largely determining how dangerous a hazard is deemed to be or a judgement of hazardousness largely determining one's level of trust. The low to moderate amount of variance in hazard estimates and evaluation explained by trust judgements evoked for specific hazard managers may be due in part to the hidden effect of this global judgement of trust; without it, the variance explained might be higher. Only careful empirical work can test either of these speculations.

The system performance thesis, however, has a second implication for trust judgements of specific hazard managers that is both more useful for understanding specific situations and that makes it unnecessary for us to rely on undirected global judgements of trust to test the thesis. If the baseline criterion for trust is HMS performance, then trust judgements of specific hazard managers might be shaped by people's conception of the members and roles of the HMS. Suppose one conceives of drinking water quality as affected only by private water providers, with no regulatory body involved. High trust in hazard management might occur if one believes the market ensures the utility's competence, care, or sharing of values. (Although, strictly speaking, water utilities are monopolies within their service areas, except for bottled water, so that market competition is largely irrelevant.) If one expects private utilities to be willing to let water quality deteriorate if this increases financial returns, one would have low trust in the HMS. Or one might cope with the cognitive dissonance of being completely at the utility's mercy for safe drinking water through denial, and report high trust (this variant response is not pertinent to the current argument). Adding members to one's mental model of the HMS could alter the dynamics of trust and risk judgements. One might, for example, see government as a guardian of the public interest or as in collusion with the private utility to hide the true risks. One who expects government regulators to be strict and competent overseers of utilities might exhibit high trust in the overall system, despite continuing to see private utilities as profit-hungry. Or perhaps the trust judge would reduce trust in the system, believing government oversight will degrade otherwise optimal performance of the marketplace.

Furthermore, judgements of trust in the utility part of this two-party HMS might rise slightly now that one does not seem solely reliant on the utility for safe water. If government and industry are seen as colluders, however, trust in HMS performance is likely to be particularly low, and perhaps reduce the individual institutions' judged trustworthiness compared to their ratings otherwise. Expansion of the HMS model to include three or more parties complicates the dynamics and the possible roles. For example, would people treat journalists or environmentalists as hazard managers in the same sense as they do (or should, according to experts) water treatment facility managers or regulators? But the hypothesized effects on judgements of trust for the overall system and for its individual members would be roughly the same no matter how large, or what the membership, of the system.

If this second proposition is true, how do people judge trust in the overall HMS? In the preceding paragraph I seem to imply a cognitively demanding approach: one has to know (or believe one knows) the aims and competence and potential interactions of each member of the imagined system to weigh their aggregate impact on the hazard. But that is the most demanding, and probably rarest, form of the HMS cognitive model; it might occur primarily among formal hazard managers themselves. A much less intensive approach would only require that people have developed an affective judgement of each member of their, perhaps much less populated, HMS model (see Slovic 1997 for discussion of the potential role of affect in risk judgements generally). If they combined these with an additive judgement process, they would simply count the number of good (eg, trying to keep water safe) and bad (not trying for, or actively opposing, safety) actors in the system, deciding trust in HMS performance on which side is in the majority. If negative news has greater signal value (Slovic 1993; see Earle and Cvetkovich 1995 for a criticism of this proposition), bad will probably win in a tie, assuming that the respective sides are deemed equal in power, while good needs at least a simple majority. For example, political scientists have suggested that negative attitudes toward the US federal government might be determined by negative views of Congress, seen as a much more central institution than the presidency or the Supreme Court, despite reasonably positive views of the latter (Hibbing and Theiss-Morse 1995). The true level of complexity in any individual's cognitive model of a HMS, and the distribution of such complexity across a population, would need to be assessed before we decide that HMS-based trust judgements are too complex and cognitively demanding to occur in real life.

My last argument for considering the role of the HMS in direct judgements of trust (as opposed to its impact on the sources of trust – see next section) is more philosophical than empirical. A plausible argument is that trust requires choice; without a choice, there is no judgement to make (Luhmann 1988). Luhmann posed this as a choice between trusting and not trusting, not as a choice between trust in one entity and trust in another. However, if a decision whether to take action to prevent harm is mandatory in the face of hazard unless one just accepts that death will come, the difference between these two choices is unclear. In other words, either I can decide to take action or not against danger, or someone else can; either I can take that action when the choice is made, or someone else can. If I choose not to trust the other entity, I am in effect trusting myself to make the choice or take the protective action. Even on the simplest level, then, we are dealing with a two-entity HMS. If in the way we study trust we implicitly assume that only one hazard manager is available to be judged for trustworthiness, by Luhmann's criterion trust, paradoxically, is not the kind of judgement our subjects are being asked to make. They are showing confidence (Luhmann 1995), or hope, self-knowledge, and retreat (Earle and Cvetkovich 1995), but not judging trustworthiness, in the absence of the choice that the HMS concept allows. This is a radical view, and chances asserting that only trust research based on the HMS approach could be valid, since other methods (see below) imply that people make trust judgements one group or institution at a time. I do not make that claim, but it forces us to be somewhat clearer about what we think people are doing when we ask for their estimate of the trustworthiness of government or industry or environmentalists.

HMS Impact on the Sources of Trust

My primary thesis concerns the direct impact of HMS understandings on trust judgements of the overall system and of its constituents. However, it is remotely possible that system understandings would affect the causes or origins of trust. In another paper (Johnson 1999) I reviewed several hypotheses advanced by scholars, including attributions of trust to judgements of competence, fiduciary responsibility, fairness, and shared values, among others. Some scholars suggest one of these factors dominates trust production (eg, Earle and Cvetkovich, 1995), while others offer more eclectic views; at least one (Metlay 1996) has suggested trust is instead only one-dimensional.

One could conceive of people judging competence and so forth entirely independently for each actor in an HMS. For example, the US Environmental Protection Agency's (EPA) judged competence, tendency to take others' interests into account (fiduciary responsibility), or degree of shared values (eg, egalitarianism; health as the sole criterion for decision-making) with the trust judge might have no connection with how the judge rates a third party's standing on these measures. If these factor judgements are indeed independent across judged actors, and these factors indeed determine trust judgements, then we should expect trust in one actor to be independent of trust in another, contrary to my earlier thesis.

However, judgements of these qualities for one actor need not be independent of judgements of others' expression of them. If the HMS is considered a team, skills one member has should either reinforce or complement others' skills, not conflict with them. If one member is the only one with a vital set of skills, its competence may be far more acceptable (if above some minimally satisfactory level) than if it was one of several with those skills, and perhaps not even the best. Fairness, to the extent that it concerns such factors as access to decision-makers (eg, see Weatherford 1992), applies a lot to one or a very few actors (those who control the structure of public participation, for example) and not at all to others, and thus would tend toward being an independent judgement (ie, not dependent on one's mental model of the HMS). Yet if fairness is conceived of as respect for each other's right to voice beliefs (as in a Habermasian decision process – see Webler 1995), then judgements of one person's fairness may depend on the mutual interaction among multiple parties. Fiduciary responsibility (acting on behalf of others' interests) or values-sharing will also be subject to interdependence, if relative positions of institutions on these factors are important to trust judgements. For example, someone might disagree with bigness, and the lack of fiduciary responsibility or shared values it implies, in both industry and government. However, one or the other institution might still rate more trust depending upon such beliefs as the immorality of profit or that the multiplicity of corporations makes them smaller threats than apparently monolithic government.

If these speculations are accurate, and people are willing to commit the cognitive resources needed for these judgements, the HMS they have in their thoughts about the issue will structure their judgements about HMS members' relative rank on whatever dimensions, whether competence or shared values, enter into trust judgements. Furthermore, to the extent that they have more than one member in their conceptual HMS, the very importance of these factors in trust judgements (as opposed to their magnitude as ascribed to different actors) may vary depending upon their attribution across the HMS. For example, if most or all hazard managers are deemed to have roughly equal competence, this factor may drop out of estimates of trust in favour of something (such as fiduciary responsibility or shared values) that does seem to discriminate among them. Alternatively, high or low judged levels of one quality in one actor may be deemed to offset high or low judged levels of another quality in another actor (see Renn and Levine 1991, who postulated such trade-offs in trust judgements of a given actor). Whether people go to such (relatively great) cognitive lengths to make trust judgements is an open question (Johnson 1999; also see Earle and Cvetkovich 1995), but we cannot test this hypothesis for the role of various attributes in judgements of trust for an entire HMS using the current research methods (see below).

CONSTRAINTS ON DOMINANCE OF HMS CONCEPTS IN TRUST JUDGEMENTS

Although I am arguing that hazard-trust researchers have neglected the systemic aspect of hazard management, I do not believe that HMS concepts will dominate trust judgements in all cases. Certain constraints might limit the applicability of my propositions: the existence of external cues and prompting; the role of culture and history; and whether judgements are of trust or distrust.

Whether trust judgements focus on the system or on individual actors is likely to depend upon the number of signals and prompting coming from others (whether the actors themselves or third parties, such as the mass media). For example, specific managers of drinking water risks are likely to come to mind on particular occasions: a bill arrives from the utility at a time when safety is salient (eg, one's water tastes bad); someone claims in the news media that one's water supply is (or is not) safe to drink, or that one or another manager has or has not done its job properly; someone proposes an activity (eg, siting a waste facility) that might seem to threaten one's water supply. Absent these circumstances, one will likely trust in the safety of the current water supply, or distrust its safety and switch to another source, without taking into account one's trust of particular water managers. Cues are also likely to vary in the range of actors that they bring to mind. For example, an announcement of industrial pollution that specifies the polluter makes that firm a prime candidate for a trust judgement; several government entities probably are potential candidates, but which ones will be considered in a given judgement may vary widely; candidates for environmental groups may not come to mind at all in some cases. In contrast to the drinking water example, nuclear radiation (whether for power plants or waste) has been subject to decades of media and policymakers' attention, including claims of mismanagement, producing nearly constant cueing. If dimensions of 'perceived risk' are pertinent to trust judgements, it is newer and has greater catastrophic potential than water (Slovic et al 1980). Under these conditions, many people might have trust judgements of specific actors (eg, the nuclear industry or the Department of Energy) already in mind when asked about these issues, in a way that they might not if asked about drinking water. This would not necessarily mean that HMS judgements are irrelevant, but under such conditions they would compete for one's attention with judgements of specific hazard managers.

Obviously the nature of the conceptual HMS (size; respective responsibilities of actors) will vary across not only hazards and individuals, but across time and nations, and in turn any effects they have on trust and risk judgements might vary as well. For example, until denationalization under Thatcher, UK water systems were owned and run by the national government; regional systems existed, but policy was set in London, with little autonomy for the regions. Thus regulators of drinking water safety and purveyors of water (who did the treatment, etc) were essentially one and the same. We should thus have expected different conceptual HMSs (and perhaps trust judgements) among UK water consumers of the time than in the New Jersey system described earlier, which has a private sector and a much more complex public sector. More subtly, historical or cultural experiences might foster aims for and expectations of hazard management systems that vary across trust judges. For example, Americans have long been known as distrustful of government, more so than among most Europeans, for example, and the architects of US national government deliberately designed a system with multiple centres of power, so that none would become too strong. This history is still fresh, in rhetoric at least: note the constant deploring by elites of gridlock in Washington, and claims that voters re-elected President Clinton because they trusted that he would offset Congressional Republicans' extremism and vice versa. Empirical research suggests that citizens are still suspicious of concentrations of power (eg, Craig 1993), but that they are also frustrated by the very debate, negotiation and compromise that such a divided system produces (eg, Hibbing and Theiss-Morse 1995). Concurrently and conversely, there have been claims that many people in the former Soviet Union and its former satellites in Eastern Europe, buffeted by radical changes and lost security in the last few years, desire rule by a strong man [sic] to assure stability. If true, these different expectations of HMS consistency should result in different trust judgements, even in otherwise identical (in number and nature) HMSs.

These observations, although speculative, imply that responses to a given HMS would vary across time and space. Just as with variation in these judgements by individuals, in some conditions a proliferation of hazard managers would be reassuring (redundancy as safety net), in others disturbing (confusion, inefficiency, power struggle – see Hibbing and Theiss-Morse 1995). In some cases people would expect, even rely upon, different actors having different goals (public good versus private profit), and build trust in the system upon this expectation; in others trust would occur only if multiple actors were seen as all pulling in the same direction. Such variations would not make HMS irrelevant to trust judgements any more than would cultural and historical differences in judgements of trust in individual hazard managers, but they would make research to understand the dynamics of such judgements more time-consuming.

The potential role of trust and distrust as constraints on the relevance of HMS is even more subtle and speculative. Suppose negative (that is, distrust-provoking) cues are indeed more common and salient than positive (trust-building or maintaining) ones (Slovic 1993). In this case one might expect global judgements of trust (that is, trust in the overall HMS) to be more common than global judgements of distrust, since the latter will occur in the presence of cues likely to prompt judgements of individual actors in the system. Given both the potential difficulty of measuring global judgements as distinct from judgements of water safety, and the effect of cueing to switch people away from global to specific trust judgements, this may not be an important constraint. Since it is a matter of dispute whether trust, lack of trust, and distrust are orthogonal concepts or lie on the same dimension (see Earle and Cvetkovich 1995, for one perspective on this debate), it is worth mentioning this likely slant of global judgements of HMS toward trusting situations. This constraint should not apply, however, to the effect of HMS concepts on judgements of specific hazard managers.

METHODS FOR STUDYING HMS TRUST

Both my primary speculations, and those dealing with constraints, on the role of HMSs in trust judgements require data for testing. However, we need new research methods to explore these hypotheses.

Most current research on trust in hazard managers asks about trust in one manager or actor at a time. Sometimes a single institution is the focus of an entire study or a section of a survey on hazards and trust (eg, 'Do you trust the government?'). It has become more common in survey-type studies of trust to ask for ratings of trust in several hazard managers in sequence. The typical approach asks research subjects something like the following: 'Now I will read a list of groups and institutions. For each of these I would like you to rate the level of trust you have in their management of [Hazard]. First, how do you rate your trust in the US Environmental Protection Agency, on a scale from

"Great deal of trust" to "Some trust" to "Little trust?" Next, how would you rate the news media?', and so forth. The wordings, scale sizes, and listed groups vary across studies, but for several hazards such research has found that apparently knowledgeable and disinterested parties usually (but not always) elicit high trust (eg, university scientists and doctors), while apparently self-interested parties tend to rank low (eg, industry).

This list approach has much to recommend it. First, it is simple compared to an alternative that I discuss below. Second, with broad enough definitions, one can use nearly the same list in every study, facilitating comparisons across hazards, locations, and time. For example, government, industry, journalists, doctors, scientists or university scientists, friends and relatives, and environmentalists are very common stimuli for trust judgement studies about environmental and energy hazards. Third, these lists help scholars interested in producing indices of trust from judgements of more than one institution (eg, Bord and O'Connor 1992), or those who recommend such communication strategies as collaborating with an entity more trusted than oneself (Vincent Covello, personal communication, 1997). Fourth, if one of these institutions sponsors such a study it is likely to want to know how trustworthy it appears.

But current research methods are highly unlikely to tap judgements of hazard management system performance. When a researcher asks about trust in a single institution, the answer *might* reflect trust in the whole system that prevents or minimizes risk in drinking water. This holistic response would have the benefit of conserving cognitive resources, rather than forcing one to reach independent judgements of trust for several competing or complementary managers of a hazard. But we cannot test this hypothesis without examining judgements of trust across several institutions responsible (or seen to be responsible) for hazard management. The list approach – which asks for trust judgements of hazard managers one by one – is no better, because we cannot tell from the answers how much trust a respondent has in the overall HMS, or measure the potential impact of HMS judgements on those of individual hazard managers. At best we might find that there are, or are not, order effects in these sequential trust judgements: a person's rating of electric utilities might depend on whether it was the first item on the list, or followed the state Public Utility Commission or an environmentalist group. I know of no trust study that has tested for such order effects, but even if one had, explaining a positive result would be very difficult using this method. Nor can we tell whether subjects' ratings of trust for a given institution mean that they expect that institution to have a role at all, much less an important one, and have the power to fully implement that role, in managing a given hazard. Without making this explicit, we do not know whether the elicited judgements are meaningful to those offering them. (The same criticism applies to a method used by Frewer et al 1996, in which English subjects picked which of three institutions offered by researchers they distrusted the most with regard to providing food information, and then proffered reasons for this distrust. This method does not tap subjects' conceptual HMS, nor does it allow for comparison of reasons for distrust of one manager to reasons for distrust of another.) Furthermore, the important role that citizens and consumers can play in managing at least some hazards, and the critical question of whether they recognize that possibility, is entirely ignored by these methods.

My suggested method requires much more work, but is more likely to be able to test my hypotheses. Imagine a simple HMS with three actors: a water provider, a regulator of the provider, and a consumer. A given person's mental model (Bostrom et al 1992) of the HMS could include zero, one, two, or all three actors; an empty model would be due to having given no thought whatsoever to what causes drinking water's quality. Trust judgements could be requested about any number of actors a researcher might offer, but we should expect judgements to be most meaningful (most clearly represent the judge's actual disposition) for actors that occur in the judge's HMS model.

Thus, assessment of trust and its role in hazard management will benefit from accounting for the place of a given group or institution in individuals' models of the HMS. The basic protocol would begin with an abbreviated version of a mental models approach to risk communication design (Bostrom et al 1992). That approach constructs an 'influence diagram' of the evolution of a potential hazard as seen by experts, which then is used to design an interview protocol for use with lay-people. This protocol has the interviewer begin by saying (for example) 'Tell me about radon', and, in a similarly non-directive way, urges the lay interviewee to talk about each concept he or she had raised in earlier responses. It is only when these interviewee-offered models of the issue have been fully plumbed that the interviewer uses the expert-influenced protocol to further explore the person's conceptions (eg, 'Now tell me about the role of ventilation').

The value of using a condensed form of this strategy is that it puts HMS concepts in the context of people's beliefs about threats to clean drinking water and how these might be forestalled (presumably what HMS members are there to do), and questions about how drinking water can be polluted or cleaned will help elicit people's mental models about the management system, thus preparing them to answer subsequent questions on that topic. Once a few questions about drinking water (or whatever the issue is) have been posed to set the scene, the researcher can then move on to ask non-directive questions about management of the issue to begin eliciting concepts of the HMS from the interviewee. As with the mental models strategy for causal attributions, one would add more probing, potentially reactive questions as the interviewee's stream of proffered concepts begins to flag. These probes will probably need to be generated from a combination of expert concepts (assuming one has asked, for example, actual HMS members about their views of the HMS and trust within it), the trust literature, and logic. (An example of the latter is the idea offered earlier that one's notions of generic institutions, such as the market and government's relation to it, might affect how one judges a two-member HMS of a firm and an agency.)

Researchers could also test the hypotheses I've proposed by asking people in a survey instrument what managers come to mind with regard to a given hazard, or providing experimental scenarios that manipulate the number and framing of HMS members. However, without the (prior) contextual validation provided by such non-directive interviews, survey and experimental results will be suspect, whether they support or disconfirm the hypotheses. The ideal, of course, would be use of all three methods in a single study; a survey in particular could reveal the distribution of particular HMS concepts and judgements in the population at large, and test whether the aggregate results explain the data on median levels of trust in a given group (eg, doctors) that most trust studies have yielded.

CONCLUSIONS

Adding HMS analyses to studies of judgements of individual actors will not resolve all questions about trust in hazard managers. As implied earlier, for example, trust judgements probably reflect in part a generic attitude toward the stimulus entity unrelated to its trustworthiness with regard to a particular hazard's management (as with people who are for or against the market or government on principle, for example). However, current research methods tend to ignore both this possibility and that concepts of the system of hazard management might affect judgements of safety and of specific managers. At worst, tests of my hypotheses will find that systemic context has no effect, and the field can continue with standard practice confident that a potential confounder has been dismissed on empirical grounds. (This finding would have gloomier implications for hazard management – people who lack a meaningful concept of such potential HMS attributes as redundancy or shared powers are less likely to recognize important failures or successes of the HMS – but that is another question.)

However, research might find that accounting for HMS concepts enriches our understanding of the dynamics of trust judgements. This would be most likely for our knowledge of the relations between judgements of trust in individual actors (whether of generic entities, such as government and industry or doctors, or more specific, named individuals, groups, and organizations). As noted earlier, the utility of thinking of trust as a global judgement of the performance of the overall HMS depends in part on whether researchers believe this concept intrudes too far on other risk-relevant measures, such as risk estimates. And the value of HMS for understanding the origins of trust remains to be seen, primarily because this entire topic has not been well-defined or well-explored to date. But thinking more inclusively about what is involved in trust judgements, regardless of the specific value of the HMS concept, is likely to benefit the field.

6 Environmental Regulation in the UK: Politics, Institutional Change and Public Trust[1]

Ragnar E Löfstedt and *Tom Horlick-Jones*

INTRODUCTION

On April 1st 1996, the UK Government launched a new agency, with 9500 employees and a budget of £550 million, and the responsibility for a wide range of environmental protection functions including the control of pollution, management of water resources and waste disposal licensing, in England and Wales (a similar body was simultaneously established for Scotland). This body, named the Environment Agency, was given a brief which comprised an amalgamation of a number of hitherto existing regulatory functions previously performed by a range of bodies such as the National Rivers Authority (NRA), Her Majesty's Inspectorate of Pollution (HMIP), local government waste regulation authorities and certain parts of central government's Department of the Environment.

The key change was one of reorganisation, forming a single body responsible for environmental regulation by integrating together pollution controls, and responsibility for pollution to air, land and water (Department of Environment 1991; Jewell and Steele 1996). There were a number of clear commercial reasons for the creation of the new agency. Firstly, convenience, in response to pressure from industrial bodies such as the Confederation of British Industry (CBI) which favoured a single 'one stop' agency administering industrial permits and licences (House of Commons 1992). Secondly, efficiency, in order to attend to multiple environmental impacts (eg sulphur pollution not only

1. The research leading to this paper was partially supported by a grant provided to the first author by the Swedish Council for the Planning of Coordination of Research. The second author is indebted to the Kirby Laing Foundation for financial support. We would also like to thank the following individuals for commenting on previous drafts of this article as well as bringing relevant material to our attention: John Handmer, Rosalind Malcolm, Roland Clift, George Cvetkovich, Christopher Foster, Timothy Earle, Laura Kelly, and Ortwin Renn. Additionally, we would like to thank a number of officials from the Environment Agency, in particular Lord De Ramsey, Jan Pentreath and David Slater for their helpful cooperation and assistance.

affects the air but also the land and the water) within one all encompassing agency. This was consistent with UK Government advocacy of the concept of Integrated Pollution Control (IPC), where all the pollutants are accounted for in a regulatory regime.

Leading up to its launch, and since, senior officials from the Agency have openly expressed their concern about the need to gain public credibility and trust. In the very first newsletter published by the Agency, for example, the Chief Executive, Mr Ed Gallagher, wrote that:

> The Agency must make a real difference to the environment that will last through the next generations. We must therefore carry public opinion with us and be as effective and efficient as the industries we seek to regulate in order to have credibility for this major task. (Environment Agency 1996a).

Similarly, the Chairman, Lord De Ramsey, a former Chairman of the UK Landowners' Association and the Cambridge Water Company, has made clear that, in his view:

> We want the public to learn to trust the agency. We want the public to see the agency as credible and competent. The Agency and its predecessors have improved environmental standards considerably – look at our rivers and our bathing waters, yet I don't think that we are getting adequate credit for it. (personal communication, 1996)

In addition, Dr David Slater, the Agency's former Director of Pollution Prevention and Control, made statements to the effect that:

> Recent examples of environmental and health concerns raised in public have highlighted the need to be aware of public perceptions in the scientific, economic and political decision-making process, and to ensure that the public can trust this process. (Slater, 1996).

It is interesting to reflect upon why these officials have felt it necessary to give such a high profile to the issue of public trust in their activities. Certainly, the Environment Agency is charged with a responsibility to 'develop a close and responsible relationship with the public (and) local communities', in spite of most of its activities being concerned with working closely with industry. We believe that there are a number of very important underlying reasons why the Agency is concerned about the public trust, which we will explore in this paper.

RISK, TRUST AND MODERNITY

Much has been written about the erosion of public trust in North American government agencies, and the difficulties this has created for technological decision-making (eg Kasperson, Golding and Tuler 1992; Earle and Cvetkovich 1995). Increasingly this phenomenon is seen as a key factor in determining the effectiveness of risk communication programmes and public tolerance of the results of decisions made by official bodies (US Department of Energy 1993; Stern and Fineberg 1996).

Significantly, Slovic (1993) has argued that trust is systematically destroyed by the impact of technological and social changes on what he describes as 'our remarkable form of participatory democracy'. Indeed, there is an emerging recognition that these cultural shifts are largely beyond the reach of what risk communication programmes can address, necessitating somewhat more modest expectations for such initiatives than hitherto (Chess, Salomone et al 1995). Public distrust, it seems, has become a fact of life, a characteristic of modernity.

This phenomenon, in which impersonal trust in experts, or what one might call 'systemic' trust, is thrown into doubt lies at the heart of a picture of modern life provided by an emerging body of social theory. In particular, the 'Risk Society' theory of Ulrich Beck and the closely associated work of Anthony Giddens (Beck 1992, 1995; Giddens 1990; Beck, Giddens and Lash 1994) provide a framework for understanding global processes that have unleashed local experiences of uncertainty and trepidation. As Giddens (1990) puts it, '[t]o live in a world of high modernity has the feeling of riding a juggernaut'.

If the erosion of trust in US institutions and scientific expertise does correspond to the corroding effects of late modernity's reflexivity, then can one detect similar effects resulting from these currents impacting on the social, cultural and political formations of Europe? A series of recent high profile controversies, including the North Sea drama of the Brent Spar oil platform (Löfstedt and Renn 1997) and the UK Bovine Spongiform Encephalopathy (BSE) 'mad cow' crisis, suggest distinct similarities. Indeed, it has been suggested that US-style 'advocacy science' may be in the process of crossing the Atlantic, resulting from a reduction in the authority and credibility of old ways of making decisions and the emergence of new, highly politicized, forms of technical expertise (see discussion in Horlick-Jones and De Marchi 1995; Horlick-Jones, in press).

We are observing, of course, the highly complex outcome of multiple social and political interactions. Bord and O'Connor (1992), for example, claim that trust in government is linked to trust in industry, and in turn to beliefs about the feasibility of controlling corresponding industrial hazards. On the other hand, regulatory bodies find themselves mediating interactions between industrial behaviour and public risk tolerability, which, it has been suggested (Horlick-Jones, Pidgeon et al 1996), 'may touch upon the very foundations of the social contract, as it has been traditionally conceived'.

Clearly the public's trust can no longer be taken for granted as recent evidence suggests that government institutions have little credibility in the eyes of the public (eg Marris et al 1996; Worcester 1995). The Environment Agency seems to view the gaining of public trust as important in order to make possible more effective and less controversial policy making. This view appears, in part, to draw upon the benefit of hindsight, as one of the predecessors to the Agency, the pollution inspectorate, was not highly trusted, and this created numerous practical difficulties (Woolf 1994).

It seems that the Environment Agency's preoccupation with public trust can be understood in these broader social and political terms. However, as we have noted, the mechanisms by which trust-eroding social processes are impacting upon the specific sociocultural, institutional and political structures of the UK are clearly of enormous complexity. Therefore there is a need to examine in some detail the political and regulatory context in which the Agency has come into being, and we consider these issues in the following sections.

ENVIRONMENTAL REGULATION IN THE UK: CONSENSUS AND CONSERVATISM

Here we will argue that recent changes in UK environmental policy-making can be attributed largely to three key influences: the growing importance of non-governmental agencies (NGOs) and pressure groups, the emergence of environmentalism as a political vote-winner in the late 1980s and the effects of structural changes that have taken place in the UK government's administrative apparatus, variously described as a 'hollowing out' of the state or the advent of 'new public administration'.

First, however, we consider the traditional role of consensual decision-making in the UK style of regulation. Unlike many other nations, the UK regulators have pursued a consensual, non-controversial relationship with industry for many years (O'Riordan 1985; Renn 1995). This regulatory approach has its roots in the 1842 pollution control laws (Ashby and Anderson 1981) and it is widely believed by regulators in other nations to be the most successful form of risk regulation (Jasanoff 1987), with regulatory standards and time frames being determined jointly on a case-by-case basis (Hawkins 1984; Reiss 1985).

Behind the 'success' of the consensual approach lies a number of arguably less attractive characteristics of UK administration, notably the secrecy of decision-making 'behind closed doors' (Hennessy 1989). Under the UK's Official Secrets legislation there is no obligation to disclose discussions between the regulator and its clients concerning the levels of acceptable risk, allowing frank discussions to be encouraged. Of late, a perceived reluctance to act by regulatory agencies has been attributed to government policy on deregulation, coupled with an approach of encouraging industry to regulate itself. As a result, in most cases where a violation has occurred the inspectors will attempt to persuade and inform the industry on how to best meet regulatory requirements. Enforcement is often only carried out in situations where there have been a series of repeated violations. This 'cosy' atmosphere is made possible by the fact that the majority of agency inspectors have previously worked in industry before joining the inspectorates and in some cases this amounts to a requirement for the job (Jasanoff 1986, 1987; McCormick 1991).

The creation of the Environment Agency has not changed government policy on consensual regulation, and the Agency is still encouraged to work closely with the industry. Hence, just as before the 1995 Environment Act, risk management is inherently flexible, with a large amount of secrecy in regulation present, and disputed site-specific decisions are handled by the courts.

The consensual approach to regulation has been carefully analysed by O'Riordan (1985), who argues that secrecy forms a necessary precondition for its operation. There are two reasons why this is the case: firstly, companies do not have to release commercially sensitive information that may influence their competitiveness, particularly with foreign firms; and secondly, confidentiality should encourage frank and honest discussion between the regulator and industry. Flexibility regarding the interpretation of standards allows the avoidance of figures and numbers, with standards being based on what is termed the 'Best Practical Environmental Option not Entailing Excessive Cost' or BPEO (Royal Commission on Environmental Pollution, 1988). This allows the regulators to account for local circumstances, the financial strength of the industry and so on.

Consensual regulation keeps prosecution to a minimum as the regulators and their industrial counterparts strive to come to an amicable agreement, so reducing the cost of enforcement. In many cases the regulator acts as an advisor to industry, so where a violation has occurred inspectors will attempt to inform and persuade the industry on how to best meet regulatory requirements. In this system prosecutions are pursued only as a last resort in situations where there has been a series of repeated violations.

Thus, the consensual style of regulation has several advantages in that it allows for flexibility, and reduces the cost of regulation. However, it possesses a number of disadvantages which seem to have a direct bearing on trustworthiness. The regulatory agencies in the UK have often been viewed by critics as being 'in the pockets' of industry and for not being stringent enough (Boehmer-Christiansen and Skea 1991; McCormick 1991). This claim stems from the fact that fines for environmental non-compliance were seldom levied, and when they were they tended to be low in comparison to other European nations, the power of the courts to impose heavy fines having been limited by Parliament. Therefore, historically, the UK pollution inspectorate (HMIP) has lacked credibility (O'Riordan 1985). Senior executives within the Environment Agency are only too aware of this view and are anxious to avoid the same criticisms transferring to the new agency. However, they face a major structural difficulty in the form of the Agency's mandate, based as it is on the 1995 Environment Act, which requires them to place as little constraint on their 'customers' in industry as possible (Jewell and Steele 1996).

Structural Changes in the British State

During the last 20 years, far-reaching changes have taken place in the nature of UK public administration. These changes have been prompted by radical political shifts associated with a series of governments controlled by the Conservative Party. It is rather too early to assess the likely impact of the recently-elected Labour government's policies. We discuss some of the associated politics in the following section below. It is important, however to appreciate that although these governments, driven by an ideological mission to create an 'enterprise economy', have introduced many reforms, such changes must be understood not only in terms of ideological zeal, but also of underlying economic constraints. Of particular importance, we suggest, have been the fiscal crisis common to many western governments with welfare states, the failure of successive UK governments to control public expenditure, membership of the European Union and the increasing globalization of markets (see Drucker, Dunleavy et al 1986; Hood 1991; McCormick 1991; Power 1994).

An important, and in many ways contradictory, aspect of these changes has been a centralization of power in the hands of the Whitehall government; for example, during the first 17 years or so of the Conservative reign some 150 Acts of Parliament became law, of which a majority have served to diminish the power of local councils (Jenkins 1995). Five main reasons for this state of affairs may be identified (Foster and Plowden 1996). First, the argument that central government was administratively more efficient than local councils, which were regarded as wasteful and incompetent (Baker 1993; Balen 1992). Second, a belief that local governments were in some ways less legitimate than the national governments; as compared to other nations, the voter turnouts in local governments were low (Widdicombe 1986). Third, the observation that during the 1970s much of local government changed from being simply administratively entitled to adopting an overt political stance on issues, and sometimes openly opposing central government. Fourth, it was claimed that local governments would overspend, causing a drain on government expenditure. This was especially true in the early Thatcher years, when government ministers were furious that local governments increased their spending, while they did everything possible to hinder it (Lawson 1992; Butler et al. 1994). Finally, centralization of government through reducing the power of the local councils reduced the ability of political opponents to gain valuable experience, and so challenge their electoral dominance.

Although centralization theoretically led to a greater burden being placed on ministers, in practice a great deal of the work previously handled by the local councils was to be performed by various forms of agency. Among these bodies, so-called quasi-government agencies, or QGAs, now accounting for more than 30 per cent of public sector administration, are single issue agencies controlled by a committee or board set up by Whitehall. The agency receives all or a large amount of funding from central government funds. Such agencies include the Arts Council and the Health and Safety Commission. QUANGOS, or quasi-non-governmental organizations, are not formally part of the public sector, although they can receive funding from the government, and include some voluntary organizations (see discussion in Dunleavy and Rhodes 1986). The Environment Agency is an example of a QGA. It is a single issue agency controlled by a board appointed by the government, whose chairman was hand-picked by the Right Honourable John Gummer MP, the then Environment Minister. Unlike local councils, whose most powerful individuals can be voted in and out of office, bodies like QGAs are not democratically accountable. Therefore the chairman of the Environment Agency is not elected. He can only be replaced by the central government in power.

This process of centralization, and the establishment of bodies like QGAs and QUANGOS, has corresponded to an important trend towards seeking to import private sector practices into public administration. As Hood (1991) has noted, the rise of 'new public administration' is 'emphatically not a uniquely British development' (for a North American perspective, see Osborne and Gaebler 1992). It is characterized by high-profile managers rather than faceless officials, a stress on performance measures, cost-cutting and performance-driven resource allocation, and labour discipline (Hood 1991; Power 1994). As noted above, these developments seem to be related not only to overt political factors but also to large-scale economic constraints on government, for example fiscal crisis, control on public expenditure and globalization. Clearly there are many forms of interaction between these factors, for example the apparent electoral appeal of tax-cutting.

These changes have resulted in the UK central administration increasingly playing a relatively small role in environmental decision-making. This development corresponds to a wider structural process of the so-called hollowing out of the state (Peters 1993; Rhodes 1994), leading to most of the hitherto publicly-owned electricity and water companies having been privatized and, indeed, some are now in foreign hands. These companies are now responsible to shareholders rather than directly to central government's environmental targets. In addition, by virtue of European Union membership, an increasing number of environmental laws, currently some 70 per cent, now originate in Brussels, thus potentially reinforcing the erosion of the credibility of government institutions.

At the political level, centralization and privatization are seen by some to have resulted in greater alienation of government from the public. There is some research evidence for this suggestion, for example a recent study conducted on the general public in Lancaster, a town in the north of England (Macnaughten et al 1995), where many members of the public clearly believed that the government was not interested in them, and did not want to hear their views.

The Environment Agency: The Product of a Time of Institutional Change

As noted above, there are two clear commercial reasons why the Environment Agency was formed. Firstly, the role of integration; as environmental pollution frequently affects more than one physical medium, one agency is needed to cope with the problems. Secondly, the importance of commercial convenience, allowing industry to have a 'one stop' agency for operational licences and permits (Jewell and Steele 1996). Ostensibly, according to the 1995 Environment Act, the key component of UK environmental policy is that of sustainable development. However, as Jewell and Steele (ibid) argue, in term of the construction of the new Agency, sustainable development is interpreted with an emphasis more on development sustainability. Moreover, environmental regulation is now to be based on strict cost-benefit and risk assessment considerations.

Therefore it would appear that the construction and mission of the Environment Agency is consistent with, and indeed extends, institutional and administrative trends that have developed over the period of nearly 20 years of UK Conservative government. As we have seen, however, accompanying social changes may pose significant political threats for the smooth operation of the Agency; challenges that, in part, may be compounded by what one might call the crisis in legitimation of such government agencies (cf Habermas 1976). It is to the politics of this situation that we turn in the next section.

ENVIRONMENTAL POLITICS IN THE UK

Until the recent election of the Labour Party under its leader Tony Blair, UK political life had been dominated by the right-wing Conservative Party since Margaret Thatcher came to power as Prime Minister in 1979. During that period the government pursued an ideologically-driven agenda trying to free-up the market, in particular by reducing regulation (Hutton 1995; Marr 1995), removing what it regarded as inefficiency in local government, privatizing national industry (including British Airways, British Gas, British Telecom and British Steel), and seeking to control expenditure of the welfare state, measures seen by some as amounting to a dismantling of such public provision. The government took the view that economic growth was the key engine for enhancing the lifestyles and improving the quality of life among the UK public (Grove-White 1995), and Mrs Thatcher and her advisors, most notably the long-standing Chancellor of the Exchequer Nigel Lawson, adopted a free market approach to economic policy in the Hayekian spirit and in so doing strengthened the power of private sector corporations (Hutton 1995).

This free market approach has led to wide-spread criticism over the years. Hutton argues that the Conservative ethos has indirectly perpetuated the rise of individual interests over social ones, with a consequent erosion of people's trust in one another (Hutton 1995; 1996). Despite social attitudes surveys seeming to demonstrate widespread public support for strong public services rather than tax cuts (Social and Community Planning Research 1995), this did not apparently translate into an electoral handicap for successive Conservative administrations, and indeed the Labour Party has now adopted a similar tax-cutting rhetoric.

It has been pointed out that the free market agenda has not led to wide-spread prosperity as predicted by some of its proponents, that there exists extensive poverty, especially in inner city areas, and that many citizens feel that their more spiritual and intellectual views cannot be captured by modern day conservative politics (Grove-White 1995; North 1996). Nevertheless, conservative commentators point out that although there may be some truth in these observations, most individuals want to increase their wages, and indeed some go so far as to argue that the UK's economic growth model is now regarded with envy by a number of countries such as Germany and Japan (Willetts 1996).

The Green Vote

Unlike most of Europe, the UK Government became interested in environmental issues at a very late stage (Boehmer-Christiansen and Skea 1991). Most commentators state that Mrs Thatcher's 1988 Royal Society speech on climate change was the point when the UK Government first truly showed concern for the environment. This led to a credible Environment Minister in Chris Patten and a more strategic view to environmental decision-making through the publishing of the 1990 White Paper *This Common Inheritance* (Department of Environment 1990) with annual updates every year since then. There are several possible explanations why the Conservative government suddenly 'went green' of which crude electoral advantage seems most convincing. This change followed an unprecedented success by green parties in the European parliament elections, and was set against a number of high-profile developments including reports of global warming originating in the US (Grubb 1990), the death of seals in the North Sea and the fate of *Karin B* and its cargo of toxic waste (Jacques 1988; McCormick 1991).

The practical success of the government 'greening' in terms of ecological protection has been mixed to say the least. Annual reports on the environment have been rather unsatisfactory in view of the few environmental targets having been set (Hill and Jordan 1993), and environment ministers are allegedly not doing their jobs because of a distinct lack of guidance from the Prime Minister's Office (O'Riordan and Jordan 1995). However, other commentators are more optimistic, with some suggesting that the framework contained in the report *Climate Change: the UK Programme* (Department of Environment 1994) has the potential to promote energy conservation for environmental goals (Christie 1994).

It therefore seems reasonable to assume that the UK Government recognizes an important political need to be seen as behaving responsibly towards the environment. In view of the extent of environmental concerns that accompanied the birth of the Environment Agency, it comes as no surprise that high in the Agency's priorities should be the need to appear credible and trustworthy in the eyes of the public.

Public Distrust

The UK public's distrust of government is, in general, extremely high (Social and Community Planning Research 1995, 1997; Worcester 1995); for example a poll conducted in 1995 revealed that only 25 per cent of the 5000 respondents expressed confidence that the government put the interests of the nation before those of the party, and a mere 9 per cent believed that politicians from any party would tell the truth when put on the spot (Social and Community Planning Research 1995).

Such distrust has been translated into overt political terms with widespread media allegations of the government's apparent lack of public concern regarding the BSE scare and Gulf War Syndrome, and the discussion around sleaze becoming one of the main topics of discussion during the period immediately before the 1997 general election. According to some commentators, public distrust in central authority has been made worse by a sense of alienation. Analysis of media coverage of the BSE scare, for example, reveals a general feeling among journalists that the government had treated the public as 'ignorant, stupid, and innumerate' (*Independent* 1996).

The Environment Agency clearly inherited a difficult task in seeking to build public trust. Moreover, certain aspects of its operational structure may actually militate against success in this area. In particular, the utilization of a cost-benefit approach to environmental regulation which, according to some, constitutes a rational process that transcends political squabbles (eg Breyer 1993), may arguably result in alienation of the public and so lead to greater distrust (see Kunreuther and Slovic 1996).

The Politics of Pressure

In contrast to many other European nations (see Löfstedt 1993), the UK's NGO sector appears to have provided important influences behind the formation of environmental policy in recent years. NGOs such as Greenpeace, Friends of the Earth and the Royal Society for the Protection of Birds have become drivers in environmental policy, setting the agenda which policy-makers have followed (Grove-White 1995). Examples include the present road building controversy which NGOs opposed as early as the 1970s (National Motorways Action Committee 1975), the high-profile public campaigning by Greenpeace in order to prevent the dumping of the Brent Spar offshore oil installation in the North Sea (Löfstedt and Renn 1997) and environmental concerns regarding the use of fossil fuels (Grove-White 1995).

The rise to power of the UK NGOs has led to their involvement in helping to formulate environmental policy for both companies and central government. These development have arguably resulted in some NGOs becoming less radical and more mainstream, leading to an identifiable tendency which suggests that the public is beginning to identify NGOs with environmental decision-making (Macnaghten and Scott 1994). The same development has also been prevalent in the US, where more radical environmental activists have left mainstream environmental organizations to form groups such as Earth First!

A central part of the political activities of NGOs involves calling into question regulatory decisions of governments. Indeed, some analysts have gone so far as to suggest that NGO activity, by its very nature, results in an active breeding of distrust in regulatory agencies and other government bodies (Earle and Cvetkovich 1995). The growth of environmental NGO strength in the UK therefore appears to pose additional challenges to the Environment Agency's trust-building initiatives, which significantly amplify the political difficulties diagnosed above.

THE AGENCY AND THE WORLD: THE VIEW FROM THE INSIDE

The discussion above provides a largely theoretical analysis of why the Environment Agency seeks public trust, and the scale of the difficulties posed by this objective. This work has been carried out in parallel with a number of empirical investigations, in which we sought the views of the Agency's officials. We carried out a series of in-depth interviews on the topic of trust and credibility with two senior directors, Dr Jan Pentreath, Director of Environmental Strategy (the same position he held at the NRA) and Dr David Slater, Director of Environmental Pollution (and previous head of the HMIP), together with the chairman of the Environment Agency, Lord De Ramsey. These interviews were conducted during the winter of 1995 and spring of 1996. This investigation was supplemented by an extensive analysis of press items, and of public statements made by Agency officials and other official stakeholders.

In the text below, we construct some sense of how the key issues of public trust and credibility were perceived by decision-makers inside the Agency in the important period leading up to the Agency's start of operations.

Competence and Credibility

All three of the policy-makers interviewed felt that trust was extremely important to the agency especially as a way to insure competence and credibility.
    Lord de Ramsey said, for example:

> We want the public to learn to trust the Agency. We want the public to see the agency as credible and competent. The Agency and its predecessors have improved environmental standards considerably – look at our rivers and our bathing waters, yet I don't think that we are getting adequate credit for it.

De Ramsey took this issue further in a recent speech to the UK Environmental Law Association, where he stated that through tough enforcement environmental credibility can be gained and that environmental groups should also not be trusted:

> There is one vital ingredient without which we will be unable to operate and that is public support. How do we gain trust of the public so that they view the Environment Agency as a 'good thing'? When I had lunch with Shell the other day, I suggested that on April 2nd 1996 they might like to arrange a major pollution incident on the Mersey for which we could prosecute them and fine them heavily. With some justification they felt that it might be someone else's turn. Conflicting information has left people distrusting experts, scientists and most of all politicians. Now Brent Spar has taught them that they cannot trust the green groups either, something most of us realized a long time ago – I call them the Intensive Scare Unit. (De Ramsey 1995)

Jan Pentreath, the Director of Environmental Strategy, agreed with this:

> The Agency must act proactively. We must be tough to show that we take the environment seriously. The best thing that happened to the National Rivers Association was that we had the Shell oil spill. That increased our credibility in the eyes of the public considerably. They saw that we were going to be tough towards industry.

Pentreath felt, however, that the public did not always understand what proper regulation was, and taking a Breyer perspective (Breyer 1993), felt that some regulation was too costly:

> Regulation is to some extent a 'game' in that it is essential for the public to have confidence in the regulator and the regulator in turn needs to test his level of confidence in those he regulates. If one over-regulates those who are usually 'good' operators and under-regulates those who are deliberately attempting to evade the law, then this is obviously an inefficient use of resources. The trick is to get the right balance.

David Slater, the Director of Environmental Pollution at the Agency, also felt that tough legislation would lead to greater credibility:

> This watch dog has teeth. We will be able to prosecute firms that do not meet tough BATNEEC standards. This should enhance credibility and we should gain praise from the environmental movement.[2]

In summary, all three individuals felt that credibility could be gained by strict regulation and two of them based this on the successful examples that they had implemented when they were active in the National Rivers Authority. In fact, the activities of the NRA did receive some praise from environmental groups such as Friends of the Earth. However, this credibility did have a price, namely that regulation was carried out on high visibility problems (unsanitary bathing water) which the public saw was important rather than more problematic less visible environmental issues (eg radon).

The role of credibility is very much a balancing act; as Ed Gallagher, the Director of the Environment Agency, pointed out in a recent interview it is 'to be seen to move more slowly than some of the more aggressive environment groups but faster than industry would like' (Gallagher 1996).

The Media

One way of enhancing trust and credibility was to be more vocal through the media. De Ramsey discussed this at some length:

> The agency must work more with the media. The media is giving parts of government a bad reputation. I don't think that this is always fair, especially in the case of the Environment Agency. We have done quite a few good things in the past . . . [that is to say the National Rivers Authority and HMIP] . . . yet I am not sure that the public finds us credible.

He was particularly concerned that parts of the media were in the hands of the pressure groups, but that this was partially due to poor proactive legislation from the government.

> I agree that we are currently in a regulatory vacuum. The pressure groups have taken on the political environmental agenda. The public trusts the pressure groups more than us. How can we then act proactively – we always have to answer to the pressure groups. Just the other day I got a letter from the Royal Society for the Protection of Birds and they were concerned about the diminishing number of one bird species in East Anglia. I looked into this and it turns out that the overall number of bird species have increased over the last few years, yet the numbers of this bird are decreasing. I mean that is not totally negative, but they would never look at the positive side of the story. I really hope that this group and others would write better things about us in the press.

Slater also acknowledged that the Agency had to communicate better with the press.

---

2. BATNEEC means 'Best Available Technology Not Entailing Excessive Cost', a regulatory concept which holds that the additional costs of avoiding environmental damage need to be justified by the benefits (Department of Environment, 1995).

The press is important and when I was the head of HMIP we did receive some bad publicity. However, I felt that by the time the agency was wound up, things improved significantly, partly due to our more frequent and open contacts with the press.

Pentreath felt that one way of overcoming the media problem would be to educate journalists some more.

Getting accurate and unbiased information into the media is difficult. The media like bad news. They also demand a 'story'. The NRA improved river quality by 25 per cent (that's 10,000 km of water) in six years but no one was interested. Thus in order to get the basic facts widely distributed the first initiative I took when the Agency was set up was to get a wide range of basic environmental information out on the world wide web, in easy readable form, and kept instantly up-to-date. It is thus available for news writers and others to check the facts. It also encourages the public, and public authorities, to draw their own conclusions.

The role of media was very much discussed by the former chairman of the NRA, Lord Crickhowell, when he said that in a proper report on environmental issues, the media can find anything it wants to find. He relates this to a document by the OECD on water quality in the UK, which is rather positive but which Friends of the Earth and several environmental journalists paint out as very negative, with headline quotes such as 'one of the fiercest criticisms ever made of the Government's policies coming from an impeccable source' or 'Britain – one of the worst polluters says the OECD' when in fact the headlines, according to Crickhowell, could have read 'Striking environmental progress in Britain – impressive series of British Government initiatives' (Crickhowell 1995).

The media, in other words, was in the eyes of the Environment Agency a very important vehicle in getting across the positive credibility enhancing messages that the Agency was grabbling with. They felt that better communication with the media would ensure that distrust was not perpetuated.

Secrecy

One problem that they all wrestled with was that of secrecy. Slater phrased it accurately when he said:

We must communicate better with the public in order to ensure trust. However, this is not always so easy as industry who take part in Integrated Pollution Control (IPC) are not particularly interested in seeing the results of their Operator and Risk Appraisal System (OPRA) published, which I fully understand. Of course, what happens then is that the public believes that we are in the hands of industry, which does not help our credibility. It truly is a fine balancing act.

De Ramsey said the same thing:

We want to remain open with the public but have confidential discussions with industry as this is the most efficient way of doing this.

Pentreath agreed as well:

> We cannot always be completely open when dealing with discharges from certain industries because the law allows them to withhold information from the public registers on the grounds of commercial confidentiality. But this does not mean that we allow them to pollute. All industries are treated the same and environmental protection always comes first. But it is inevitable that this can be difficult for the public to understand. At the end of the day, public trust in the Agency can be only be built on the totality of what we do, and nowadays the public, quite rightly, expect us to be as open as we possibly can. The biggest risk, usually, is the leaking of early draft documents which contain information which is simply wrong. Once new stories break, even if based on completely wrong information, it can be very difficult to get the truth back into the press. One interesting new duty for the Agency is that of gathering information to form an opinion of the state of pollution of the environment. I intend to use this duty to consult the public and to form honest straight 'opinions', with all of the evidence publicly available. This approach is essential in order to get the public on our side. We cannot improve the environment by ourselves; we must convince the public that it is in their best interest, and their children's interests, that this be done.

In sum, some form of secrecy should be maintained, but they all agreed that the price of such secrecy could be high indeed in lost credibility leading to distrust. This latter point is something that the outgoing NRA chairman, Lord Crickhowell, mentioned in his leaving speech; that the new organization may be too secretive, which will severely impact its public credibility (Schoon 1996).

CONCLUSION: THE ENVIRONMENT AGENCY – REGAINING PUBLIC TRUST?

As we have seen, in order to understand the Environment Agency's preoccupation with public trust it has been necessary to consider in detail the impact of trust-eroding social currents upon the UK's institutional and political structures. We have begun to explore the complexity of these processes in UK environmental regulation, traditionally characterized as it has been by a consensual nature and by the role of confidentiality and secrecy. The self-declared openness of the new Agency, the prominent role of risk assessment, portrayed as an apolitical arbiter of decision-making, and, above all, the search for public trust may be seen as direct responses to this crisis.

An important factor behind the institutional changes associated with the birth of the Agency has been the succession of Conservative ideology-driven governments in the UK, with their enthusiasm for deregulation and freeing up of the market. The construction of the Agency may be seen as part of this programme, minimizing the inconvenience of regulation for industry and, in the words of the Agency's Chief Executive, 'helping to implement the Government's deregulation initiative' (Gallagher 1996).

These developments have taken place against a rich background of political, economic and social changes including the ongoing crisis in UK public expenditure, the politically-potent consensus for tax cuts, the fashion in many countries for the importation of private sector-style administration into government via the construction of agencies, the emergence of 'the environment' as a powerful political issue and the impact of European Union membership.

It is important to recognize the enormous significance of recent environmental controversies on UK government thinking. NGO activity seemed suddenly able to transcend simple protest politics and to gain significant credibility in the eyes of the general public, prompting shifts in consumer behaviour with potentially catastrophic economic impacts for some. Official pronouncements of safety by austere officials no longer seemed to be regarded as trustworthy as in the past. These changes in the relationship between official expertise and public have been compounded by structural changes in UK legal practices, making it possible to challenge environmental developments via judicial review. Against these developments it is perhaps not surprising that the Environment Agency is seen by government to have an important public relations function; indeed, as its Chief Executive has stated, 'Our job in a lot of cases is a public relations and political fix' (Gallagher 1996).

The importance of public relations and the role it plays in trust and credibility was also raised in the interviews that we conducted with the policy-makers from the Environment Agency. They all felt that the media had a very important role in enhancing their credibility and they were worried that the media might not do this; this was especially well illustrated by the speech by Lord Crickhowell. What was interesting to note was their concern about the 'burden' of secrecy, which has played such an intricate role in UK consensual decision-making. They felt that secrecy was important to maintain, but the price of this secrecy could be the erosion of public trust.

Our analysis seems to suggest that in order to achieve the objective of gaining public trust, the Agency has a very difficult task ahead. Given the history of people's perceptions of quangos, agencies and other such bodies in the UK, building trust from the outset will not be easy. Elsewhere in Europe, however, for example in Sweden, bodies with similar responsibilities for environmental regulation and status with respect to government seem to be able to engender public trust. In fact the Swedish Environmental Protection Agency is seen as a highly trustworthy organization, mainly due to its reputation as a fair but firm regulator. There may be lessons here for the UK agencies.

A number of factors may be identified at this stage that may compromise the Agency's ability to attract public trust. Centralizing the Agency in one location, for example, might work against the cultivation of local publics. However, some Agency officials feel that centralization enables an assessment of the UK environment as a whole rather than adopting 'distorted' local views (Lascelles 1996).

The transparency of the Agency has also been questioned. The outgoing chairman of the NRA, Lord Crickhowell, in his leaving speech said that the new organization may be too secretive, which will severely impact its public credibility (Schoon 1996). In stressing the need for the Agency to be independent, the Chairman, Lord De Ramsey, has said that this could lead to disagreements with the government but that these should be kept out of the public eye as 'this is the most productive way of doing things' (Environment Agency 1996b).

As noted above, there has been much discussion of cost-benefit analysis (CBA) and the role it will play in environmental regulation. CBA has become the cornerstone of the new Agency, and it has been used in every regulatory decision taken by the Agency. This move endorses an approach calling for a move away from involving the 'irrational' public and focusing more on risk assessment and sound science (Breyer 1993). This has been widely criticized by several commentators as only through more participatory democracy and greater public involvement can trust be maintained or increased (Kunreuther and Slovic 1996; Renn et al. 1995; Stern and Fineberg 1996). Strict risk assessment may only alienate the public and cause greater distrust.

The most direct influence on whether the Agency gains public trust is the performance of its immediate predecessors, as it will initially be judged on the basis of the public's experience of the environmental bodies that have been integrated into the Agency, and many of the staff of the new Agency came from NRA and HMIP. As the public trust in these agencies was low, the Agency starts from a defensive position. In this context the new Agency needs to act, and be seen to act, credibly and forcefully in its first months of existence. As yet, it is not clear whether this has been the case.

7 Perceived Competence and Motivation in Industry and Government as Factors in Risk Perception[1]

Lennart Sjöberg

Trust has been mentioned as an important factor in a comparison of risk perception in France and the US (Poumadère 1995). In that study trust was related to lower perceived risk within countries, but between countries a paradoxical relationship was found. The French were more trusting than the Americans, yet perceived larger risks. This is a paradoxical result since one would expect higher trust to be associated with lower perceived risk.

Trust may differ between countries for, among other factors, historical reasons. Sweden is a relatively well integrated society with a long history of peace and successful resolution of conflicts, both internal and external. Authorities are considered, by the public, to be competent and non-corrupt, even if politicians are seen in a different light, including how they view their colleagues (Sjöberg 1996b).

In addition, previous research has shown that trust is an important factor in risk perception and risk tolerance (Earle and Cvetkovich 1994, 1995; Flynn et al 1992; Freudenburg 1993; Frewer et al 1996; Frewer et al 1994; Frewer et al 1993; Kasperson et al 1992; Renn and Levine 1991; Slovic 1993; Slovic et al 1991; Slovic et al 1991). Most of this work has been concerned with trust in the government and authorities, and in media. Indeed, trust is a main factor in a common approach to understanding risk perception, termed 'outrage' by Sandman (1993). In this approach, psychometric dimensions (Fischoff et al 1978) are combined with trust in order to understand risk perception and risk tolerance or risk acceptance.

Many papers on trust and risk perception treat the matter mostly as a theoretical problem and present no data. It seems to be simply assumed that

1. This is a study within CEC project RISKPERCOM (Contract FI4PCT950016), supported also by the Swedish Council for Planning and Coordination of Research (FRN), the Swedish Council for Humanistic and Social Science Research (HSFR), the Swedish Nuclear Power Inspectorate (SKI), and the Swedish Radiation Protection Institute (SSI).

the relationship is very strong. I have located a few examples of empirical investigations of the matter. Pijawka and Mushkatel (1991/92) studied risk perception of nuclear waste and trust in federal government, agency and state and local government. They specified trust as trust that decisions taken will protect public safety (probably in general). The correlations with risk perception expressed about 5–10 per cent explained variance in perceived risk on the basis of trust. The same level was reported by Bord and O'Connor (1992) in a study of a hazardous waste site. Trust measures were general. Hallman and Wandersman (1995) investigated a hazardous waste landfill, with specific measures of trust and risk. They obtained about 16 per cent explained variance. An unusually strong relationship was found (specific risk and trust factors) in a study of a high-level nuclear waste repository (Biel and Dahlstrand 1995), about 35 per cent. Rather strong correlations (about 35 per cent) were also found in a study by Bord and O'Connor (1990), with specific risk and trust items concerning food irradiation.

Hence, the data so far indicate that trust in general is less clearly related to risk perception than specific trust. Furthermore, there is a suggestion that policy attitudes may be more clearly related to trust than risk perception per se. This work has been of great importance and is a pioneering effort. Much surely remains to be done, however, when it comes to understanding risk perception (Drottz-Sjöberg 1991). The traditional psychometrics trust approach accounts for, at the most, some 25 per cent of the variance of perceived risk (Sjöberg 1996). In addition, trust has possibly many other aspects to it not yet investigated thoroughly. The present paper is an attempt to develop a multi-dimensional concept of trust.

If there are hazards in society, they are to some extent man-made. If they are man-made, somebody is responsible. They are due to lack of competence, negligence, indifference or malevolent intent (Sjöberg 1991). I now develop this notion further and specify four facets. One primary aspect is the image of man that is subscribed to. Is man good or bad? Are people in general honest and to be trusted? The first trust dimension is *perception of general honesty*. A second aspect is the state of society. Is it relatively harmonious or is it full of conflicts? The second trust dimension I propose is the *perception of social harmony*. There are also actors which may or may not be seen as having some responsibility for hazards. The first is that of politically responsible persons. *Trust in politicians* is my third trust factor. The fourth and final[2] trust factor treated here is trust in corporations and businessmen. Corporations are responsible for running much of society and surely they contribute to the hazards that we encounter.

The primary purpose of the present paper was to develop measures of these trust dimensions and to test their relationship with perceived risk. In addition, I wanted to compare their explanatory power with that of Cultural Theory (CT) scales developed by Dake (Dake 1990; Wildavsky and Dake 1990), since they constitute an important attempt at measuring concepts assumed by many to provide explanations of perceived risk (Douglas and Wildavsky 1982).

2. Trust in media was also investigated but is excluded here since it had no relation to risk perception.

METHOD

The gross sample of respondents consisted of 250 persons who had taken part in earlier surveys of risk perception, as members of the general public in Sweden and selected at random. They had at that time indicated their willingness to participate in further studies. Of the 250, 169 or 67.6 per cent returned a filled out questionnaire. Data were collected in May–June 1996. Of the participating respondents 59.3 per cent were men, 40.7 per cent women. Mean age was 44 years (range 18–75).

Questionnaire

The questionnaire was printed in A5 format, and had 31 pages. It asked for the following judgements:

1. Personal risk of 35 hazards, judged on category scales from 0 to 7 and with an explicit 'don't know' category.
2. Same as A, but general risks.
3. Probability of harm, judged on category scales with eight steps, plus a 'don't know' category.
4. Severity of consequences of injury, seven-category scale as in A and B.
5. Demand for risk mitigation by the government (national and local), judged on seven-category scales, a 'don't know' category, and a category explicitly denying the government's responsibility for mitigating risks.
6. 130 attitude items written for the present study to measure, in a very broad sense, perceived social conflicts and trust, plus Dake's (1990) 53 CT items. These were all judged on five-category scales from 'agree definitely' to 'disagree definitely'.
7. Dake's 33 social concerns, judged on seven-category scales, from 'no problem at all' to 'a very extreme problem'.
8. Background data and assessment of the questionnaire.

The median time to respond to the questionnaire was 60 minutes.

RESULTS

Scaling

Four scales were constructed on the basis of item and factor analysis:

1. Trust in corporations, (=0.84) α
2. Trust in politicians, (=0.92) α
3. Perceived social harmony, (=0.67) α
4. Perceived general honesty, (=0.84) α

These values are very satisfactory with the exception of the social harmony scale which needs some more items, especially for inferences about individual

Table 7.1 *Intercorrelations among the trust scales*

	A	B	C	D
A. Trust in Corporations	1			
B. Social Harmony	0.45	1		
C. General Honesty	0.69	0.53	1	
D. Trust in politicians	0.55	0.48	0.70	1

Table 7.2 *Correlations between trust scales and CT scales*

	Hierarchy	Egalitarianism	Individualism	Fatalism
Trust in Corporations	−0.15	−0.47	−0.20	−0.60
Social Harmony	0.03	−0.12	−0.01	−0.32
General Honesty	−0.08	−0.16	−0.25	−0.60
Trust in politicians	−0.04	0.04	−0.34	−0.52

Table 7.3 *Intercorrelations among the CT scales*

	A	B	C	D
A. Hierarchy	1			
B. Egalitarianism	−0.11	1		
C. Individualism	0.48	−0.25	1	
D. Fatalism	0.22	0.19	0.29	1

scores (not at stake here). The CT scales were scored according to Dake's keying instructions.[3]

Intercorrelations among the trust scales are given in Table 7.1, between the trust scales and the CT scales in Table 7.2, and intercorrelations among the CT scales in Table 7.3.

Only the Fatalism subscale had any sizeable correlations with the trust scales.

Trust and General Risk

Correlations between ratings of general risk and the trust factors, as well as educational level, were computed. The mean proportion of explained variance was 0.087. The level of explanation of risk perception achieved by the trust factors was quite modest. This level seems, however, to be rather typical of attitude-type measures.[4] The findings were quite clear when it came to the differences between the trust dimensions. Only Trust in Corporations and Social Harmony showed a consistent pattern of correlations with perceived

---

3. Reliabilities (Cronbach's) for egalitarianism, individualism, hierarchy and fatalism were, respectively, 0.77, 0.72, 0.48 and 0.74. Clearly, the hierarchy scale needs more items.

4. The CT scales explained a little more of the variance of general risk perception, 0.102.

risk. Beliefs about General Honesty and Trust in Politicians did not correlate much with perceived risk. Separate analyses of personal risk and probability of harm gave similar results to the ones presented for general risk above.

Societal Concerns, Trust and Cultural Theory Scales

The 33 societal concerns used in testing cultural theory were correlated with CT and trust scales. These concern items were the ones used by Dake in his test of CT. It should be noted that only very few are explicitly concerned with technology or the environment; most are social, political or economic. The correlations between CT scales and concerns were rather low. The mean R^2_{adj} was 0.066. This value is normal for CT scales and social concerns data (Sjöberg 1997, in press), maybe even a little on the high side. The data show, on the other hand, stronger correlations between social concerns and trust dimensions; the average R^2_{adj} was 0.098, clearly better than the CT scales.[5] It is to be noted that Trust in Politicians and beliefs about General Honesty, which did not correlate strongly or almost not at all with perceived risk, did correlate with social concerns.

There is clearly a possibility that demographic factors (sex, age, and educational level) and political attitudes (left/right) account for all or some of these relationships. Hence, I decided to compute partial correlations between trust and concerns, and between CT scales and concerns. The demographic variables accounted on the average for 6.7 per cent of the variance of trust scales and for 13.4 per cent of the CT scales. The highest values were 28.1 per cent of the egalitarianism scale and 16.2 per cent of trust in corporations. Political attitude and educational level were the most important factors, and also age for the hierarchy scale.

These results are disturbing for the claims of the CT scales in particular. It is well known that egalitarianism is the scale that works best in accounting for risk perception of all the CT scales; part of this success may thus be due to background factors and political attitude. For each set of explanatory scales 132 correlations with social concerns were computed, with background factors and political attitude partialled out. For trust scales, 70 correlations remained statistically significant but for CT scales only 45 did so. Hence, CT scales not only correlated more weakly with social concerns than the trust scales; what correlations there were seemed also to be more strongly due to the influence of demographics and political attitude. Some explained variance remained, however, and hence CT scales do seem to measure, albeit very weakly, some unique sources of risk perception (Marris et al 1996).

DEMAND FOR RISK MITIGATION

Demand for risk mitigation was only marginally correlated with trust and CT scales. The average R^2_{adj} for trust was 0.059, and for CT scales it was 0.042.

---

5. For some reason, CT scales seem to correlate with concerns with an R^2_{adj} of about 0.1 in American data, considerably lower in European applications (about 0.05).

Table 7.4 *Regression analyses of demand for risk mitigation*

	Personal risk	General risk	Probability of harm	Severity of harm	R^2_{adj}
Smoking	−.13	.25*	.15	.26**	.219
Alcohol	.05	.11	.17	.23**	.130
Motor vehicle exhausts	.04	.17	.26*	.11	.192
AIDS	.09	−.06	.13	.33***	.112
Air pollution	.31**	.00	.02	.22**	.166
High voltage transmission lines	−.01	.34**	.04	.31***	.307
Green house effect	.17	−.15	.29*	.40***	.335
Domestic radon radiation	−.12	.13	.31**	.44***	.382
Inadequate dietary habits	−.14	.11	.14	.38***	.239
Irradiated food	.09	.07	.18	.44***	.417
Traffic accident	.16	.32*	−.17	.27**	.200
Lightning	.07	.09	.20	.12	.067
Depletion of the ozone layer	−.10	.21	.21	.40***	.328
Domestic nuclear power	.17	.25	−.12	.22**	.143
West European nuclear power	−.07	.15	.28	.25**	.213
East European nuclear power	−.13	.13	.29	.27**	.203
Natural background radiation	−.10	.20	.26	.31**	.322
Nuclear waste	.09	−.09	.12	.26**	.076
Genetic engineering	−.12	.18	.10	.41***	.218
Contaminated drinking water	.03	.18	−.25*	.43***	.178
Terrorist attacks	.05	.14	.08	.15	.073
Spoiled food	.09	−.09	.10	.42***	.187
Food contaminated by radiation	.01	.21	−.04	.36***	.189
X-ray diagnostics	−.05	.22	.03	.41***	.214
Sun rays	.07	.16	.03	.24*	.131
War	.07	−.02	.01	.37***	.126
Chemical waste	.01	.04	.19	.32***	.169
Dangerous goods transportation	.01	.00	.11	.54***	.338
Nuclear arms	.07	−.02	.17	.21*	.079
Floods	.16	.08	.13	.22*	.161
Radioactive fallout from the Chernobyl accident	−.08	.13	.30*	.32***	.304
Inadequate medical care	−.08	.05	.05	.55***	.294
Violence and aggression	.17	−.01	.11	.27	.152
Unemployment	−.07	.01	.18	.58***	.456
Mad cow disease	−.06	.22	.20	.35***	.273

Ratings of risk, probability and severity of consequences are explanatory variables, (ß weights given in the table. R^2_{adj} gives the proportion of variance explained on the basis of the four trust dimensions.

(Perceived severity of consequences also was very little explained by risk dimensions and CT scales.) What, then, accounts for demand for risk mitigation? See Table 7.4.

It is very clear from these results that severity of consequences is the most important factor in demand for risk reduction. The same result has been reported earlier in several data sets (Sjöberg 1994). On the other hand, trust does not seem to be a good explanatory variable for understanding demand for risk mitigation or severity of consequences; it is more clearly related to perceived risk or probability of harm.

Is the effect of trust on risk acceptance asymmetric? It has been argued that low trust is especially detrimental to risk acceptance. If so, low trust might be sufficient to be a determinant of low risk acceptance while high trust may be necessary for risk acceptance, but not sufficient. In turn, such a trend should be possible to discern in contingent means or probabilities of risk acceptance, given low or high trust.

In order to test this possibility, I computed an index of demand for risk mitigation by taking the mean of all demand ratings, and an average trust index by averaging the four trust and harmony scales. These indices were then transformed into quantiles and the lowest and highest 25 per cent in the trust scale were singled out. The distributions of ratings of demand for risk mitigation of these subjects show the expected lack of symmetry, although it is rather weak. Consider the extreme values of low trust and high demand for risk mitigation and its opposite, high trust and low demand for risk mitigation. In the former case, 35.7 per cent of the low trust respondents are found, in the latter 24.4 per cent of the high trust respondents. The high trust respondents spread their ratings of demand for risk mitigation more than the low trust subjects did – hence the low trust subjects appeared to be more inclined towards an extreme (low) demand response than the corresponding tendency for the high trust subjects to give an extremely low response with regard to demand for mitigation.

If high trust is necessary for low demand for risk mitigation, the corresponding trends should be discerned in contingent probabilities calculated for groups high or low in demand for risk mitigation. However, the data did not show the expected reverse trend, but rather, again, that those rating a high level of demand for mitigation had the smallest dispersion of trust and a concentration of subjects with low trust. The correlation between trust and demand for risk mitigation at this level of indices was -0.15, still a low value. The analysis of contingent distributions showed, however, that the scatter was not uniform, and the simple over-all correlation coefficient does not tell the whole story of the relationship between trust and risk acceptance.

Because the analysis of causal structure of trust and demand for risk mitigation showed lack of symmetry, but not the expected type, it was decided to run a cluster analysis of the data, including standardized indices of trust, expected severity of consequences of harm and demand for risk mitigation, as well as a standardized index of mean perceived general risk. The means for a five cluster solution (the K-means procedure of SPSS was used) are given in Table 7.5.

Clusters 1 and 3 have expected patterns of means: demand for mitigation is associated in a logical manner with trust and risk perception. The small cluster 2 has low means in all four variables and may be an effect of response bias (acquiescence); these subjects also had a low average educational level. Cluster 5 may be seen as exhibiting a fairly reasonable pattern; the high level of demand for mitigation in that cluster can be explained by the high level of expected severity of consequences of harm. Cluster 4 gives paradoxical results: a low

Table 7.5 *Means of trust and risk indices in a five cluster solution*

	Cluster no.				
Variable	1	2	3	4	5
Demand for risk reduction	−0.36	−1.42	0.58	−0.65	0.68
Trust	1.24	−0.65	−0.95	−0.26	0.59
Perceived general risk	−0.85	−0.64	1.04	−0.47	0.10
Severity of consequences	−0.83	−1.88	0.22	0.21	0.71
N	27	12	44	38	44

All variables were standardized

Table 7.6 *Correlations between demand for risk mitigation and trust and risk indices in a five cluster solution*

	Cluster no.				
Variable	1	2	3	4	5
Trust	−0.25	−0.05	−0.24	−0.08	−0.14
Perceived general risk	−0.03	−0.05	−0.06	−0.03	−0.19
Severity of consequences	−0.01	0.00	0.29	0.00	0.27
N	27	12	44	38	44

level of demand for mitigation and low trust and high severity of consequences, together with low perceived risk. Clearly, clusters 2 and 4 exhibit non-logical patterns of data which presumably must be understood with reference to phenomena not readily inferred from the data at hand.

The correlations between demand for risk mitigation and the three trust and risk indices are given in Table 7.6. The table shows that demand for risk mitigation was virtually uncorrelated with trust and perceived risk in clusters 2 and 4, while there was some correlation in the other clusters – the ones that had more logical mean profiles in Table 7.5. A multiple regression analysis with data from clusters 2 and 4 only gave an R^2_{adj} of 0.064 (trust had no significant ß-value), while the corresponding analysis for clusters 1, 3 and 5 pooled data gave an R^2_{adj} of 0.029. In the latter analysis, trust and severity of consequences both had highly significant ß-values of −0.31 and 0.44, respectively.

A series of regression analyses was run for both general risk and demand for risk mitigation as dependent variables, for each hazard and with the trust and harmony scales as independent variables. General risk was much better explained in the reduced data set containing only clusters 1, 3 and 5 – 16.2 per cent (twice the value in the whole sample). On the other hand, demand for risk mitigation was only slightly better explained, on average. Here the value was 0.061 as compared to 0.059 for the whole sample.

SPECIFIC AND GENERAL FACTORS IN
PERCEIVED RISK AND RISK TOLERANCE

Previous research has shown that perceived nuclear waste risk is well accounted for by three major factors: general risk sensitivity, fear of radiation, and attitude to nuclear power (Sjöberg 1996). Some further explanatory power is provided by background factors, and a dimension of unnatural and immoral risk. The model achieved about 60 per cent explained variance in several data sets (see also Sjöberg and Drottz- Sjöberg 1994). A special analysis of perceived nuclear waste risk is called for in the present context. An index of general risk sensitivity was constructed by pooling all items having to do with non-nuclear and non-radiation risks; this is my measure of general risk sensitivity. In a similar way, items measuring non-nuclear risk of ionizing radiation (eg X-ray diagnostics) were pooled. Analogous measures were constructed for demand for risk mitigation. Four regression analyses were carried out, two with trust dimensions as added explanatory variables, the other with CT scales. Results are given in Tables 7.7 and 7.8 below.

Table 7.7 *Regression analyses of nuclear waste ratings with trust dimensions added*

Explanatory variable	Perceived general risk	Demand for risk reduction
Radiation (non-nuclear)	0.43***	0.08
Risk sensitivity	0.36***	0.64***
Trust in Corporations	–0.14*	0.01
Social Harmony	–0.01	–0.05
Trust in politicians	0.08	0.03
General Honesty	0.06	0.09
R^2_{adj}	0.608	0.518

The table gives ß weights and R^2_{adj}

Table 7.8 *Regression analyses of nuclear waste ratings with CT scales added*

Explanatory variable	Perceived general risk	Demand for risk reduction
Radiation (non-nuclear)	0.41***	0.10
Risk sensitivity	0.34***	0.66***
Egalitarianism	–0.17**	0.06
Hierarchy	0.04	0.01
Fatalism	0.00	0.05
Individualism	–0.01	–0.02
R^2_{adj}	0.626	0.516

The table gives ß weights and R^2_{adj}

The results show that specific fear of radiation and general risk sensitivity are most important in accounting for perceived risk and corresponding measures are most important when it comes to demand for risk mitigation. In the case of perceived risk, trust or CT add a marginal amount of explanatory power in addition to the two major explanatory factors.

Perceived risk of nuclear waste could be very well accounted for by the simple models, while risk intolerance was somewhat more difficult to account for. Whatever caused this difficulty could not be caught with trust or CT dimensions. Adding specific variables of severity of consequences and probability of injury did not improve on the models. A clue is given by the rank order of the means of the variable of demanded risk mitigation. The lowest three hazards were lightning, natural background radiation and dietary habits. These are perhaps hazards where the government cannot or should not interfere, being natural hazards or lifestyle phenomena. The three highest values belonged to nuclear waste, unemployment and inadequate medical care. It seems that such hazards may be among those where the government is perceived as having both special responsibility and competence. Hence, data on responsibility and competence are called for in the further study of demand for risk mitigation.

DISCUSSION

Four facets of trust were identified and measured: trust in corporations, trust in politicians, belief in social harmony and belief in general honesty. Only trust in corporations and beliefs in social harmony correlated with perceived risk. On the other hand, concern over social problems was correlated with all four trust dimensions.

CT scales were little correlated with trust dimensions, with the exception of fatalism. Trust dimensions were more efficient in accounting for concerns than the CT scales, which, however, probably work better on US data. Perhaps the CT scales need to be revised and adapted more thoroughly for applications in different countries. On the other hand, they explain on average no more than 10 per cent of perceived risk even when they work best, in US applications (Sjöberg 1997, in press).

The average level of explanatory power achieved by the trust dimensions was modest, about 10 per cent. The nuclear power and waste risks were explained at a level somewhat higher than the average of the 35 hazards investigated. Perceived level of nuclear waste risk was well accounted for by a simple model including general risk sensitivity and specific fear of radiation, trust dimensions or CT scales adding only a marginal amount of explained variance (although statistically significant). I conclude that trust plays a role, albeit a rather modest one, in risk perception. These results agree well with previous studies of the relationship between general trust measures and risk perception. Specific items is perhaps another matter, but here it was considered to be of the most immediate interest to study trust at the general level. Demand for risk mitigation was harder to explain on the basis of trust dimensions, and still harder using CT scales. Here, a factor of a general tendency to demand risk mitigation was the only efficient general explanatory variable. At the level of specific hazards, severity of consequences was by far the most important explanatory variable of demand for risk mitigation.

There was some support in the data for the notion that low trust is sufficient to create a high demand for risk mitigation, while high trust is not sufficient to create the opposite, only necessary. In turn, this means that simple correlations are not sufficient to analyse the relationship between trust and risk acceptance. Cluster analysis enabled me to identify about 30 per cent of the subjects as having different dynamics than the postulated one between risk acceptance, trust and risk perception. When these subjects were deleted, trust had a stronger impact on demand for risk mitigation. In addition, perceived risk was much better explained by trust scales in this subgroup than in the whole sample. In turn, this could mean that trust is quite important for a majority of subjects even if it is not for a large minority.

Hazards may be seen as caused by various agents and circumstances. Here I have dealt with such agents at three different levels: people in general or human nature, the state of society and corporations/government. There could be other sources of hazards, such as individual people or ways in which they are affected, eg by drugs. There is also the possibility of ill will or even evil intentions, not covered here.

When it comes to demand for risk mitigation it is also likely that responsibility and competence of the government must be measured if that variable is to be better understood. However, it is quite clear that risk perception per se is insufficient to cover the policy implications of beliefs and attitudes about hazards.

8 Institutional Trust and Confidence: A Journey into a Conceptual Quagmire[1]

Daniel Metlay

What are we to make of the recent explosion of academic research focusing on trust relationships? At the very least, these studies signal that trust plays a number of central roles in the civic culture. For example, trust seems to influence how individuals perceive technological risks (Flynn et al 1992); it appears to catalyse regional economic development (Putnam 1993); it likely provides a 'lubricant' for interactions within organizations (Meyerson et al. 1996); and it probably is linked to the level of political legitimacy enjoyed by democratic regimes (Inglehart 1990). But, at the same time, the notion of trust comes in so many flavours, packages, and subspecies that it seems to have been swallowed up in a conceptual quagmire. Scholars have presented us with 'calculus-based trust', 'knowledge-based trust', and 'identification-based trust' (Lewicki and Bunker 1996). They have argued about 'characteristic-based trust', 'process-based trust', and 'institutional-based trust' (Zucker 1986).

For researchers, these conceptual puzzles and mysteries are challenging and stimulating, offering as they do an almost endless supply of grist for contemplation, speculation, and conjecture. But for me, an academic turned practitioner, this intellectual quagmire makes it hard, if not impossible, to respond persuasively to policy-makers' simple, yet quite pragmatic, requests for help: 'What can I do to increase the public's trust and confidence in my agency? What changes in organizational behaviour must I institutionalize to make a difference over the long-term? Given limited resources, which of those changes ought I try hardest to secure?'

Elsewhere I have tried to provide some answers to those questions for the particular case of the Department of Energy (DOE) and its management of radioactive wastes generated by commercial reactors and by the production of nuclear weapons (SEAB 1993). In this chapter, I would like to take a very modest first step in exploring a much larger question – whether those prescriptions might be generalized and applied to other situations and circumstances.

1. The views expressed in this paper do not necessarily represent the views of the US Nuclear Waste Technical Review Board, a presidentially appointed independent federal agency charged by Congress with evaluating the scientific and technical validity of the Department of Energy's radioactive waste disposal efforts.

To do so, I shall address the following issue: what meaning can be attached to an individual's assertion that she has trust and confidence in a particular institution? I conclude that trust is not a complex and multifaceted concept. Rather it is quite simple, depending on two distinctly different components or dimensions: (1) a tightly interconnected and intertwined set of affective beliefs about institutional behaviour and (2) how competent the institution appears to be. I then investigate the implications of this finding for two recent analyses of trust. This chapter ends with some thoughts on the challenges policy-makers face in restoring public trust and confidence.

GIVING MEANING TO TRUST AND CONFIDENCE

In the corpus of research just alluded to as well as many other works, it is striking just how often 'trust' is either an undefined term or a term defined using concepts that circle the reader back to the notion of trust. Indeed attempting to attach meaning to trust conjures up former Justice Potter Stewart's oft-quoted reference to pornography – it is something that cannot be defined precisely but one knows it when one sees it. Settling on a common definition may, of course, be premature, given the notion's richness and reach. But the fuzziness that unfortunately surrounds the concept does impede efforts to make claims either about its antecedents or its consequences.[2] Nevertheless, despite the poorly delineated ground where terminological assertions become blurred with empirical propositions, a set of proto-hypotheses have been advanced that attempt to imbue with meaning the notion of institutional trust and confidence. I will attempt to summarize them briefly.

- *Trust and confidence is related to whether an institution is seen as being open and forthcoming.* Ouchi (1981) details the prominent role that trust plays in the functioning of Theory Z organizations, especially with respect to maintaining openness. Based on the discussions held in a focus group that was evaluating the DOE's proposed radioactive waste repository in Nevada, Mushkatel and his colleagues (1992) report a close connection between trust and openness.
- *Trust and confidence is related to whether an institution is seen as being reliable and consistent in its actions.* Trust carries an element of risk; those who trust have to be willing to be vulnerable to other individuals' (or institutions') actions.[3] The more those actions are seen as predictable, the less the risk and the greater the willingness to trust. McGregor (1967) puts it most directly, 'Inconsistencies between words and actions decrease trust.'

---

2. As the sociologist C Wright Mills put it: 'When we define a word, we are merely inviting others to use it as we would like it to be used; for the purpose of definition is to focus argument upon fact, and the proper result of good definition is to transform argument over terms into disagreements about facts, and thus open arguments to further inquiry.' (Mills, 1959)
3. When we can count on someone *doing the opposite* of what he says, we remark ironically, 'I can really trust him to do that.'

- *Trust and confidence is related to whether an institution is seen as having integrity and being honest.* Slovic (1993) identifies events that are quite likely to decrease trust in those running a hypothetical large nuclear power plant. Of the six events most destructive of trust, three involved a lack of integrity and dishonesty: officials lying to government, covering up problems, and falsifying records.
- *Trust and confidence is related to whether an institution is seen as being credible.* Although Renn and Levine (1991) believe that credibility followed from trust, other students of the subject suggest that the causal arrow is reversed. For example, economic studies that are not subjected to rigorous peer review may be viewed as self-serving rather than credible. An institution that appears to have a history of such behaviour is less likely to be trusted. Fromer and colleagues (1995), for example, use credibility to understand public reactions to the transportation of nuclear waste.
- *Trust and confidence is related to whether an institution is seen as being fair.* One party will be more likely to trust another if it believes that it will not be unfairly taken advantage of (Bromiley and Cummings 1993).
- *Trust and confidence is related to whether an institution is seen as being caring and concerned.* The assessment of political institutions, which depends on the trust of the electorate, is, in part, based on their concern for the broad 'public' interest (March and Olsen 1989).
- *Trust and confidence is related to whether an institution is seen as being competent.* Gabarro (1987) and Kirkpatrick and Locke (1991) observe how the trust relationship between managers and subordinates depends on perceptions of competence. Sako (1992) relates how buyer organizations will often forgo quality inspections once they become convinced of suppliers' competence.

These propositions clearly specify what at least some researchers believe to be the *core elements* of trust and confidence. Unfortunately none of those investigators have subjected their claims to an especially rigorous empirical test. We are therefore at a loss to know whether the elements are linked *in fact* to some relatively valid measure of trust and confidence. Furthermore we do not know how or even if the elements are related structurally to each other. The next section of this paper will address both of those issues.

DATA AND METHODOLOGY

In 1990, Secretary of Energy James D Watkins established a task force[4] to provide him with advice on steps the Department of Energy might take to increase public trust and confidence in its programmes for managing radioactive waste generated by commercial reactors and by efforts to produce nuclear

---

4. The author served as director of that task force

weapons (SEAB 1993).[5] Among the activities undertaken by the task force was the development of a survey to measure attitudes relevant to trust held by those who had a demonstrated interest in or who were affected by those programmes. The survey was first administered in 1992 to a group of 351 respondents. Succeeding Watkins in 1993, Secretary of Energy Hazel R O'Leary decided to use the survey to measure the Department's progress in establishing public trust and confidence. The survey was therefore readministered in 1994 to 452 respondents.[6] (Details about the design and administration of the survey appear in the appendix to this chapter.)

What distinguishes this survey from many, if not most, other studies of institutional trust is that all respondents had to pass a threshold test of *actual involvement* with the DOE; they had to interact in some fashion with the Department or its contractors for at least an average of one hour per week over the course of a year.[7] Thus, when they were asked questions having to do with trust and confidence in the DOE, individuals' answers were less likely to be labile, spur-of-the-moment responses and more likely to reflect relatively well-established attitudes. Moreover, for a sizeable fraction of those interviewed, their relationship with the DOE was a significant aspect of their professional lives; consequently their answers were grounded in substantial and direct experience and in a relatively high degree of knowledge about the complex work taking place at the agency.

Whenever possible, questions (items) that had been well validated were incorporated into the survey. For example, the key dependent variable, trust and confidence, was measured using a question that had been included in various Gallup polls for nearly a quarter of a century:[8]

I am going to read you a list of institutions in American society. Would you tell me how much confidence you, yourself, have in each one – a great deal, quite a lot, some, or little. . .?

5. The United States is not the only country where lack of trust created difficulties for siting and developing nuclear waste repositories. A similar tale, for example, unfolded in the spring of 1997 in the United Kingdom. Nirex, the company charged with the responsibility for managing Britain's waste, was dealt a major blow when the Secretary for the Environment disapproved a plan to construct an underground laboratory near Sellafield in Cumbria. Critics of the plan were suspicious that the laboratory would become a 'Trojan horse': once it was built, it would be much harder to stop the construction of a repository at the site. In fact, the former chairman of Britain's Radioactive Waste Management Advisory Committee stated that before Nirex starts looking for another site it would have to learn 'to operate in a transparent manner and be responsive to the need to gain public confidence.' (*Nature*, vol 386, April 3 1997, p. 424.)

6. Obviously some individuals were interviewed both times. The survey was also administered in 1996, but those data are not yet available.

7. In addition, the individual could not be employed by the federal government or by a contractor of the DOE.

8. An alternative item is used in the Harris Poll and by the National Opinion Research Center: '*As far as the people running [various institutions] are concerned, would you say that you have a great deal of confidence, only some confidence, or hardly any confidence at all in them?*' This formulation was rejected because it personalized trust and confidence and because it appeared biased toward lack of trust and confidence.

- US military
- Nuclear Regulatory Commission
- Organized religion
- Department of Energy field offices
- Banks
- National Academy of Sciences
- Department of Energy headquarters
- Environmental Protection Agency
- Nuclear power industry
- Congress
- Department of Energy contractors
- News media
- National environmental groups
- Electric utilities.

One important issue had to be addressed when first analysing data from these items: do those interviewed evaluate the three organizational units of the Department of Energy – headquarters, field offices, and private-sector contractors – in a common fashion? The answer, it turns out, was clearly yes. The level of trust accorded one unit correlated very highly with the level of trust accorded another unit.[9] Moreover, although a factor analysis of responses to all 14 institutions sorted them into three distinct groups,[10] each of the units of the Department of Energy fell into only *one* of them.[11] Supported by these findings, a Likert scale was constructed using the respondents' perceptions of trust for all three units. This scale, which I shall call DOEPTC, represents public trust and confidence in the Department of Energy as a whole.

Developing items to measure the core elements of trust and confidence was not nearly as straightforward. None of the relevant studies furnished specific wording for items that could be used. Thus an effort had to be undertaken from scratch to construct questions that had at least *face validity*. Discussions were held with many of the researchers in this field.[12] Then different wordings were reviewed by small focus groups composed of individuals similar to those who might be asked to participate in the survey. Nineteen items were finally adopted and included in a much larger questionnaire. They are grouped

9. In 1992, the associations were: Headquarters/field – 0.644; Headquarters/private-sector contractors – 0.628; and Field/private-sector contractors – 0.539.

10. Factor analysis is a methodology for assessing whether there is an underlying structure in respondents' answers to a series of items. In the classical factor analysis model, an item is expressed as a linear combination of underlying common factors or hypothetical constructs. The technique estimates the *coefficients or loadings* of each of the factors. See Harmon (1967).

11. The principal components technique was employed. Only three factors had eigenvalues greater than one. (This is the convention normally used to pare down the number of factors that will be analysed further.) In the 1992 data set, the three factors account for nearly 55% of the variance. A varimax rotation yielded these loadings: DOE field offices – 0.798; DOE headquarters – 0.783; DOE contractors – 0.701. In the 1994 data set, the three factors account for nearly 52% of the variance. A varimax rotation yielded these loadings: DOE field offices – 0.744; DOE headquarters – 0.693; DOE contractors – 0.722.

12. None of those researchers are responsible, of course, for the final wording of any of the items.

by the element of trust and confidence they attempt to measure and are presented below.[13]

Do you strongly agree, somewhat agree, somewhat disagree, strongly disagree that the Department of Energy. . .?

Openness
■ Provides all relevant unclassified information to the public
■ Does not explain the reasons for the decisions it makes
■ Tells the whole truth about important activities

Reliability
■ Does not take its commitments seriously enough
■ Changes policies without good reason
■ Tries hard to keep its promises

Integrity
■ Takes actions that are consistent with its words
■ Rarely acknowledges the mistakes it has made
■ Pursues relevant studies even if the research may call into question some aspects of a program
■ Is too influenced by politics

Credibility
■ Ignores the views of scientists who disagree with them
■ Has difficulty explaining its studies before independent peer review panels
■ Distorts the facts to make its case

Fairness
■ Is committed to impartial process for making decisions
■ Makes a good faith effort to treat everyone even-handedly

Caring
■ Can be counted on to do the right thing
■ Does not listen to concerns raised by people like you

Competence
■ Has the necessary skills to carry out its job
■ Is generally staffed by first class scientists and engineers.

An exploratory factor analysis on these items was performed on the data from the 1992 survey. Three components, which accounted for nearly 62 per cent of the total variance, were extracted employing the principal components technique followed by a varimax rotation.[14] But only one item, 'too influenced by politics', loaded at a level of greater than 0.600 on the third component. Its correlation with DOEPTC, moreover, was the lowest of any of the 19 items; just 0.252 in 1992 and 0.170 in 1994. For these two reasons, the item was eliminated from any further analysis.

---

13. These items were *not* asked in this order.
14. Their eigenvalues were 9.680, 1.129, and 0.965 respectively. The fourth highest eigenvalue was 0.763.

A second exploratory factor analysis was carried out with the remaining 18 items using the 1992 data set once again.[15] This time just two components, which accounted for over 59 per cent of the total variance, emerged.[16] To demonstrate that this simpler factor structure was more than a statistical artifact, a confirmatory factor analysis was performed on the 1994 data set. As before, just two components, which accounted for 54 per cent of the total variance, emerged. The items' loadings on each component and their correlations with DOEPTC are presented in Table 8.1.

THE STRUCTURE OF INSTITUTIONAL TRUST AND CONFIDENCE

The interpretation of the results of the 1992 data analysis is unambiguous. The 16 items that tapped what might be called the *affective elements* – openness, reliability, integrity, credibility, fairness, and caring – only fell along the first component. The two items that spoke to *institutional competence* fell along the second.[17]

The findings using the 1994 data set are not quite as clear cut. Compared to the earlier data, the loadings of the items that fell along the first, affective, component were somewhat lower overall, while the corresponding loadings on the second, competence, component were somewhat higher. One item that fell along the affective component in the 1992 data set – 'pursues relevant studies' – clearly fell on the competence component in 1994. These structural shifts however are not unexpected. Investigators who routinely deal with this kind of data, such as survey researchers and psychological test designers, are very familiar with the truism that drawing meaning from factor analyses is more often an art than a science.

Yet in this instance, one does not have to be a Picasso or even a Wyeth: a very strong case can be made that the *underlying structure of attitudes and beliefs* about trust and confidence is virtually the same in 1994 as it was in 1992. Out of the 16 items that clearly fell along the affective component based on the analysis of the first data set, all but four clearly fell along it based on the analysis of the second data set. And three out of those four were just barely lower than the 0.600 conventional cut-off level for inclusion in a particular component.

The strong congruence between the 1992 and 1994 results is further reinforced when the relationship between the two components and the constructed variable DOEPTC is examined. Using factor scores to weigh the contribution of each item to the underlying component, scales measuring affect and competence were built. The results of regressing the component scales against DOEPTC are presented in Figure 8.1. In each year, the affective component

15. A principal components analysis followed by a varimax rotation was used.
16. Their eigenvalues were 9.570 and 1.027 respectively. The third highest eigenvalue was 0.864.
17. The two items that use 'studies' as a vehicle for assessing integrity and credibility – 'pursues relevant studies' and 'has difficulty explaining studies to independent peer reviewers' – have the lowest loadings on the first component. But it is significant to note that those interviewed still did respond strongly to the affective character of these two items.

Table 8.1 *The components of trust and confidence*

Elements of Trust and Confidence	Components 1992		Components 1994		Correlation with DOEPTC	
	1	*2*	*1*	*2*	*1992*	*1994*
Openness						
Provides all relevant unclassified information	**.687**	.284	**.671**	.194	.598	.482
Does not explain reasons for the decisions it makes	**−.738**	−.019	**−.702**	−.204	−.502	−.404
Tells the whole truth about important activities	**.751**	.311	**.742**	.218	.680	.543
Reliability						
Does not takes its commitments seriously enough	**−.632**	−.342	**−.627**	−.246	−.526	−.423
Changes policy without good reason	**−.709**	−.208	**−.588**	−.282	−549	−.448
Tries hard to keep its promises	**.719**	.363	**.574**	.485	.629	.467
Integrity						
Takes actions that are consistent with its words	**.708**	.383	**.658**	.460	.614	.597
Rarely acknowledges mistakes it has made	**−.575**	−.312	**−.630**	−.071	−.533	−.396
Pursues relevant studies even though the research may call into question some programs	**.588**	.308	.347	.507	.531	.384
Credibility						
Ignores the views of scientists who disagree with them	**−.723**	−.279	**−.670**	−.226	−.579	−.487
Has difficulty explaining its studies before independent peer review panels	**−.596**	−.110	**−.640**	−.124	−.385	−.473
Distorts the facts to make its case	**−.777**	−.268	**−.726**	−.281	−.636	−.539
Fairness						
Is committed to an impartial process of decision making	**.736**	.249	**.593**	.448	.676	.475
Makes a good faith effort to treat everyone even-handedly	**.710**	.384	**.630**	.390	.653	.543
Caring						
Can be counted on to do the right thing	**.714**	.395	**.639**	.453	.735	.613
Does not listen to concerns raised by people like you	**−.718**	−.225	**−.714**	−.339	−.524	−.545
Competence						
Has necessary skills to carry out the job	.214	**.847**	.197	**.780**	.471	.479
Is generally staffed by first class scientists and engineers	.231	**.816**	.083	**.823**	.468	.334

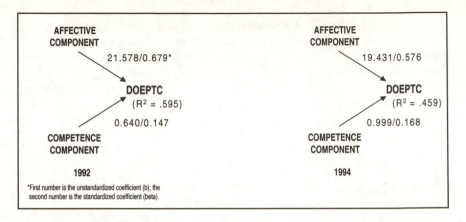

Figure 8.1 *Relationship between the two components and DOEPTC*

had roughly four times the impact of the competence component in predicting DOEPTC.

COMPARISON WITH OTHER RECENT ANALYSES

These findings suggest that some central claims about institutional trust and confidence may have to be reconsidered. In particular, they present the strongest evidence for revising the conventional wisdom about the number and meaning of the components or dimensions that constitute trust. These findings also speak, albeit less definitively, to the role values play in engendering trust.

The Dimensionality of Trust

Over the past two decades, scholars have speculated on and tried to discover the number and the meaning of the components or dimensions embedded within the notion of trust. Barber (1983) was the first to posit a two-dimensional concept: the expectation of technical competence and the expectation that fiduciary responsibilities will be fulfilled. Many of those cited above supplemented Barber's concept with new shades of meaning. Mushkatel and his colleagues (1992), for instance, contend that trust may have as many as seven distinct dimensions. Still others sought to investigate the question empirically. Butler (1991) summarizes a number of such studies, some of which claim that trust has as many as four dimensions. Butler's own research leads him to conclude that there are ten dimensions. Mishra (1996) argues that there are four dimensions.[18]

18. He further contends that they 'combine multiplicatively in determining the overall degree of trust that one party has with respect to a given referent.' I tested this claim using the survey data from both 1992 and 1994 and discovered no support for it. I first estimated a multiplicative model of the affective and competence components. It explained less variance than did a linear model. I then added a multiplicative term to the linear regression and found that its coefficient was not statistically significant.

A study by Peters and his colleagues (1997) most directly challenges the findings of this chapter. Based on surveys examining public knowledge and perceptions of chemical risk in six communities, they hypothesize and claim to demonstrate that 'perceptions of trust and credibility' in a number of institutions are dependent on three factors: 'perceptions of knowledge and expertise, perceptions of openness and honesty, and perceptions of concern and care'. This work, however, suffers from significant conceptual and methodological flaws.

Some of the conceptual problems are evident in the way the hypothesis is framed. Notions that are at least arguably distinct – trust and credibility, openness and honesty, and concern and care – are merged. This conceptual fuzziness extends to the construction of the single item used to measure each of the key dependent and independent variables.[19] In particular, the respondents are asked to evaluate trust but not credibility, openness but not honesty, and concern but not caring.

The methodological problems however are more troubling. Rather than using a statistical approach that is designed to reveal dimensionality, such as factor analysis, Peters and his colleagues opt for linear regression. They justify the choice of this technique by asserting that the intercorrelation among the independent variables is too small to introduce biases caused by multicollinearity.[20] Although it is true that, under conditions of perfect multicollinearity, the relevant independent variables almost certainly will fall along the same dimension, the contrapositive does not necessarily hold true.[21] Put more simply, Peters and his colleagues used the wrong tool to substantiate their claims.

In contrast, the analysis reported here seems quite robust even though it would be reckless to propose that these findings hold for all populations that might be surveyed or for all other institutions. Nevertheless the analysis does suggest that, rather than being a richly complex and multidimensional notion, trust may be actually quite simple and two-dimensional. The competence component is identical with Barber's first element of trust. But the affective component is different than and not as straightforward as fiduciary responsibility. In fact wrapped up in the affective component are a wide variety of highly correlated attitudes and beliefs. They resist separation statistically. But the more one thinks about these affective elements, the clearer it becomes that they are also conceptually difficult to separate as they are constantly rubbing up against each other across vague and diffuse boundaries. At

19. Personal communication to the author from Richard G Peters, October 17, 1997.

20. In the classical normal linear regression model, it is assumed that none of the independent variables are perfectly correlated with any of the others or with any linear combination of the others. When this assumption is violated, the condition of perfect multicollinearity arises. When all of the independent variables are uncorrelated with each other, there is complete absence of multicollinearity. Thus multicollinearity is a matter of degree, not kind. If it is too high, the estimates of the regression coefficients will be biased. See Kmenta (1971).

21. I replicated the analysis reported by Peters and his colleagues using the items and data from the two SEAB surveys. For both years, when knowledge, openness and honesty, and concern and caring were regressed against DOEPTC, statistically significant coefficients were generated. This result occurred notwithstanding the fact that the last two independent variables were shown to fall along a single dimension. For a more generalized statement of this point, see Kmenta (1971).

the end of this essay, I discuss the implications for policy-makers of this circumstance.

What about Values?

In a major research effort, Earle and Cvetkovich (1995;1997) explicate what is essentially a normative theory of social relations. They look to supplant pluralist society with a cosmopolitan one, thereby attenuating the cleavages that now divide groups. This transition is facilitated by social trust. In the course of explicating their ideas, they advance very different claims about the under-pinnings of trust and confidence.[22] In their view, basing trust and confidence either on some perceived level of institutional competence or on affective reactions to specific institutional behaviours is cognitively too demanding. Instead they contend that what counts is whether there are *shared values* between the 'truster' and the 'trustee'. They consider as especially powerful the cultural values associated with Douglas and Wildavsky's (1982) ideal types, the hierarchist, individualist, and egalitarian.

How does the perspective Earle and Cvetkovich bring to bear fit with earlier research on institutional trust? Their empirical investigations provide some indirect, but not full, support for their claims. And because their book was published several years after the SEAB survey was developed, data unfortu-nately could not be collected that might inform this issue with a high degree of methodological and theoretical precision and rigour. But fortuitously two questions were included in both the 1992 and 1994 surveys:

> Would you say that, over the last four years, your level of trust and confidence in the way the Department of Energy deals with the management of radioactive wastes has greatly increased, somewhat increased, stayed about the same, somewhat decreased, or greatly decreased?

> Based on your experience in dealing with the Department of Energy on issues related to the management of radioactive wastes, please tell me whether you strongly agree, somewhat agree, somewhat disagree, or strongly disagree with the statement that the DOE has lately become more sensitive to the environmental consequences of its actions?

Because of a natural experiment that took place at the DOE, these items may provide a vehicle for at least roughly evaluating claims by Earle and Cvetko-vich. In January 1993, six months after the first round of interviews, President Clinton was inaugurated. Watkins left office, and O'Leary took his place as Secretary of Energy. Joining her were a number of very senior-level appointees drawn from public interest and national environmental groups. Many of those individuals had been prominent critics of the DOE's radioactive waste manage-ment programmes. Among the changes that O'Leary promised was renewed attention to compliance with a broad range of environmental laws. When the second round of interviews was conducted in September 1994, O'Leary had

---

22. For example, they are strongly critical of both the fundamental premises as well as the prescriptions that were adopted in the report of Watkins' task force (SEAB 1993).

been in office for more than 18 months, probably enough time for any mark she might have made to have been felt.

Approximately 20 per cent of the survey respondents were members of public interest and environmental groups. For these individuals, who Douglas and Wildavsky assert are archetypal egalitarians, the item tapping the perception of increased environmental sensitivity may be a reasonable (unbiased) surrogate or proxy for measuring the degree to which the DOE shares the respondent's commitment to environmental protection. (The logic here is that, because all of these respondents are likely to have a strong commitment to environmental protection, the more they see the DOE pursuing such a course, the more they believe that they share important core values with the agency.) In contrast, the rest of the respondents, presumably, are not as uniformly committed to the egalitarian value of environmental protection, and therefore the impact of shared values will be attenuated for them. Our faith that the sensitivity item is, in fact, a reasonable surrogate or proxy for shared values will be bolstered if it can be shown that changes in the level of trust and confidence are more strongly associated with the perception of increased environmental sensitivity for egalitarians than for the rest of the sample.[23]

Using the 1994 data set, Pearsons' correlation between the perception of increased environmental sensitivity and the change in the level of trust and confidence was calculated. For the egalitarians, the association was 0.415; for the rest of the sample, it was 0.266. The difference between the two measures of association appears to be substantively as well as statistically significant.

If one is prepared to accept that, for members of public interest and environmental groups, the sensitivity item can be used as a reasonable surrogate or proxy for shared values, then the Earle and Cvetkovich conjecture can be explored. In particular, their claim will be supported if it can be shown that the perception of increased environmental sensitivity on the part of the DOE plays a more central role in predicting the absolute level of trust and confidence for egalitarians than for rest of the respondents.

Using the 1994 data set once again, separate regressions were run for members of public interest and environmental groups and for the rest of the respondents. In each instance, DOEPTC was the dependent variable. The independent variables were shared values (increased environmental sensitivity), the affective component, and the competence component. The results are presented in Table 8.2.

On the surface, it would appear that the regression analyses generally support Earle and Cvetkovich: the unstandardized coefficients (bs) for shared values behave exactly as the two researchers would predict. But the interpretation of these findings is seriously complicated by the fact that the regression coefficient for 'shared values' is not statistically significant for egalitarians. I can posit at least three reasons why this result might arise.

23. A t-test of means on the environmental sensitivity item indicated no difference at all between the two subsamples. Thus, it would appear that whether or not the individual represented a public interest or environmental group made no difference in how she *perceived* (as opposed to evaluated) the behaviour of the DOE.

Table 8.2 *The impact of values in predicting DOEPTC*

Dependent Variables	Egalitarians		Rest of the Sample	
	b	*β*	*b*	*β*
Shared values	0.468[†]	0.201[†]	0.186[†]	0.072[†]
Affective component	9.963	0.377	21.510	0.604
Competence component	1.056	0.209	0.743	0.124
Sample size	77		304	
Multiple R^2	.401		.502	

[†]Not significant at $p < 0.05$

1. *There is, in fact, no relationship between shared values and DOEPTC.* This explanation would imply that claims by Earle and Cvetkovich are not correct.
2. *The sample size is too small to yield a statistically significant estimate.* This explanation would suggest that shared values is not the dominant direct influence in producing DOEPTC. Based on the B's, shared values has about the same impact as the competence component but only about one-half as much as the affective component.
3. *The surrogate or proxy for shared values contains too much measurement error.* This explanation leads one to defer making any judgment whatsoever about the arguments advanced by Earle and Cvetkovich.

Although the data do not favour any particular explanation, none is especially supportive of the Earle and Cvetkovich thesis.

IMPLICATIONS FOR POLICY AND THEORY

Leaders of major public and private institutions increasingly appear to recognize that trust and confidence is a valuable commodity that can improve internal operations as well as facilitate interactions with actors outside of the organization. Energy Secretary O'Leary, for example, termed it a 'critical success factor' in the DOE's strategic plan (DOE 1994). For good reason. Trust and confidence legitimates institutions' activities. The more the DOE was trusted, for example, the more an individual believed that the agency should retain its radioactive waste management functions. (The Pearsons' correlations were 0.572 in 1993 and 0.457 in 1994.)

But trust is not a panacea that can cure all ills. In particular, it seems to 'lubricate' relationships, but it does not lead individuals to accept 'good' processes in place of acceptable performance. Two survey items provide some insight into this claim:

Do you strongly agree, somewhat agree, somewhat disagree, or strongly disagree that. . .

- The substance of a decision is more important than the process used to make it.
- You would be more likely to accept a decision you did not agree with if you were involved in the process that made it.

Pearsons' correlation between DOEPTC and the first item was just 0.150 in 1992 and 0.115 in 1994. For the second item, the correlations were 0.228 and 0.013 respectively.

Notwithstanding the limits to what trust can accomplish, most governmental policy-makers still ask the question that launched this chapter: what can be done to increase public trust and confidence? O'Leary certainly undertook a number of initiatives designed to achieve that end.[24] But as Slovic (1993) continues to remind us, it is extremely difficult to restore lost trust and confidence.

The survey data seem to confirm this view. With the exception of the item 'has difficulty with peer reviews', the mean value of *every element* belonging to the affective component shows a positive and statistically significant change between 1992 and 1994. The amount of improvement ranges from a low of about 7 per cent to a high of about 17 per cent. Items such as 'provides relevant unclassified data' and 'distorts the facts' scored some of the largest gains. In contrast, the mean value of *none of the elements* belonging to the competence component changes over the two year period. Given the rather strong impact – shown in Figure 8.1 above – that the affective component has on public trust and confidence, one might reasonably expect that there would be more or less a commensurate increase in DOEPTC. Yet the mean value of that measure is virtually the same in 1992 as it was in 1994.

Perhaps one ought not be surprised at this finding since roughly half of the variance in DOEPTC is not accounted for by either the affective or competence components. Nonetheless it is impossible to avoid asking why O'Leary was not more successful. The survey, unfortunately, does not include items that provide a ready or clear explanation. All I can do is to advance two plausible possibilities.

First, the affective and competence components may interact in ways that are not easy to model statistically. There may, for instance, be some threshold that one or the other component must rise above before the level of trust rises. Alternatively each of the tightly interconnected and intertwined elements of the affective component must show improvement at the *individual level* for trust to be recovered. Indeed, the SEAB task force seems to understand implicitly the potential for some kind of interactive effect between the affective and competence components when it observes (SEAB 1993):

24. O'Leary's major effort was the so-called Openness Initiative, launched in December, 1993. Through it, she released massive amounts of previously classified information about nuclear weapons testing, the stockpile of fissionable materials, and studies of the effects of exposing often unsuspecting human subjects to radiation. These actions placed her on the front page of national publications such as the *Washington Post* and the *New York Times*. They also put her on the covers of *Time* and *Newsweek*. ABC News chose her to be the 'Person of the Week'.

[Our] recommendations are not simply choices on a *menu* – something from Column A can be picked to go along with something from Column B; rather they represent the panel's *recipe* for what the Department should do to strengthen public trust and confidence: put another way, they are threads of roughly comparable importance that make up a fabric.

For policy-makers, of course, this prescription suggests just how difficult it will be to recover trust.

Second, there may be an important relationship between trust and power. When power is distributed relatively evenly, trust is not essential, particularly when exchanges take place over short time horizons and involve clear feedback measures. Each party is in a position to protect its interests either in the absence of trust or if the trust relationship breaks down. Ironically, being able to does seem to make it easier to trust. In the 1992 survey, the Pearsons' correlation between change in the level of trust and a measure of how satisfied the respondent felt about being able to influence the Department of Energy was 0.374. In 1994, it was 0.345.

However when power is distributed unevenly, the trust relationship is more essential for the more dependent and less influential party. Yet maintaining it is more problematic because the more powerful party may believe that its interests will not be adversely affected if trust breaks down. I suspect that we will not make much further progress in escaping the conceptual quagmire that we find ourselves in with respect to institutional trust until we can understand better why those who are weak nevertheless may trust.

APPENDIX: SURVEY DEVELOPMENT AND ADMINISTRATION

Questionnaire Design

A working group composed of DOE officials initially specified the types of information they hoped the survey would gather. Focus groups were conducted with members of various stakeholder organizations to get their views on: a) what factors influenced public trust and confidence; b) what measures might be adopted by the Department of Energy to increase trustworthiness; c) how public trust and confidence might be conceptualized; and d) the utility of various mechanisms for public involvement. Researchers from the Social and Economic Sciences Research Center (SESRC) at Washington State University then developed several drafts of a questionnaire. To keep the instrument to a manageable length, the working group selected those questions that were of greatest importance. SESRC sought peer reviews on a preliminary question-naire from stakeholder groups, academic researchers, and private sector polling experts. The final questionnaire contained a total of 96 items, of which eight were completely open-ended, seven were semi-structured, and the rest were close-ended.

Sample

Stakeholder organizations located throughout the US who were known to have frequent and direct communication with the DOE or its contractors with regard to the Department's environmental restoration and civilian and defence radio-active waste management programmes comprise the population from which a sample was drawn to conduct this study. (Only non-federal and non-contractor organizations were included.)

A database of stakeholders that was created included 949/1282[25] organizational contacts derived from the following sources: a) organizational representatives appearing on Department of Energy Field Office community relations mailing lists; b) organizational representatives who had commented on the Environmental Restoration and Waste Management Programmatic Environmental Impact Statement; c) organizational representatives who commented on the Environmental Restoration and Waste Management Five-Year Plan; d) a national stakeholder list provided by the Office of Civilian Radioactive Waste Management; and e) names provided by organizational representatives who were either replacements for themselves or additional representatives of their organizations. (In cases where an individual was a representative of two organizations, they were called to ask which one they wanted to be associated with and whether they could provide an alternative or replacement contact for the other organization.)

The database contained many local government representatives. If possible, the city manager was chosen as the city representative rather than the mayor. Mayors were included if the city manager was unavailable. The chairman of the county commission was chosen as the county representative. If the chairman was unavailable, a member of the country commission was included. One representative was selected from each of the tribal or Native American organizations listed.

Survey Implementation

Prior Letter

Each person in the data base was sent a letter announcing the study. This letter explained the purpose of the study and indicated why it was important for respondents to participate. The letter also assured respondents that participation was voluntary and that the information provided would be kept confidential.

Interview Procedures

Interviewers received four hours of interviewer training and four hours of training on the telephone questionnaire. The average length of interview was 34/32 minutes. The longest interview conducted was 57/60 minutes. Up to 8/5 attempts were made on 8/22 separate days. Approximately half of the calls were place during morning hours and half in the afternoon for all time zones in the US. The calling period spanned 24/20 business days and 34/28 calendar days. Respondents were provided with an opportunity to reschedule a call if the contact was at an inconvenient time. They could reschedule any time during the day or evening and on any day of the week. Altogether 4,535/3,446 phone calls were made during the interview period.

---

25. Where two numbers appear in the text, the first refers to the 1992 survey administration and the second refers to the 1994 administration.

The interviews were conducted out of the Public Opinion Laboratory of the SESRC. The interviewers used the micro-computer assisted telephone interviewing (MATI) software to aid in the telephone interview. This system displays each item on a monitor; the interviewer then can read the questions to the respondent and enter the response directly into a networked personal computer.

Response Rates

Of the 941/1282 representatives in the data base, 340/444 completed interviews and 11/8 partially completed interviews were conducted. The cooperation rate (the ratio of the number of completed interviews to the number of completed plus refused interviews) was 85.0/91.2 per cent. The completion rate (the ratio of completed interviews to the total number of potential respondents) was 56.4/47.2 per cent The response rates were affected by both the high ineligibility of respondents (insufficient interaction with the DOE) and by interviewers not being able to reach respondents.

9 Trust and Public Participation in Risk Policy Issues

Judith A. Bradbury, Kristi M. Branch and *Will Focht*

INTRODUCTION AND OVERVIEW

Recent social science literature has paid increasing attention to the concept of trust, albeit with differing definitions of the term and its constituents and also with differing emphases on its societal origins, functions, and implications. Many of the early contributors to the literature focused on the role of trust in establishing and maintaining political legitimacy. More recently, discussion has shifted to the role of trust in hazard management and, more broadly, to the fundamental role of trust in modern society.

Over the past decade, we have assisted several federal agencies in their attempts to institutionalize public participation as part of their organizational response to risk policy issues. In large part, these agencies have introduced public participation as a means of addressing public distrust and enhancing their ability to make decisions that can be implemented. In some cases, such as the Secretary of Energy's Advisory Board, public participation was explicitly identified as an organizational response that was needed to re-establish public trust and confidence in the Department of Energy (DOE). However, our review of the literature on both trust and public participation and our experience in developing criteria for evaluating public participation initiatives have resulted in our questioning the wisdom of establishing trust as a goal of public participation and caused us to examine the relationship between trust and public participation.

In this chapter, we provide answers to the following questions, in an attempt to refocus the discussion and identify a more productive research approach to the relationship of trust and public participation in risk policy issues:

- What is trust? What are the differing conceptions and dimensions of trust that have been identified in the literature?
- What are the social functions of trust?
- What is the relationship between trust and public participation in risk policy issues? Why is trust particularly important for agencies such as the

Department of Energy (DOE) that are responsible for development and implementation of policies involving technological risk?
■ How should we define the research problem in examining the relationship between trust and public participation in risk policy issues? What are the key research questions to be addressed?

What is Trust?

Trust is a social construct and an abstraction. Defining the term and delineating the distinction between trust and related concepts such as confidence and legitimacy have proven difficult for both scholars and lay-persons,[1] with definitions varying over time and across authors. In addition, discussions of trust frequently are confused by authors' failure to distinguish the difference between trust and distrust and to clarify causality, in particular to identify what creates trust on the one hand and what trust creates on the other.

Two particular contributions provide a helpful road map, or framework for examining the various concepts, dimensions, and bases of trust that are presented in the literature and that we review briefly in this section: specifically, Lewis and Weigert's (1985) observation that trust, as a social-psychological and relational construct, involves all three fundamental dimensions of social relationships – cognition, effect, and behaviour; and Luhmann's (1979) distinction between trust and distrust.

Lewis and Weigert (1985) emphasize that trust is a social, as well as an individual, psychological process and that it involves reciprocity and therefore social relationships. They delineate trust as a multi-faceted concept that incorporates cognitive, affective, and behavioural dimensions. This analytic distinction helps clarify the three dimensions that have received differing emphases in the literature.

As a cognitive process, trust involves a choice based on reasoning about the available evidence and is based on a degree of cognitive familiarity with the object of trust. This knowledge is necessarily incomplete and incorporates an element of doubt or risk. The affective component involves an emotional bond among participants in a relationship; violation of that bond implies damage to the relationship per se. The behavioural component reflects the actions undertaken in the belief that others will act in a similar manner. Though analytically separate, the three dimensions are combined in actual human experience and, indeed, serve to reinforce one another. For example, one person's or organization's behavioural display of trust may increase both cognitive and affective trust in another, ie, it helps to create evidence of trustworthy behaviour to the other (cognitive aspect of trust), which also reinforces positive sentiments (affective aspect of trust).

---

1. For example, responses to a 1992 survey of representatives of organizations that deal with the US Department of Energy (DOE) radioactive waste programme revealed that almost one-third had difficulty articulating an answer to the question. 'What does the term *trust and confidence* mean to you?' (*See:* Secretary of Energy Advisory Board (SEAB), *Earning Public Trust and Confidence: Requisites for Managing Radioactive Wastes*, US Department of Energy, 1993).

Luhmann (1979) emphasizes the distinction between trust and distrust. He argues that distrust is not the opposite of trust and that the two concepts should be viewed as functional equivalents in their role of reducing complexity. This distinction is important in clarifying the literature, which frequently confuses discussion of the two concepts.

Earle and Cvetkovich (1996) also argue that trust and distrust should not be viewed as falling on a continuum but should be viewed and analysed as separate items. They criticize past work that has treated distrust as a loss of trust ie, that social trust has been incorrectly treated as if it were 'inherent at the beginning' and that 'then things go wrong'. In their view, distrust has been a core value in US political culture from the very beginning: 'In America . . . we learn to *distrust* social trust . . . [and] are taught to *trust* distrust'. Bradbury et al. (1994), in their study of community members' views of the Chemical Weapons Stockpile Disposal Program, found that trust and distrust are closely linked to questions of openness and accountability.

Although interwoven in human experience and combined in various ways in the literature, the dimensions and associated bases for trust are grouped in the discussion below under the cognitive, affective, and behavioural dimensions identified by Lewis and Weigert (1985). Among the cognitive dimensions of trust – or perhaps more accurately viewed as attributes of trustworthiness – expertise and technical competence have been empirically identified with trust and legitimacy (Hollander 1958; French and Raven 1959; Barber 1983; Kasperson 1986; Golding and Tuler 1992). Similarly, Covello (1992) and Peters, Covello and McCallum (1997) propose that competence and expertise, and knowledge and expertise, respectively, be included among trust's dimensions/attributes. Kasperson (1986) suggests adding absence of bias, indicating that the neutrality and impartiality of the trustee is also important in judgements of trustworthiness. Renn and Levine (1991) agree with Kasperson, adding objectivity to the list of attributes.

Other dimensions identified in the literature as affecting judgements about trust include honesty and openness, indicating that trustworthiness is affected by forthrightness and willingness to disclose information (Covello 1992; Peters, Covello and McCallum 1997). Several authors emphasize procedural fairness as a key dimension of trustworthiness. These include Renn, Webler and Kastenholtz (1996) who argue that in pluralistic societies where disagreement exists over what constitutes a fair outcome, procedural fairness is favoured over substantive fairness (Tyler 1988; Tyler and Lind 1992).

Affective dimensions emphasize trust as a social commodity and a relational, group identity-based construct. From this perspective, trust is based on emotional bondedness between the truster and trustee, with emotional bonds enhanced, or determined, by the existence of a perception that the trustee shares important values with the truster. Kramer and Tyler (1996) and Earle and Cvetkovich (1995), for example, present cogent and comprehensive discussions of the relationship between shared values and social trust. Both differentiate two kinds of trust. The first kind is cognitive or rationally constructed (Kramer and Tyler's instrumental social trust or Earle and Cvetkovich's pluralistic or traditional social trust) and is based on rational calculations of perceived competence and attribution of motive (judgments about meeting fiduciary obligations), as were discussed above.[2] The second is socially constructed (Kramer and Tyler's relational trust or Earle and Cvetkovich's cosmopolitan trust) and is based on shared values and group identification. In this view, judgements as to the nature of the social bond between the government institutions and the public are central to judgements of trustworthiness and thence to policy acceptability and legitimacy.

Behavioural dimensions (which are closely linked to the affective) include the element of fiduciary responsibility. Arendt (1968) views a legitimate government as one that is seen as pursuing the interests of the public rather than having interests of its own. Barber (1983) also emphasizes fiduciary responsibility, while Kramer and Tyler (1996) allude to fiduciary responsibility in their identification of 'moral obligation to others'. Bradbury et al. (1994), in their study of community members' views of the Chemical Weapons Stockpile Disposal Program, found that a key reason for residents' distrust of the army was the army's behaviour that demonstrated it could not be trusted to act in the interests of the community. Kasperson, Golding and Tuler (1992) similarly include dedication and commitment to a goal: a public institution is judged as trustworthy when it is seen as acting in the best interests of the public. Covello (1992) and Peters, Covello and McCallum (1997) expand this dimension to caring and empathy, and care and concern, respectively.

WHAT ARE THE SOCIAL FUNCTIONS OF TRUST?

Scholars who have examined the social functions of trust in society have highlighted several features of the concept that are relevant to our discussion of trust in relation to public participation. These are: the discussion of system trust; the role of trust in reducing complexity; the role of trust in fostering collaboration; the element of risk that is involved in trust; and the linkage between trust and public feelings of dependency on technical expertise.

First, is the distinction between *system*, or macro-level trust, and trust based on interpersonal, micro-level relationships. Misztal (1996), who conducts a detailed historical review and analysis of contributions to the trust literature, attributes the interest in system trust to the conditional and transitional nature of modern society. She points to globalization and the absence of commonly accepted standards related to institutions such as the church, family, and work as having led to 'a search for bases for social solidarity, cooperation, and consensus'.[3] Giddens argues that as society has become more complex and differentiated, trust increasingly is required in the form of 'faceless commitment, in which faith is sustained in the workings of knowledge of which the lay person is largely ignorant' (Giddens 1990).

2. Earle and Cvetkovich (1995) note Annette Baier's observation that the traditional formulation of trust is very male-dominated (focusing on descriptors such as competent, responsible, rational, abstract, distanced from life, that are associated with power relationships) and does not include concerns, like caring and shared values.

3. Whether these institutions did, indeed, provide a foundation of trust is an open question. Wynne's insights about the relationship of trust and dependency (discussed in a later section of this paper) may be pertinent here.

Other authors have emphasized the importance of recognizing that trust operates at both an interpersonal (micro) and system (macro) level (Luhmann 1979, 1988; Earle and Cvetkovich 1995; Misztal 1996). Micro-level and macro-level trust are seen as playing a mutually reinforcing role: system trust appears to establish the context within which specific social relationships occur, while establishment of trust on the micro level may also contribute to confidence at the system level. Putnam (1993), for example, distinguishes between the intimate interpersonal trust generated in close-knit groups and the impersonal trust of complex societies, arguing that a general trust in the broader social system develops out of experience with interpersonal trust. In his view (similar to that of Tocqueville), networks of civic engagement at the interpersonal level generate social trust, as social capital.

Second, is the role of trust in reducing complexity. Luhmann (1988), for example, has emphasized the need for trust because of two interdependent changes that are occurring in modern society: increasing complexity and contingency ('the increasing replacement of danger by risk'). He views trust as a medium of communication such as money or power that reduces the complexity of the world. Earle and Cvetkovich (1996) adopt and expand on this viewpoint, arguing that social trust, which is based on shared cultural values, 'developed in tandem with complexity in society'. They state that 'social trust is a simplifying strategy that enables individuals to adapt to complex social environments and thereby benefit from increased social opportunities'.

Third, is the role of trust in fostering collaboration. Misztal (1996) identifies three key, social functions of trust in contributing to (1) reduction in complexity – to the predictability and reliability of interactions (eg., through roles and routines); (2) cohesion – to the formation of the basis of self-identity and, hence, relationships with the wider world; and (3) to collaboration – to the fostering of mutual respect and solidarity among persons with different perspectives, a form of social capital that benefits the larger community. She places particular emphasis on the importance of trust in generating social cooperation in this complex world – providing a background that sustains the smooth running of cooperative relations, solving the free-rider problem, helping reconcile different interests, and securing communication and dialogue by keeping minds open to all evidence. She advocates greater attention be given to conditions under which these mutually reinforcing forms of social capital can be created and sustained.

Fourth, is the recognition that trust involves an element of risk and uncertainty. Misztal (1996), following Luhmann (1979, 1988), emphasizes that to trust is 'more than believing'; it involves 'expectations about something future or contingent' or having 'some belief as to how another person will perform on some future occasion'. She defines trust as 'believ[ing] that the results of someone's intended action will be appropriate from our point of view', and clearly distinguishes between *trust* and *confidence* on the basis of the degree of confidence that is attached to the expectations. Trust is a 'matter of individual determination and involves choosing between alternatives (I decide to take a risk and trust my new colleague), while confidence is more habitual expectation (I am habitually confident that my milkman will deliver milk to my doorstep tomorrow)'. Luhmann (1988) further emphasizes that the distinction between confidence and trust includes a difference in attribution, with trust carrying an internal attribution that leads to the possibility for 'disappointment that depends upon your own personal behaviour'.[4]

Earle and Cvetkovich (1995) similarly define social trust as a 'risk judgment that assigns to other persons (agencies, organizations, institutions, etc.) the responsibility for working on some necessary task', where the person or institution to be trusted may be widely separated from the person making the decision. These authors identify risk management as an example of an area where most tasks are too complex for one individual to address and require that responsibility be assigned to many others.

The final feature of trust highlighted here is the linkage between trust and feelings of dependency. Similar to Luhmann, Wynne (1996) criticizes the treatment of distrust as loss of trust; however, his criticism is from the perspective of the lay person's distrust of technical expertise. His insights are especially relevant to understanding the relationship of trust and distrust to expert and public interpretations of risk in policies involving hazardous technologies and substances. Wynne argues persuasively that an observed lack of overt public opposition or alienation does not necessarily indicate the existence of public trust. He draws on evidence provided by Welsh, and by McKechnie and Welsh, to demonstrate that public concern about excess childhood leukaemias near the Sellafield nuclear reprocessing complex in northern England was evident in the earliest days of the nuclear programme and is not simply a feature of the more recent, post-1970s era as frequently assumed – that before the debate among experts occurred, lay people were already challenging the scientists' expertise and also their enforced dependency upon it to control the physical risk in which they were unavoidably situated. This dependency includes dependency on the experts' framework for defining the terms and language of the debate and is frequently exacerbated by economic dependency.

Wynne (1996) emphasizes that, when accidents or negative incidents occur, the public is likely to feel more than the betrayal of a trust relationship – such events make explicit and force recognition of an 'implicit and long-standing sense of self-denigration at "allowing" their own dependency' on an untrustworthy institution. As he points out:

> There is ample sociological evidence supporting a different theoretical conception of this relationship [between trust and overt dissent], one which recognizes ambivalence and also the clustered problems of agency, identity, and dependency. In other words, the reality of social dependency should not be equated with positive trust, when it could be better characterized as 'virtual' trust or 'as-if' trust . . . [This sociological work] shows how people informally but incessantly problematize their own relationship with expertise of all kinds, as part of their negotiation of their own identities. They are aware of their dependency, and of their own lack of agency even if the boundaries of this are uncertain; and awareness of this causes anxiety, a sense of risk, and an active interest in evidence, for example about the basis of their unavoidable as-if 'trust' in those experts.

---

4. These definitions of *trust and confidence* differ from those provided in the 1993 report of the Secretary of Energy Advisory Board (SEAB), op cit.

What is the Relationship of Trust to Public Participation in Risk Policy Issues?

The detailed review and analysis by Misztal (1996) of the functions fulfilled by trust provide a useful foundation for examining the relationship between trust and public participation in risk management policy. Her emphasis on the role of trust in fostering collaboration offers valuable insights into the linkage.

The role of trust in reducing complexity and generating social cooperation is particularly relevant to our examination of the role of trust in organizations whose risk management policies impact communities and the environment, including agencies such as the DOE. Many of the issues facing DOE as the agency makes decisions related to site cleanup and the storage or disposal of hazardous wastes reflect the difficulties of modern governments in developing and implementing policy. The difficulties are compounded for such agencies, however, by the need to develop policies on highly complex issues that are both technically and socially feasible – where there is frequently both disagreement about the evidence provided by technical experts and a lack of commonly accepted values and standards. The literature indicates that development of cooperation on matters that are of concern to communities surrounding the sites, along potential transportation routes, and across the DOE national complex, requires building an adequate level of trust and lowering the level of distrust among persons with differing perspectives. Communication plays a key role, both in sustaining and being sustained by mutual trust and reducing distrust among different groups, or in Misztal's (1996) words, 'trust is both the fruit of good communication and its necessary precondition'. In the terms of Earle and Cvetkovich (1995), an important aspect of effective communication is a greater appreciation and more effective use of narratives to create and interpret emergent group values.

Misztal's (1996) view of trust and communication is consistent with Funtowicz and Ravetz's (1985) discussion of the need for political debate among different perspectives – for a 'civilized dialogue of risks' – in science-policy controversies and with Earle and Cvetkovich's (1995) discussion about the need for transformational exchange among multiple cultural perspectives. These scholars recommend dialogue, discourse, or narrative as a more appropriate approach than a traditional one based on a view of science 'as the facts' for issues involving uncertain facts, disputed values, high stakes, and a need for urgent decisions. This view is consistent, also, with Habermas's (1973) concept of *communicative rationality* as a means of overcoming an overreliance on technical-scientific knowledge and restoring democracy. In an ideal speech situation envisaged by Habermas, citizens interact through language (what Habermas terms *communicative competence*) to develop mutual understanding and agreement. The goal is to 'provide orientation about right action . . . the realization of the good, happy, rational life.'

Viewing communication as discourse or dialogue and appreciating the importance of shared cultural values to communication and social trust have significant implications for the theory and practice of public participation. As emphasized by Bradbury (1994), this view represents a very different approach than the linear view of communication – as transmission of a message from source to receiver – that has long been the dominant model underlying much of the discussion in risk management and risk communication.[5] It shifts the focus from the effect of the transmission on a recipient to a focus on relationships and the mutual nature of communication; and it emphasizes the long-term, interactive nature of communication as a transaction *process* among groups with different bases of experience and frames of reference and hence differing ways of judging the validity and relevance of knowledge. It also shifts the focus from differences between expert and lay-person (whose attitudes and behaviour have typically been deemed to be in need of change) to differences in expertise and experience among all stakeholders, indicating different contributions that various parties bring to the communication process. Moreover, a convergence rather than a linear view of communication highlights the iterative nature of the process, indicating that the experience and understandings that the participants bring to the process are continually in the process of change.

The multi-way communication envisaged above is, in effect, the essence of public participation. Such communication, which is based on mutual trust, coordinates political and social action. Our own and others' research into a variety of environmental issues has demonstrated that government agencies' failure to acknowledge the legitimacy of differing viewpoints and to engage their representatives in meaningful discussion and negotiation contribute to escalating controversy and to their own inability to build the necessary societal consensus to effectively implement policy.[6] Public participation can thus be viewed as a means of developing this consensus among policy makers, technical experts, and the range of affected stakeholders. The challenge is to develop a context that allows participants to establish and maintain effective dialogue. As discussed by Earle (1997), 'Trust can be understood . . . to be more primitive than cooperation, earlier to evolve and sooner to develop. . . . Cooperation builds on trust.'

Earle and Cvetkovich (1995) emphasize that increasing public participation does not ensure success in reducing distrust or enhancing and creating trust. They cite challenges posed by the need for public participation to move beyond the prevailing pluralistic, competitive, and defensive framework to one that allows creativity and synthesis. They note the difficulty of achieving the necessary forums for communication and participation, pointing out several flaws in the traditional model of public participation: the expectation

5. Bradbury draws on Roger's work in communication theory to distinguish between the traditional linear model of communication and a convergence model of communication. It should be noted that the National Research Council's recent publication, *Understanding Risk* (National Academy Press, 1996), represents a change in emphasis away from linear terminology as compared with its previous publications.

6. Work completed in 1994 by the authors for the US Army Chemical Stockpile Disposal Program, for example, showed a pervasive distrust among many citizens living in communities near to the stockpile sites. No effective mechanism for communication between the Army and community citizens existed and thus there was no opportunity for the parties to develop a common understanding of the problem. The army continued to narrowly define the problem as purely technical, while failing to recognize as legitimate and address the broad scope of community concerns. The ensuing cycle of distrust resulted in delay and escalating costs as the opposed public worked through their State and congressional representatives and the State regulatory programme to halt programme implementation (Bradbury et al 1994).

of participation from everyone, the lack of acknowledgement of the division of labour, failure to acknowledge the limits of human capacities, and failure to recognize the need for leadership. Moreover, structuring the process inevitably involves addressing issues of dependency and empowerment, which, as Wynne (1996) has shown, are closely linked to trust.

Focht (1995, 1996), who argues that the determination of which form of stakeholder involvement is most appropriate depends on the policy context, calls for *transformative* involvement strategies in dealing with controversial science-policy issues. Such strategies must be capable of transforming conflict into consensus by negotiating value differences, addressing factual uncertainty, and building social trust among stakeholders and between stakeholders and the agency. In this context, Focht recommends also the dialogue envisioned by Funtowicz and Ravetz (1985), by Renn, Webler and Wiedemann (1995) and by Webler (1995).

HOW SHOULD WE REDEFINE THE RESEARCH PROBLEM IN EXAMINING THE RELATIONSHIP BETWEEN TRUST AND PUBLIC PARTICIPATION IN RISK POLICY ISSUES?

The DOE, which, as noted above, is one of the primary agencies involved in developing and implementing policy issues involving technological risk, has been in the forefront in supporting research on trust. Two offices have played a key role in this research: the Office of Environmental Management (EM), which is responsible for remediating former nuclear weapons production and testing sites, and the Office of Radioactive Waste Management (OCRWM), which is responsible for implementing the requirement of the Nuclear Waste Policy Act to dispose of high-level radioactive high waste. The two offices have jointly funded a series of stakeholder surveys of opinions on trust and confidence in DOE (DOE conducted surveys on trust and confidence in 1992, 1994 and 1996). In addition, EM has included questions about trust in its 1996 and 1997 evaluation surveys of the Site-Specific Advisory Boards (SSABs) (citizens' advisory boards), established at 12 sites around the complex since 1992.

The SEAB research was preceded by an extensive review of the trust literature and the survey included stakeholders who had been identified as dealing frequently with DOE programmes. It is noteworthy that SEAB respondents identified citizen advisory boards as the activity that would most increase public trust and confidence. The SSAB evaluation surveys were developed in collaboration with an Evaluation Steering Committee, composed of DOE and SSAB representatives, who helped develop a framework to clarify the goals of the evaluation from the perspectives of the key players and establish criteria for evaluating the effectiveness and value of the SSAB initiative. Significantly, several SSAB members did not believe that increasing trust in DOE should be included as one of the six SSAB goals to be measured.

Although the SEAB reports, in particular, have produced valuable data on trust and confidence in DOE, the research has provided little in the way of guidance of the link between trust and public participation.[7] Indeed, I would argue that the research has approached the issue of trust from a problematic perspective. The focus on whether and how public trust in DOE is increasing assumes that increased trust in the agency is the desired goal and that different types of public participation are possible means to that goal. The reluctance of SSAB representatives to identify increasing trust in DOE as one of the SSAB goals may reflect discomfort in this instrumental, and potentially manipulative, use of trust.

Moreover, the issue of trust is broader than developing trust between the agency (in this case, DOE) and the public. Rather, as the SSAB evaluation research has shown, the challenge for several SSABs has been to build a sufficient level of trust among members from diverse perspectives – to learn how to accommodate a variety of viewpoints (ie, not simply 'expert' versus 'lay' views). In some instances, Boards have experienced considerable difficulty in establishing informal as well as formal processes that enable them to work effectively as a group. The polarization among different subgroups on a Board may reflect a deeper community conflict that 'spills over' into discussion of cleanup issues, resulting in stalemate or resignation from membership of key representatives of a viewpoint that differs from that of the dominant community group(s).

Renn, Webler and Wiedemann (1995) identify a possible approach to enhancing dialogue among groups with diverse perspectives. These authors, whose view of public participation as dialogue is consistent with the views outlined in this paper, argue that public participation can be fruitfully examined from the perspective of providing a 'means to realize critical awareness' by offering opportunities for individuals to enter into social relations that encourage personal development through critical self reflection and engagement. Webler (1995), in the same publication, builds upon Habermas' (1973) critical theory of communicative action, where public participation is viewed as a communicative act in which the emphasis is on providing processes that are fair and competent. The strength of Habermas's normative theory of human interaction lies in its emphasis on the need for a dialogue which permits the participants freedom to define their collective preferences, interests, and values, and also enhances their ability to reflect on and develop changing needs and responses. Webler accordingly defines participation as 'interaction among individuals through the medium of language' and sets forth criteria of fairness and competence for examining public participation.

Developing an empirical basis for evaluating the role of trust in establishing and maintaining an effective public participation process or dialogue along the lines suggested by Webler, may prove to be a more productive approach, both in furthering our understanding of trust and also in improving the quality

7. The findings from the SSAB surveys showed that, despite stakeholders' beliefs (reported in the 1994 SEAB survey) that establishment of SSABs would be the most important activity to increase trust and confidence, little change occurred in trust and confidence in DOE, as compared with 1996. In large part, the SSAB results can be explained by the very limited number of questions and an insufficient coverage of the various dimensions of trust. (These deficiencies will be addressed in future iterations of the survey.) In part, also, the results may reflect SSAB members' reluctance to view increasing trust in DOE as one of the goals of the SSAB Initiative.

of the public participation dialogue and achieving a working consensus on policy.

We would therefore suggest an alternative research focus to that of the SEAB report in defining the research problem of the relationship between trust and public participation. In our view, increasing trust and reducing distrust should be viewed primarily as a basis for initiating and sustaining a more effective dialogue with the goal of developing consensus on risk management policies. This perspective allows us to reframe the research question in terms of effective intervention. The essential research question in the relationship between trust and public participation thus becomes: What is the role of public participation as an intervention strategy in creating and maintaining a context in which effective dialogue can occur?

If public participation is used as an intervention strategy, it raises several specific questions. A first, key question is: what effect does initiating and implementing a fair, open process (such as that advocated by Webler (1995) and public participation advocates) have on levels of trust, distrust, and cooperation and on development of a working consensus among diverse participants? Second: how do we create a context in which the transformation identified by Focht (1995, 1996) and by Earle and Cvetkovich (1995) can take place – what specific actions can be taken to reduce a cycle of distrust that prevents effective dialogue? Third: is the establishment of personal relationships critical to the establishment of interpersonal trust – and is interpersonal trust, in turn, critical to the establishment of system trust? And finally: how does the provision of mechanisms for accountability affect levels of trust and distrust? In our view, studies designed to answer these questions would provide valuable information about the relationship between trust and public participation that could be used to achieve a working consensus on risk policy issues.

10 Social Trust, Risk Management, and Culture: Insights from Native America[1]

M V Rajeev Gowda

INTRODUCTION

The last few decades have witnessed significant controversy over the societal management of health and environmental risks – those arising from natural sources as well as by-products of technological developments. In attempting to manage these risks, governments, industries, and scientific experts have been unable to measure up to the public's expectation of safety. Consequently there has been an increase in public dissatisfaction with risk management efforts, rejection of proposals which entail risk, and the emergence of sharp differences between the public's and experts' attitudes towards risks and their management. Scholars attempting to understand these developments from different intellectual foundations have moved toward a focus on social trust as central to the resolution of risk management controversies. The essential idea is that if social trust could be developed, risk management controversies would disappear and society would arrive at a balanced and judicious portfolio of risks and risk management strategies.

How do scholars conceive of social trust? Do these conceptions reflect empirical reality and historical experience? Are they culturally bound to industrialized, western democracies or do they offer a theoretical framework to understand risk management conflicts more generally? In order to address these questions, this chapter examines how various theories of social trust and risk management measure up when subject to tests drawn from the cultural settings and historical experiences of Native American peoples. The specific contexts examined include the management of health risks among the Mvskoke (pronounced Muskogee) tribe of Oklahoma and nuclear waste siting proposals

1. I am grateful to George Cvetkovich, Tim Earle, Doug Easterling, Rick Farmer, Will Focht, Morris Foster, Jeff Fox, Pam Innes, Robin Magelky, Claire Mays, L. A. Wilson, II, and to participants at the Bellingham International Conference on Social Trust in Risk Management for their assistance and comments. This research was partly supported by National Science Foundation grant SBR 9320991.

among the Mescalero Apache of New Mexico and the Sac and Fox Nation of Oklahoma.

SOCIAL TRUST AND RISK MANAGEMENT: AN OVERVIEW

Controversies over the management of health, energy, and environmental risks have been receiving increasing attention as more groups have contested experts' risk management strategies. Traditionally, risk managers have attributed these differences to the public's irrationality and lack of knowledge. However, research on the public's perception of risks – termed the psychometric paradigm – showed that the public had a rich conception of risks which took into account values and qualitative factors while experts typically focused on quantitative or technical dimensions of risks (Slovic 1992). The public also emphasized issues of procedural and substantive equity. People care whether they are exposed to risks involuntarily, whether those risks entail potentially catastrophic outcomes, whether those risks trigger dread due to their novel or unnatural nature, and whether risk managers can be trusted to manage risks in a competent and caring manner (Slovic 1992). Thus, psychometric researchers emphasize that lay-people's views are worthy of attention and need to be respected and integrated in risk-related decision-making. However, psychometric researchers do acknowledge that lay-people's perceptions of risks are sometimes mistaken because of their use of mental shortcuts or psychological ' heuristics and biases' (Slovic, Fischhoff, Lichtenstein 1979). Separating the influence of values such as equity from the influence of heuristics and biases remains a challenge for researchers working to integrate public perceptions of risk into the decision making about risk management.

The overall recognition that public concerns about risk are legitimate and reflect a broader notion of rationality has led scholars to urge their incorporation in risk-related decision-making. Integrating public viewpoints will help resolve risk-related conflicts because it will build trust between parties with different perspectives on risk management. For example, Pildes and Sunstein (1995) emphasize that:

> To build the trust necessary to find acceptable regulatory solutions, agencies should recognize the conflict between expert and lay assessments, pay attention to lay evaluations of risk, and seek to communicate risk information effectively. . . . policy-makers should view lay and expert reasoning as two distinct styles of rational risk assessment, neither of which has a monopoly on rationality.

What, then, is trust, and how can it be built? One definition of trust puts great emphasis on process, credibility, and competence. Trust is defined as 'a person's expectation that other persons and institutions in a social relationship can be relied upon to act in ways that are competent, predictable, and caring (Kasperson, Golding and Tuler 1992). These authors argue that their definition captures the multiple dimensions of trust – cognitive, emotional, and behavioural. Further, this definition is able to capture both interpersonal trust, which arises in small, cohesive, less complex social units, and system trust, which is critical to the functioning of large complex societies with their governmental and market systems. Trust, then, is the basis for cooperation and community cohesion.

A corollary to this perspective is that trust and distrust become two sides of the same coin. Flynn et al. (1992) argue that there is a continuum between trust and distrust and that as long as people's perceptions of risk managers lean more toward the trust end of the scale workable solutions to societal problems may be obtained. Trust is inherently fragile and there is an asymmetry between trust and distrust. This is because negative, trust-reducing events are more available and carry more weight than trust-enhancing events (Slovic 1993). Kasperson, Tuler and Golding (1992) point out that distrust arises from broken expectations, and that when expectations are broken in one setting, distrust and attributions of hostile intentions can arise in other contexts and spheres of interaction.

An alternative approach to the role of trust in resolving risk management controversies is put forward by Wildavsky and Dake (1990). They suggest that society is composed of groups of people with different world views, for example, egalitarians, individualists, and hierarchists. These world views affect not only how they perceive risks but also affect what they consider to be legitimate risk management solutions, ie, processes that are worthy of trust. The implication of Wildavsky and Dake's (1990) 'cultural' argument is that trust is difficult to build if society is composed of groups with different world views because these groups will differ in their definition of what risks are worthy of society's attention and also over how these are to be resolved. For example, egalitarians may view a hazardous waste siting process that locates a waste site in a poor, minority community as unjust and worthy of redress by society. In contrast, individualists may consider this outcome to be legitimate if it resulted from the workings of market forces. From Wildavsky and Dake's (1990) analysis, we may pessimistically conclude that unless there is societal consensus over one world view, distrust and conflict are inevitable.

Earle and Cvetkovich (1995) try to arrive at an improved conception of social trust in risk management by going beyond both the psychometric and cultural theories of risk. They accept the psychometric school's argument that lay-people's conceptions of risk reflect a richer and broader rationality but reject the school's emphasis on *dis*trust. Similarly, they accept the cultural school's argument that there are different world views or value systems in society. Indeed these world views or value systems justify a society's existence and organization, and can be inferred from narratives such as founding myths. But Earle and Cvetkovich (1995) strongly disagree with Wildavsky and Dake's (1990) pessimistic conclusion that the presence of multiple world views within a society dooms efforts to arrive at social trust and thereby a resolution of risk management conflicts.

Instead Earle and Cvetkovich (1995) argue that social trust can be achieved through a process they term the 'cosmopolitan synthesis'. They begin by suggesting that societies typically reflect a situation of 'pluralistic' social trust where multiple sets of values or world views coexist. This can result in conflict between people with different value systems over issues of risk management. However, instead of remaining in this static, pluralistic mode, societies can move toward a resolution of these conflicts through the interaction of world views aimed at deriving a meta-value system that transcends the limitations of the previously existing value systems. When this synthesis is achieved, society will have created 'cosmopolitan' social trust which reflects the new set of values shared by the entire society. Earle and Cvetkovich (1995) acknowledge that this process of achieving the cosmopolitan synthesis is difficult because it involves complex and dynamic interaction between value systems, is very demanding of human resources, and involves leaders taking the best of the values present in different world views to create a newer, improved set of consensual values. But once this cosmopolitan synthesis is achieved, conflicts should disappear. This chapter will use a historical perspective on social trust and risk management in Native America to explore how the above perspectives fare in these contexts.

SOCIAL TRUST IN NATIVE AMERICAN CONTEXTS

Native American groups constitute relatively unique entities in that they have historically developed alternative paradigms for dealing with life. Studying risk in Native communities raises interesting questions about the influence of traditional cultural norms and ideas on how risks are perceived. Studying risk management in Native American communities is inherently useful because many Native Americans approach risks through alternative conceptualizations of health and environment. For example, many Native Americans conceive of 'environment' broadly and as highly related to 'health'. These paradigms, and their resulting cultural practices, have been affected by contact with Euro-American cultures and technologies, but still are retained to different extents within Native groups. Therefore, these settings provide a useful test of whether constructs and conclusions from the literature on social trust and risk management apply to other cultural paradigms.

Another development which underlines the need for risk-related research to pay attention to non-mainstream cultural perspectives is the increased salience of the problem of 'environmental injustice'. This refers to the disproportionate risk burdens borne by minority groups in the US (see Vaughan 1995 for a review). Vaughan and Seifert (1992) point out that the introduction of an environmental justice frame to environmental conflicts poses significant challenges to societal risk management, especially because the non-minority participants in the conflict adopt 'technical-rational' perspectives which stress economic efficiency and scientific appropriateness, rather than equity and civil rights. Even in this area there has been very little research on Native Americans.

Pre-Contact Social Trust: Health Care among Mvskoke

American history is replete with clashes of values among competing groups. Native American tribes had very different values and 'ways of life' prior to the arrival of Europeans in the new world. Some of these cultural patterns are still evident today despite the influence of the west. One example is the pattern of health risk management among the Mvskoke tribe of Oklahoma. Among the Mvskoke, there is a general focus on traditional methods of care which have been sustained since the pre-contact era. This is true despite the existence of some heterogeneity within the Mvskoke where some members prefer western biomedicine while others prefer traditional medicine. This traditional approach to health risk management involves an interaction between social organization and risk management beyond that conceived by risk and culture theorists like Dake (1992) and Rayner (1992).

The Mvskoke community is organized around the concept of ensuring the physical, mental and spiritual care of its members (Foster 1996). The tribe's social structures, mores, behaviours, values, and shared symbols transform care from an individual concern into a collective practice. Community rituals and activities are centred around concerns for care and wellness, and their perform-ance helps perpetuate the community's well-being and contributes to social solidarity and interdependence. There is a shared awareness of risk factors and trust in the medicine men charged with ensuring care. Faith, confidence, and credibility are all central to the community. Traditional medicine requires that people believe in the medicine man's diagnosis and cures as a prerequisite to their efficacy. However, this does not result in blind faith as information about traditional illnesses and cures is common knowledge to tribal members, and is passed on through verbal narratives.

The Mvskoke conceptualization of health risks and their management stands in contrast to western views of medicine because it emphasizes 'process'. The western paradigm essentially sees wellness as an event to which one responds when it disappears, rather than as a central life process. The Mvskoke notion of care stresses the importance of an integrative or holistic view of health, with emphasis on disease prevention and overall mental, spiritual, and physical health as a way of life. This makes previous distinctions between medical activities and social activities artificial and creates less of a setting for the generation of distrust. And because care is the core of communal life, it cannot be bought and sold to the highest bidder, or reserved only for the wealthy. It is a way of life in which all participate. Table 10.1 contrasts western and a generalized version of the Native approaches to health risk management developed by JT Garrett, a Native American health care professional (Native North American Almanac 1994).

Variations in social structures and traditional practices within the tribe reflect differences in the amount of resources various subgroups among the Mvskoke are willing to devote to the provision of care. The integrated nature of Mvskoke social life and health care explains how social cohesion is maintained con-currently with variations in time and place. This suggests that, in the Mvskoke context, risk and culture interact to create a dynamic equilibrium which sustains the community over generations. It is an equilibrium where values and trust are interwoven into the multihued fabric of care.

Contact and Social Trust: Values in Word and Deed

Contact with Euro-Americans set the stage for a clash of values. This is evident in the historical record of the federal government's policies toward Native

Table 10.1 *Native American (Indian) and Modern Western Approaches to Health Risk Management*

Indian Medicine	Modern Medicine
Is wellness oriented	Is illness oriented
Patient treated in family or community setting	Patient is treated alone and isolated from family
Focuses on 'why' illness occurred	Focus on 'how' illness occurred
Includes natural and supernatural causes	Emphasizes natural causes
Expects multiple causalities	Usually links illness to a single cause
Treatment approach is primarily holistic	Treatment approach is primarily physiological
Treatment is personal and reciprocally oriented	Treatment is often impersonal and complaint oriented

Source: Native North American Almanac (1994).

Americans. These have fluctuated over the years, marked by idealism in the post-revolutionary periods, by the forcible relocation of numerous tribes under President Andrew Jackson, by positive efforts in the 1930s aimed at tribal government revival, and by the dissolution of the federal-tribal relationships and land annexations which affected many tribes in the 1950s.

The Euro-American value system, as espoused in the US Constitution, can be thought of as representing values which the Native peoples could conceivably hold in esteem. However, the Native experience with the rule of western law and the lack of western morality left them viewing these grand structures as mere empty shells. American institutions failed to live up to their promises and were often subverted to achieve outcomes different from their exalted purposes. These failures occurred even when western values were ordered to be extended to Native Americans. For example, in the nineteenth century, the Supreme Court (led by Chief Justice Marshall) was rendered impotent when President Jackson refused to enforce its decision in the case of Worcester v Georgia. As a consequence, many tribes were relocated to Oklahoma. Alexis de Tocqueville observed:

> The conduct of the Americans of the United States with respect towards the aborigines is characterized . . . by a singular attachment to the formalities of law . . . [It] is impossible to destroy men with more respect for the laws of humanity (quoted in Strickland 1992).

Western capitalist values did not live up to their stated promise of economic growth and prosperity when implemented in Native America. Using the rationale of providing Natives with the 'benefits of private ownership', the Dawes Act of 1887 mandated that tribal lands be broken up into smaller pieces which were then allotted to individual tribal members. Rather than enhancing the prosperity of Native Americans, this act merely 'provided a mechanism for land hungry whites to obtain access to reservations and for bureaucrats to expand their domains' (Anderson 1995).

The conflict between value systems continues today. But resource management conflicts are not amenable to solutions based on economic analysis because Natives do not regard land as an alienable commodity. This prevents them from parting with land or engaging in market transactions. This conception of the land goes beyond the simplistic idea of 'being one with nature' (Jorgensen 1984) and may arise because of how Natives invest themselves in the environment through site-specific rituals (Momaday 1976). Indeed, Stoffle and Evans (1990) use the term 'triage' to incorporate the anguish felt by Natives when forced to indulge in trade-offs involving their lands.

If we regard this situation from the perspective of Earle and Cvetkovich's (1995) notion of the interaction of value systems to achieve a cosmopolitan synthesis, perhaps this historical outcome could have been avoided. In the context of land ownership, the implication of their work is that Native American values are oriented toward respect for land and its care. Similarly, the underlying economic argument for private ownership is that it gives owners an incentive to take efficient care of land. A cosmopolitan synthesis could therefore be achieved centred on the common value of land stewardship. Unfortunately, however, such a synthesis was not the historical outcome.

Instead, as these examples demonstrate, the Native American experience with the western value system has been one of duplicity, where grand words translate into sordid outcomes, where instead of amalgamation of values, one system triumphs over the other through the exercise of power. The interaction of value systems was characterized by the use of brute force. Further, value systems in theory are different from value systems in practice. Thus, if Native peoples were to try to achieve a synthesis of value systems, they would face the dilemma of choosing which values to address – the idealistic values of intentions or the ignoble values represented by actual outcomes.

Post-Contact Social Trust: Nuclear Waste in Native America

The historical record of abuses by the government against Native Americans has led to a lack of trust which remains today. This can be seen in current controversies over nuclear waste disposal (Gowda and Easterling 1996). The federal government designed a process to identify volunteer communities which would host a temporary nuclear waste storage repository, termed the Monitored Retrievable Storage facility (MRS). This process was explicitly oriented toward achieving goals of procedural fairness. However, its ironic outcome has been that the only potential recipients of nuclear waste remaining after the process worked itself out were Native American tribes. This outcome is particularly interesting, given that Native American tribes have historically borne a large share of the costs associated with the nuclear industry, for example, through health effects suffered by uranium miners predominantly drawn from the Navajo tribe who are only now receiving compensation (Schneider 1993).

The US Congress set up the Office of the Nuclear Waste Negotiator to find a volunteer host community for the MRS in exchange for significant compensation. Along with cities and counties, Native American tribes were invited to volunteer in recognition of their status as sovereign entities. The Nuclear Waste Negotiator, with the stated goal of fairness, provided state governors with the right to veto proposals by cities or counties within their states. When governors concerned about hostile constituent perceptions exercised their vetoes, the only participants left in the nuclear waste siting process were Native American tribes.

The elected tribal government of the Sac and Fox Nation in Oklahoma applied for and was awarded a study grant from the Office of the Nuclear Waste Negotiator, using established procedures for tribal decision-making. However, a group of tribal members organized a petition for a special meeting of the entire tribe to vote on the issue of participating in the MRS process, and accused the tribal leadership of being secretive about the process. The outcome of the tribal meeting was that the Sac and Fox rejected the study grant and withdrew from the MRS process. The Sac and Fox opponents' rationales for rejection of the study grant included a strong distrust of the federal government as a partner and as a risk manager. Citing historical repudiation of treaties, opponents questioned the temporariness of the MRS facility. While recognizing that tribal governments were involved in the process because of their sovereign status, opponents perceived this as exploitation of their status, and suggested that sovereignty would erode as the federal government took a greater role in the management of the MRS facility. The historical record of the federal government's interactions with Native Americans thus fuelled significant distrust among Sac and Fox opponents of the MRS siting process. This response was typical of the reactions of most Native American tribes.

Meanwhile, a unique development occurred among one tribe, the Mescalero Apache, which volunteered to host the MRS. The Mescaleros' willingness to host the MRS provides a contrasting perspective on social trust and risk management in Native America. More importantly, because this case illustrates how the Mescalero were able to adapt and transform the values of the dominant culture to their own advantage, it serves as a test of the concept of cosmopolitan social trust (Earle and Cvetkovich 1995).

The Mescalero Apache obtained a study grant from the Nuclear Waste Negotiator in 1991 and announced their intention of beginning negotiations to host the MRS in 1993. When it began to seem that the MRS programme would fall through, the Mescaleros signed an agreement with Northern States Power in 1994 to host a private holding facility in exchange for approximately $50 million per year over 20 years (Border and Weiss 1994). The Mescaleros made it clear that they would accept some but not all of the waste from each utility which participated in the project (Nuclear Review 1995).

A referendum on the issue in January 1995 resulted in the proposal being defeated by a margin of 490 to 362. The defeat was credited to distrust of the federal government and the work of Rufina Marie Laws, a tribal member, who undertook a door-to-door campaign against the proposal. Laws provided a rationale for opposition which invoked traditional Apache narrative form: she spoke of her vision of 'glowing liquid flowing down the slopes of the sacred Sierra Blanca, wiping out everything it touched' (Satchell 1996). The tribal government supported a requisition for a new referendum, based on the

allegation that the first was tainted by misinformation from non-tribal environmentalists. The new referendum resulted in the adoption of the nuclear waste
facility siting proposal by a margin of 593 to 372 (Satchell 1996).

A significant feature which led to the strong support for the MRS facility
among the Mescalero was the advocacy of the long-serving tribal president,
Wendell Chino. Chino argued that the nuclear waste facility would serve the
tribe's economic interests and provide high-technology jobs for educated youth.
Further, he pointed out that because Native Americans have a historical and
cultural responsibility to Mother Earth, they would provide the best guardians
for nuclear waste. Finally, he assured tribal members that they would not end
up as the sole repository of wastes, because he would ensure that, through a
strategy reflecting his political cunning, only a fraction of the wastes would be
taken from each utility; the rest would remain on the utility's premises as is
currently the case. It is probable that the Mescalero Apaches' trust in Chino's
leadership influenced the outcome of the second referendum. Under Chino,
the Mescalero Apache not only run a ski resort, Ski Apache, but have also
taken advantage of their sovereign status to establish a flourishing casino
complex, The Inn of the Mountain Gods. These ventures have increased the
self-confidence among tribal members in their ability to manage complex
ventures, thus leading to their support for the facility. Social trust in the
Mescalero case is tied to historic evidence of competence on the part of the
tribal leadership, and this, combined with the narrative of self-confidence, led
the Mescalero to conceive of a private sector version of the MRS as a business
proposition rather than a risk-imposing venture.

IMPLICATIONS FOR SOCIAL TRUST CONCEPTS

On the whole, these cases reveal that the theoretical conceptions of the risk
and culture paradigm are somewhat limited. First, the Mvskoke case reveals
that culture is more than just a world view in the Wildavsky and Dake (1990)
sense. Culture is an intricate web of institutions and activities – a way of life
that sustains the community rather than being merely a common outlook or
set of beliefs. Mvskoke society is organized around the provision of care –
both physical and spiritual – and all community activities are oriented toward
enhancing this process and outcome in an ongoing manner.

Second, the case studies of health risk management among the Mvskoke
and nuclear waste siting among the Sac and Fox and Mescalero Apache reveal
the centrality of concepts of social trust developed by scholars in the psychometric paradigm. These scholars emphasized the importance of competence
and historical performance as central to the construction of trust. Clearly, in
the Mvskoke case, the faith in the medicine men would not be sustainable if
their competence was questionable, ie, if they were unable to provide results.
Similarly, the Mescalero Apache were willing to go along with the proposals
advocated by their leader, Wendell Chino, in part because of his successful
record in economic development.

Further, scholars in the psychometric paradigm have pointed out that trust
can be fragile and that a record of failures could easily transform trust into

distrust. This is glaringly evident in the Sac and Fox case. There the historical record of the federal government's interactions with Indians was cited as overwhelmingly negative by opponents of the MRS, and this led to significant political activity to overturn the tribe's study grant with the Nuclear Waste Negotiator. However, trust in medicine men and Chino may be more difficult to lose, because they could attribute any failures to other entities, eg, western doctors or the federal government respectively.

Third, these case studies suggest that Earle and Cvetkovich (1995) are on the right track when they emphasize values and suggest that these are embedded in narratives. Certainly, the Mvskoke case reveals that values and narratives are central to the very organization and sustenance of these communities. Further, in the economic development context, Cornell and Kalt (1992) argue that these narratives are persistent in their effects. They suggest that the economic success of tribes today is determined by whether their current organizational and leadership structure matches their historical structure. They argue that only those tribes which have achieved such a congruence will be successful, thus crediting these narratives with a potency that has stood the test of time. Given the importance of narratives, social trust research needs to transcend the limitations of psychometric methods of inquiry to identify and study these narratives and their implications. Ethnographic methods of inquiry may well be the appropriate research methods that need to be utilized.

Fourth, the value of Earle and Cvetkovich's (1995) conception of cosmopolitan social trust is evident in the way the Mvskoke deal with health risk management today. They are offered the opportunity of utilizing western medical services provided by the Indian Health Service (IHS) while being faced with the gradual decline of the availability of medicine men and their practices. Mvskoke people today draw on the resources of both the western IHS and the traditional medicine men, and try to achieve an effective integration of these two health systems. For example, many Mvskoke classify some diseases as western and others as traditional and use treatments accordingly. Mvskoke people contrast the medicine men, who are prized for their attention to the overall history of the patient (including mental factors) before diagnosis and treatment, and IHS doctors who work on a rotation and do not serve long enough in the IHS to develop cultural awareness or personal relationships. The ability of Mvskoke respondents to bridge western and traditional paradigms and draw from each when appropriate, suggests that this is cosmopolitan social trust in action.

Fifth, these case studies illustrate that the process of achieving the cosmopolitan synthesis envisaged by Earle and Cvetkovich (1995) is not necessarily a benign process, characterized by honourable motives on the part of the participants. Indeed, in the Native American experience, if a cosmopolitan synthesis was ever achieved, it was arrived at through the use of force and power, with the western set of values driving out and nearly exterminating the Native set. In the health care context, it is far from clear that the end result is superior. The western allopathic framework is even now discovering the value of a more holistic approach which pays attention to wellness and process issues.

Sixth, the Earle and Cvetkovich (1995) conception of cosmopolitan social trust is value neutral and does not distinguish between the articulation of values and how they are translated into action. Consider Earle and Cvetkovich's (1995) definition of cosmopolitan social trust:

> Cosmopolitan social trust is a demanding process; it requires that people unchain themselves from their pasts and move into uncertain futures. It demands change. To make change easier, cosmopolitan social trust relies on leadership. The role of the cosmopolitan leader is to encourage people to think about their pasts as contingent and to consider beneficial uses of the new. The cosmopolitan leader encourages the creation and discussion of possible futures. . . . The art of leadership is in story telling. And the basic tool of the cosmopolitan leader, the means by which she encourages cosmopolitan social trust, is narrative.

Wendell Chino fits this description, but is he the model cosmopolitan? He has been able to lead the Mescalero to grapple with their changed historical circumstance and to adopt economic development imperatives so crucial for success in a market economy. More than anything, he has been able to exploit the values of the dominant order by taking advantage of sovereignty to establish a gaming operation, regardless of whether or not there is a traditional foundation for this in the Mescalero world. He has even created a narrative to support the entry of the Mescalero into such profitable activities: witness his statement that, ' the Navajos make rugs, the Pueblo make pottery, the Mescalero make money' (Satchell 1996). His willingness to play a political game with the utilities, by taking only a fraction of their wastes, bespeaks of an ability to exploit political situations. Similarly, he tweaked the federal government by taking on its suggestion of a voluntary process, taking the money, and side-stepping the federal government altogether. Finally, he has been able to create new narratives to link his agendas with traditional Mescalero thought, as exemplified in his spin on the responsibility to Mother Earth.

Is this cosmopolitan social trust in action? Is this the creation of new values systems? We do not have a normative standard by which to judge the appropriateness of any value system which results from the cosmopolitan encounter. Therefore, we are left unsure which interpretation of Native American traditions concerning nuclear technology we should view as legitimate and acceptable, that of Chino or Rufina Laws, the Mescalero opponent of the MRS. This problem also continues when we address other tribes. Some tribes have specific teachings about the impropriety of nuclear technology. For example, Wallace Black Elk, an elder among the Lakota Sioux, argues that the atomic force that binds the nucleus together is a sacred force; splitting the atom and transmuting matter is viewed as an intrusion into the realm of God and invites retribution (Black Elk and Lyons 1990). Without a normative standard for evaluating cosmopolitan social trust, we are unable to accept one argument over the other. The major problem is that ultimately all of these arguments may merely be narratives that justify actions pushing particular political agendas and designed to exploit whatever edge can be obtained according to the rules of the dominant value system. If so, then from the perspective of Earle and Cvetkovich (1995), Chino is far from the cosmopolitan, since he is only capitalizing on differences rather than transcending them, and is opportunistic with regard to values.

While these case studies have provided insights into social trust and risk management in the Native American context, care should be taken to avoid sweeping generalizations from these specific tribal contexts to all Native American tribes. The term Native American is an umbrella term for hundreds of unique tribes which differ significantly from one another in terms of ethnic origin, cultural practices, institutions, and geographic location. Yet, it is also clear that historical experiences transcend tribal boundaries. The effects on Native America since contact with the Western European world seems to sweep across tribes; the marginalization of Native peoples on the North American continent is a general phenomenon. Thus, while further research in other tribal contexts is definitely needed to enhance our understanding of how social trust and risk management interact with culture, these case studies provide a useful indication of the nature and impact of these interactions.

11 Who Calls the Shots? Credible Vaccine Risk Communication[1]

Ann Bostrom

Trust is a key component of the exchange of information at every level, and overconfidence about risk estimates that are later shown to be incorrect contributes to a breakdown of trust among public health officials, vaccine manufacturers, and the public. (Institute of Medicine, 1997b)

INTRODUCTION

This paper attempts to characterize the evolution of social trust in the vaccine context through analysis of vaccine policy developments, along with an assessment of current communications, decision-making, and institutional arrangements for risk management. Changes in judgements of acceptable risk and estimates of the efficacy of some vaccines are among recent developments that have increased the complexity of vaccine risk management and the importance of social trust therein.

Vaccines are widely considered to be among the most cost-effective and successful health interventions this century (see Table 11.1). For vaccine policies to be effective, people need credible vaccine risk communication and trust in vaccine risk management (IOM 1997b), possibly more now than ever.

However, some research suggests that anti-vaccine movements and sentiments may be rising in the US, corresponding to a decline in trust in allopathic doctors and government authorities who manage vaccine risks (Gangerosa, Phillips, Wolfe and Chen 1996). In the last decade, parent groups (eg, National Vaccine Information Center) with strong interests and concerns about vaccine safety have become more visible. A recent issue of *Mothering* magazine

1. The research leading to this paper was partially supported by the National Immunization Program of the Centers for Disease Control and Prevention (CDC). The author is indebted to Ragnar Löfstedt and the other participants in the 1996 Bellingham International Conference on Social Trust in Risk Management for comments on earlier versions. The author bears sole responsibility for the contents.

Table 11.1 *Reported Cases of Vaccine-Preventable Childhood Diseases in the US*

Disease	Maximal No. Of Cases (year)	1993 Cases	Reduction%
Diphtheria	206,939 (1921)	0	–100 %
Pertussis	265,269 (1934)	6,132	–97.7%
Tetanus	1,560 (1923)	9	–99.4%
Poliomyelitis	21,269 (1952)	0*	–100 %
Measles	894,134 (1941)	277	–99.9%
Rubella	57,686 (1969)	188	–99.7%
Congenital rubella syndrome	20,000 (1964–1965)	7	–99.9%
Mumps	152,209 (1968)	1,630	–98.9%

Data from the National Immunization Program, Centers for Disease Control and Prevention, Atlanta, GA.
*Excludes an estimated four cases of vaccine-associated paralysis
Rubella first became a reportable disease in 1966.
Mumps first became a reportable disease in 1968.
Table data taken from Fedson, DS (1994)

(Summer 1996, Vol 79) was devoted entirely to the issue of vaccination; the impetus for this was a perceived lack of credible vaccine risk communication. This issue sold out. Recently, the Institute of Medicine (IOM) held several workshops – including one on vaccine risk communication – under the umbrella of the Vaccine Safety Forum, on request from the National Vaccine Program Office of the US Public Health Service (IOM, 1997a,b). One of the main conclusions of the workshop was that trust is at issue.

Johnson (Chapter 5, this volume) suggests that trust is a function of competence, care and consensual values. If so, changes in vaccine policies that affect trust should correspond to changes in these three attributes. While US vaccine risk management policies appear to have been relatively adaptive and constructive, alternative institutional arrangements for risk management might be more conducive to building and maintaining trust.

DISEASE AND VACCINE POLICY DEVELOPMENT IN THE US: RAPID CHANGE

The horrendous smallpox epidemics of the early 19th century (Swales 1992) and AIDS in the present both illustrate that diseases can have devastating effects, which vaccines may be able to reduce or prevent. Table 11.1 provides disease incidence statistics that are often cited by the Centers for Disease Control as illustrating the public health benefits of vaccines. Dramatic drops in reported cases of disease, for example measles, that coincide with vaccine licensure are used as evidence that vaccines have caused these declines (CDC 1996), as are increases in disease incidence in other countries where vaccination rates have fallen (see Box 11.1). However, because these are observational data and do not control for other possible influences, the attribution of these declines to vaccines requires trusting that other simultaneous changes in the nation, such as improvements in health and hygiene, did not cause the declines.

Data from the CDC on tetanus refer to deaths, not cases; CDC does not have information on the numbers of reported tetanus cases before 1947. The number of reported deaths refers to 1992. Mortality data for 1993 are not available. The provisional number of tetanus cases reported for 1993 is 42.

Smallpox vaccination is reported by some as early as the 6th century (Watson 1996), and was common at the end of the last century. In 1980, announcements were made that smallpox had been eradicated (Hinman and Orenstein 1994). By the end of the last century, vaccines and sera for rabies, tetanus and diphtheria had been developed (Parkman and Hardegree 1994).

In the last few decades, development and widespread use of vaccines has continued at an increasing rate. Investigational New Drug submission requests for vaccines more than doubled from 1986 to 1993 (NIAID 1995). A summary of the licensure dates of vaccines (Table 11.2) now recommended for US children makes it evident that many vaccines have only been in widespread use in the US relatively recently (ie, no very long term experience). The increasing number of vaccines required for children has left many with concerns, including concerns about the mere numbers of shots children must receive – the pincushion effect (see Table 11.2). Combined vaccines are one solution to the pincushion effect that is being pursued aggressively (cf Hinman and Orenstein 1994). However, the effects of combined vaccines are among many unknowns that accelerated research on and introduction of vaccines have thrust into the health policy arena.

Public health agencies would like to address other disease increases with vaccines, for example, those of pneumonia and influenza: from 1979 to 1992, the age-adjusted death rate from pneumonia and influenza increased from 20.4 to 24.8 per 100,000 population. The crude death rate increased from 1979 to 1994 by 59 per cent, from 20.0 to 31.8 deaths per 100,000 (Morbidity and Mortality Weekly Report, Vol 44, No 28, 1995). Most of this increase was in pneumonias of unknown etiology. But influenza vaccines have had mixed reception by the public. In one recent study, the most common reason (34.3 per cent of all reasons) elderly patients who had received an influenza vaccination previously failed to do so annually was fear of side effects and shots (Ganguly and Webster 1995; cf. Fiebach and Viscoli 1991).

What Vaccine Risks?

At the turn of the century, 13 children in the US died from an unsafe vaccine: the diphtheria antitoxin they took was contaminated with tetanus bacilli. As a result, the Biologics Control Act was introduced and signed into law in 1902. Many other incidents have raised alarm over time and, in many cases, caused changes in vaccine policies.

Box 11.1 *Disease description, vaccine policy development and recommendations*

Diphtheria. In the 1920s 100,000 to 200,000 cases (140–150/100,000 population) and 13,000–15,000 deaths were reported each year. The number of cases fell gradually to about 15 per 100,000 in 1945. More rapid decrease began with widespread use of toxoid in the late 1940s. Diphtheria antitoxin first used in US in 1891. Booster doses (Td – together with tetanus toxoid) are required every 10 years to maintain antitoxin levels. Recent outbreaks in the former Soviet Union (Ukraine, Russia) have been attributed in part to low vaccination coverage.

Tetanus, first described by Hippocrates, is an acute disease, fatal in 30 per cent of cases. Tetanus toxoid was introduced into routine childhood immunization in the late 1940s.

Pertussis (whooping cough) outbreaks were first described in the 16th century. Pertussis vaccine was introduced in the 1940s in the US. This whole cell pertussis vaccine has been the source of much controversy in the last decade. As of 1996 acellular pertussis (aP) vaccine is recommended in the US, as described below.

Poliomyelitis. The first outbreak of polio described in the US was in 1843. In 1952, 58,000 cases of poliomyelitis were reported in the U.S. Inactivated Salk vaccine was introduced in 1955 and used extensively until the 1960s. In 1961–63 oral polio vaccines were introduced and largely replaced IPV use. Recent changes in these policies have also been suggested and are discussed below.

Measles references are found as far back as the 7th century AD. The first live attenuated vaccine was licensed for use in the US in 1963. A goal was set to eliminate measles by 1983, but this was not met. There was a resurgence of measles in 1989–1991, with a total of 136 measles-associated deaths reported; 98 per cent of fatal cases had no history of vaccination. The resurgence is attributed to low vaccination coverage by the CDC. However, large outbreaks during this time were also reported in several other countries in the Americas. Recommended administration of measles vaccine has changed over time:
    1963 Single dose at 9 months
    1965 Single dose at 12 months
    1976 Single dose at 15 months
    1989 Two doses; 15 months and school entry.
    1994 Two doses; 12–15 months and school entry.*
    * AAP recommendation differs from ACIP recommendation: 12–15 months and entry into middle/jr high school.

Mumps were described by Hippocrates in the 5th century BC. Mumps can cause deafness (1/20,000) and orchitis (testicular inflammation – in 20–50 per cent of postpubertal males). Mumps became a reportable disease in the US in 1968. An inactivated vaccine was developed in 1948, but provided only a short immunity and so was discontinued in the mid-1970s. Live attenuated mumps virus vaccine was licensed in December 1967.

Rubella virus was first described as a disease distinct from scarlet fever and measles in 1814. Congenital rubella syndrome (CRS) results from maternal infection with rubella during pregnancy. Rubella vaccine was licensed in 1969. Prior to vaccine licensure, epidemics of rubella occurred every 6 to 9 years.

Hepatitis B is an established cause of acute and chronic hepatitis, cirrhosis, and primary hepatocellular carcinoma. In the US, the most important route of transmission is sexual contact with an infected person. Only 0.1 to 0.5 per cent of the population are chronic carriers. Hepatitis B vaccine has been available in the US since 1981. This first vaccine was plasma-derived from human carriers, 'not well accepted' and removed from the US market in 1992. Recombinant hepatitis B vaccine licensed in 1986 in the US (the first vaccine licensed in the US that was produced by recombinant DNA technology). In 1988, ACIP and AAP recommended that all pregnant women should be routinely tested for hepatitis in an early prenatal visit.

Hib (Haemophilus influenzae) causes bacterial meningitis and other invasive bacterial diseases among young children (<5 yrs). A pure polysaccharide vaccine licensed in the US in 1985 (HbPV) was not effective among children younger than 18 months; estimates of effectiveness in older children included negative effectiveness (greater disease risk for vaccinees than nonvaccinees). Used until 1988, it is no longer available in the US. The first Hib conjugate vaccine was licensed in 1987. Four additional conjugate vaccines were licensed in 1990 for use in infants as young as six weeks.

Varicella (chicken pox) was not differentiated from smallpox until end of 19th century. A vaccine for varicella was licensed in the US in March of 1995. Widespread use was recommended by Red Book committee in May of the same year. There is some controversy about this recommendation, as chicken pox is generally a mild disease in healthy children.

Most recently, the press reported widely on the Edmonston-Zagreb (EZ) measles vaccine trials in Los Angeles. In short, a few years ago, the EZ measles vaccine, a vaccine that had been used widely internationally, was thought to be effective, but was not licensed in the US, was tested by the Centers for Disease Control at several dose levels in the Los Angeles area, mostly among vaccinees of lower socioeconomic status. Early in the field trials, epidemiological studies in other countries reported the possibility of higher mortality among female infants who had received the EZ vaccine. For this reason, the trials in Los Angeles were interrupted. Eventually it became apparent that the consent forms used for the trials did not explicitly state that the EZ vaccine was not licensed for use in the US. While no increase in mortality has been detected in the vaccinees in LA, who have been followed for several years now, this oversight has recently caused the CDC some significant discomfort and bad publicity. Given the public exchanges, it appears that the incident may have caused a loss of trust in CDC among those of lower socioeconomic status, due to the apparent lack of care. The CDC has issued an apology and promised to make appropriate changes.

Table 11.2 *Vaccine licensure dates*

1940s	Diphtheria
	Tetanus
	Pertussis
1955	Polio
1961–63	Polio
1963	Measles
1967	Mumps
1969	Rubella
1986	HB
1990	Hib
1995	Varicella

Recent progress in immunization was and is considered revolutionary, but by the mid-1980s it had also created a liability crisis and a 'perceived disarticulation of the vaccine efforts'. In 1986, 255 lawsuits were filed against domestic DTP (diptheria-tetanus-pertussis – pertussis is whooping cough) manufacturers (Task Force on Safer Childhood Vaccines 1995). While some other countries had stopped pertussis vaccinations (with consequent increases in pertussis incidence), or adopted acellular pertussis vaccines, US policies continued to include whole cell pertussis vaccine (in DTP), despite many reported or alleged adverse neurological events from whole cell pertussis vaccination in the US. One argument was that acellular pertussis vaccines were not as effective as whole cell pertussis vaccines, and so should not be substituted, despite the expectation of lower adverse event frequencies.

National and international trials concluded in the last year or two provide substantial evidence that adverse event frequencies are much lower for acellular pertussis vaccines, but also that efficacy rates are potentially (much) higher than those for whole cell pertussis vaccines. Policies have now changed accordingly (CDC, 1997).

Alleged adverse events from whole cell pertussis and documented cases of poliomyelitis from oral polio, along with earlier documented vaccine problems, raise the issue of what is an unacceptable risk, and when decision-makers, be they parents, providers, or policy-makers, might choose not to vaccinate or not to recommend vaccination. This raises the question of what specific conditions should appropriately contraindicate vaccination.

Recent surveys of physicians, parents and adult patients provide evidence of widespread concerns about vaccination, and disagreement with current policies. However, it appears likely that providers and patients do not always realize that they disagree with vaccine policies. For example, presented with a set of vaccination scenarios, physicians chose not to immunize in over two-thirds of cases for which the American Academy of Pediatrics or the Advisory Committee on Immunization Practices recommends immunization, because the physicians judged as contraindications conditions not so recognized by those bodies, or they judged the risks of vaccines as outweighing the benefits

(Campbell et al. 1994; see also Loewenson, White, Osterholm and MacDonald 1994; Salsberry, Nickel and Mitch 1995). Another recent study of immunization (Woodin et al 1995) found that more physicians than parents had concerns about giving very young children three injections (ie, multiple injections), while nearly a third of parents had concerns about a single injection for their child (Woodin et al. 1995). Consistent with these findings, a study by Askew, Finelli, Lutz, DeGraaf, Siegel and Spitalny (1995) found that 30 per cent of private physicians interviewed agreed with the statement that 'giving more than one injection at a time increases the likelihood of side effects (even more so than the combined risk of side effects if the injections were given separately)'. These views are not consistent with the views of the ACIP and AAP.

Two small studies have explored more generally how parents think about vaccines. A small, ongoing study of the mental models of African American parents in Pittsburgh has found some suggestive differences between the mental models of parents whose children receive DTP3 immunization in a more timely fashion and those whose children are immunized later (Trauth et al 1996). Those whose children are immunized more on time appear more likely to mention direct exposure to the disease and a weak immune system as risk factors; more likely to say that shots strengthen the immune system, and that a series of shots is needed to get full protection from pertussis; and less likely to say that poor health is a risk factor or that shots act as medicine. In a much earlier, similarly open-ended study of 34 mothers about whooping cough in England (Harding and Bolden 1983), knowledge of the effects of the disease was very limited, including not knowing that the disease could be fatal. Some mothers appeared unaware of vaccine risks; most were unfamiliar with contraindications for vaccination and with the concept of herd immunity.[2] This study also looked at sources of information and whether mothers wanted more information before making their decision. A majority did, but without much consensus regarding what that information should be; statistics on the risk, after-effects of the vaccination, and effects of the disease were all mentioned.

These limited findings on vaccine risk assessments and perceptions illustrate several points. First, medical risk assessment can be a source of non-compliance with vaccination. Both providers' and parents' mental models or common sense understandings of illness (cf Leventhal, Diefenbach and Leventhal 1992) may not be consistent with expert recommendations for vaccination, and are a source of potential disagreement and lack of shared meaning, which may affect perceptions of care and competence, and reflect a lack of consensual values. So both interpersonal trust (with the medical provider) and social trust (in health care establishments and public health) influence the parent facing vaccination decisions.

Second, providers, who may be regarded as 'experts' by parents or patients, may also fail to share with immunization experts a common understanding of

---

2. If a large proportion of the population is vaccinated, even those who are not vaccinated may be protected, because those who are vaccinated are not likely to transmit the disease. It follows that one does not need 100 per cent vaccination to eliminate a disease from a population, 90 per cent may be enough.

the hazardous processes underlying disease and vaccine risks. This, which is related to competence, can lead to vaccine policy failures, even without overt loss of social trust. For example, providers who feel that vaccinations should be withheld if an infant has a fever may miss opportunities to vaccinate and leave children exposed to diseases unnecessarily.

Third, there are many kinds of specialists in the US who are considered health experts by some but whose expertise is not consistent with standard medical policy or practice. Chiropractors and homeopaths are examples. But even these groups are not homogeneous in their beliefs about vaccines, with most recommending at least some vaccines and some abhorring all (eg, Swales 1992). Consensual values are missing. Trust based on one health model, such as homeopathy, seems likely to preclude trust in allopathic medicine providers, should the patient or parent perceive these to be competing and inconsistent sets of beliefs.

REGULATORY HISTORY AND STRUCTURE OF
VACCINE RISK MANAGEMENT AND POLICY

Changes in the regulatory structure for vaccine policy reflect attempts to institutionalize care, competence, and consensual values. By providing compensation for adverse events, increasing adverse event surveillance, requiring increased communication efforts, and becoming more flexible, the system reflects attempts to respond caringly to adverse events. Strict safety regulations and increased research on safety enforce competence. By requiring interagency or multi-party advisory groups in addition to other communications, policies attempt to foster consensual values.

There are multiple national actors in vaccine risk management and policy, including the Food and Drug Administration (FDA), Centers for Disease Control (CDC) and the National Institute of Health (NIH), each of whom are involved in various aspects of the regulation, development, evaluation, and safe delivery of vaccines. Additionally, there are numerous advisory committees and working groups, such as the Task Force on Safer Childhood Vaccines, which include representation of many perspectives. While there are coordination attempts, many of these groups appear to operate fairly autonomously (although there is overlap in memberships on these various committees). Although policies are recommended by national advisory groups, vaccine requirements differ from state to state. There are, however, broad similarities between most states' requirements.

The most recent changes in recommended vaccination policies are for polio, pertussis, and varicella (chicken pox). Vaccine changes were proposed recently by the Advisory Committee on Immunization Practices (ACIP) for polio and pertussis, with inactivated polio vaccine being substituted for the live oral vaccine for the first two of four doses, and acellular pertussis vaccine suggested as a substitute for the whole cell pertussis vaccine that has long been used in the US. In March of 1995 the FDA licensed a live attenuated varicella vaccine, which was endorsed for all children by the American Academy of Pediatrics (the Red Book committee) two months later, in May (Napoli 1996). The ACIP and the Red Book committee are the two most prominent policy-making groups for childhood and adult immunizations in the US.

As mentioned above, the first regulatory structure for vaccines in the US was the Biological Control Authority, which was established with the Biologics Control Act of 1902. In 1937 the Laboratory of Biologics Control was formed within NIH. It was incorporated into the National Microbiological Institute and later renamed the National Institute of Allergy and Infectious Disease. After the Cutter incident, in 1955 the Surgeon General established the Division of Biologics Standards. It was eventually transferred to the FDA and in 1987 renamed the Center for Biologics Evaluation and Research (CBER) (Parkman and Hardegree 1995).

In response to pressures from parent groups, such as the National Vaccine Information Center, as well as vaccine manufacturers, among others, the National Childhood Vaccine Injury Compensation Act was passed in 1986 (NCVIA – Public Law 99-660, enacted Title XXI of the Public Health Service Act). The NCVIA established the National Vaccine Program (NVP) to 'achieve optimal prevention of human infectious diseases through immunization and to achieve optimal prevention against adverse reactions to vaccines'. The National Vaccine Advisory Committee (NVAC) was established to serve as a technical advisory committee to the NVP. With 1987 amendments the Act also established the National Vaccine Injury Compensation Program (NVICP) to compensate those injured by vaccines, and included several activities that bear on improving the safety of and risk communication about vaccines (see Sections 2126–2127, 312–314, described in Task Force on Safer Childhood Vaccines 1995).

The NCVIA also established the Vaccine Adverse Event Reporting System (VAERS), which is a passive surveillance system for adverse events. However, VAERS cannot be used to estimate frequencies of events in the general public, because the system is passive and reporting rates are not known. VAERS has been criticized highly because it is a passive system, but it has also attracted much attention – because there is otherwise a deficit of information about adverse events.

Thus, vaccine management structures have changed in response to vaccine-related injuries. But as criticisms of VAERS show, risk communication attempts are still judged inadequate by some. Such information deficits leave room for disagreement and open conflict about the effects of vaccines and whether vaccine risk managers are competent or caring.

DECISION-MAKING ABOUT VACCINES

Government can, in the US, compel vaccination. Most states require a standard set of childhood immunizations for school entry, although some require fewer than others and permitted exemptions vary (CDC, 1994).

Should vaccines be mandated? Medical decisions, because they can involve technologies regulated by the government, unfamiliar members of the medical profession, and familiar medical providers, may be influenced by trust at several levels, including interpersonal trust, trust of expertise, trust of government – and, in the case of bandwagoning, as described below, social trust broadly.

The decision research on this topic illustrates that there are a broad range of influences on vaccine risk decisions, and that decision-making styles differ. Stephen Pauker of the New England Medical Center and Tufts University offers a continuum of models for medical decision making, from the doctor's perspective (1995 AAAS meeting). These range from MDMG 'Me Doctor Me God', the classic decision-making model, in which the doctor makes all decisions unilaterally, and its successor – informed consent – to various forms of increasingly shared decision-making, including the use of in-depth videos regarding the nature and outcomes of specific medical interventions to inform patients before they decide, the use of decision analysis, in which the doctor would actively elicit the patient's values as well, and support multi-attribute decision-making, and the extreme case in which the doctor only provides guidelines for the medical decision, so that the doctor plays a smaller role, if any. Clearly preferences among these models vary, depending on the context and the people. One can regard these models as representing a scale from least to most participative. Doing so highlights the potential – and even likely failure – of participative decision-making strategies to support cognitive simplification.

In other countries, several common circumstances related to decision-making appear to have led to increases in anti-vaccine movements and resulting disease outbreaks due to falling immunization rates (Gangerosa, Phillips, Wolfe and Chen 1996). These include outspoken and articulate advocates of non-vaccina-tion, some apparent decrease in advocacy of vaccines by medical practitioners due to concerns about vaccine safety and efficacy, and salient cases of neuro-logical reactions following vaccination (Gangerosa et al 1996). Most vaccination decisions are made in consultation with or by pediatricians, family doctors, or public health providers. Parents are likely to follow the recommendations of their physician (eg, Binkin et al 1992), or some other trusted source, which fact highlights the critical role of providers, and both social and interpersonal trust, in determining immunization rates.

Although surveys show that people tend to trust physicians more than other sources of expert advice (eg, McCallum et al 1991), participation by the public in medical decision-making is likely to continue to increase. Where patients are required to give informed consent (cf Merz et al 1993), or decide for themselves how to use over-the-counter treatments (see Jungermann, Schütz and Thüring 1988), some participation in the decision is inevitable. When they do, some kinds of biases or tendencies are predictable.

Decision-making studies have identified an 'omission' bias in hypothetical vaccination decisions (eg, Asch et al 1994; Meszaros et al 1996; Ritov and Baron 1994, 1995), as well as other decision contexts. The bias is essentially a percep-tion that actions are riskier than inactions (omissions of actions), and that vaccination, because it involves taking an action, is riskier than disease, even if the expected mortality and morbidity rates are lower with the vaccine. These results are consistent with the general observation made by some groups that vaccination of a child is a 'physical intrusion into a healthy body' (Pilgrim and

Rogers 1995), and with physicians' preferences to 'do no harm'. Free-loading (relying on herd immunity and choosing not to vaccinate) and altruism (vaccinating to protect others) may play some role in vaccine decisions, but researchers have found that 'bandwagoning' – that is, doing what everybody else seems to do – appears to be a much stronger influence (Hershey et al 1994).

Several ethical principles have been identified as important in the decision-making research on environmental and medical risks, including the omission bias, as described above, and the 'do-no-harm' bias (Baron 1995). According to the do-no-harm principle, people are reluctant to harm some people to help others, even when the harm is less than that which would result from not acting. Such attempts to be fair to groups, even when they are unidentifiable, can result in unjustifiable judgments (Baron 1995). While members of the medical profession may regard a decision not to vaccinate as unethical (because it increases risks to the rest of the population, for example, especially if it threatens herd immunity – compare with Hardin's (1968) discussion of the tragedy of the commons) – others may regard compulsory vaccination as unethical, and consider informed consent the only viable ethical policy. And risk communication is a key component of informed consent.

CURRENT VACCINE COMMUNICATION

The NCVIA also mandated the development of vaccine information materials to be distributed by providers to parents and patients receiving any childhood vaccine. Materials are supposed to include information on the diseases, vaccine reactions, possible ways to reduce the risk of major adverse reactions, contra-indications, information on groups at high risk for vaccination, availability of the NVICP, and federal recommendations about immunization schedules. CBER collaborates with the CDC in the development of this information (Parkman and Hardegree 1995).

The first set of materials produced in response to this were the Vaccine Information Pamphlets, which were widely criticized for being too lengthy (eg, Fitzgerald and Glotzer 1995). Their successors, the Vaccine Information Statements (VISs), have only recently been produced. Less to do with the VISs themselves than the management strategy they imply is that the statements provide a unnuanced response to an audience that is extremely diverse in its information needs and wants. Insufficient attention to the audiences' prior beliefs and information processing needs (eg, cognitive limitations) are among the criticisms one can make of the VISs (cf IOM 1997b).

Relative to what is known about many kinds of environmental risk perceptions, little is known about vaccine risk perceptions (Bostrom 1997). This is despite a large vaccine literature, active vaccine groups, and a recent attempt by the CDC to address what in this literature and on hotlines appear to be common misconceptions about the risks of vaccines (CDC 1996). These 'common misconceptions' include beliefs related to the disappearance of diseases regardless of the use of vaccines, the relative risks of vaccines and diseases, the potential existence of 'hot' lots of vaccine, misunderstanding of base rate issues related to disease incidence among vaccinated and unvaccinated children, and concerns about overloading the immune system with multiple vaccinations given at the same time. This document was distributed widely before it was empirically evaluated (an evaluation is underway), evoked criticisms from several sources, but has also been in great demand (by, for example, those whose job it is to implement state vaccine policies).[3]

Other sources of information about vaccines are the ad campaigns sponsored by the CDC to increase vaccination rates, the package inserts required with all vaccines, and hotlines to federal agencies. The ad campaigns are designed with the sole intent of increasing vaccination rates, and do not address risks. While vaccine package inserts do provide extensive information about risks, they are not designed to simplify or provide easily comprehensible narratives about vaccines. One informal study of telephone calls to the CDC about vaccines found that most of the calls came from providers (Hatcher 1993).

Earle and Cvetkovich (1995) provide evidence that credibility is more a consequence of trust values, which lead to social trust, than a cause of social trust. Thus for information to be useful in risk management, it must not only be designed effectively, but it must be credible, which means that it must build on trust (see also Renn 1991).

INSTITUTIONAL AND ORGANIZATIONAL OBSTACLES TO TRUST

At least two conditions appear to threaten credible vaccine risk communication. First, those involved in maximizing immunization rates should not be in charge of risk communication and management. Conflicts between communication objectives and agency goals for current governmental managers make it unlikely that risk communication from those sources will be perceived as credible. The CDC has as its stated goal to increase immunization rates. It would be difficult for the CDC to communicate credibly about vaccine risks as long as perceived vaccine risks are seen as a potential obstacle to high immunization rates, despite the separation of vaccine safety from other immunization activities at CDC. Second, the training and professional affiliations of these agencies' staffs, such as the CDC in which many are MDs, may be perceived as an obstacle to credible risk communication.

Several parallels between vaccine risk management and environmental risk management are evident. For example, the tendency for a dominating professional culture to drive current activities and potentially prevent change – lawyers at EPA, doctors at CDC. There are also some differences, such as the evidence of continual change in vaccine management policies, regulations, and institutional arrangements. Whether by design or because of the immediacy of health tragedies, public health agencies appear to respond relatively quickly to trust-endangering events.

3. These conclusions are based on multiple discussions during 1996-7 with members of VARICO, a loosely organized vaccine risk communication group that holds conference calls regularly under the auspices of the National Immunization Program at the Centers for Disease Control.

For policies to be effective in the long run, they must be flexible or reflect some of the diversity of values in public. Some people who trust US public health policies may want only to know what the majority of their community is doing (do others vaccinate?). Others, who can serve a watchdog function, will become alarmed and distrustful if their questions about vaccine safety are not addressed.

Lack of trust appears central to immunization policy critics' arguments, resulting from first, uncertainty and disagreement about what the risks are and how to control them; second, policy-makers' apparent preferences for compulsion (ie, involuntary risk); and third, relatively sparse information about risks and even some withholding of information (eg, vaccine lot sizes, which manufacturers do not have to reveal).

Thus for vaccine risk policies to succeed, they must in some regard take into account the range of beliefs, prior experiences, and specific circumstances of publics and medical providers (cf Kunreuther, Slovic and MacGregor 1996). At a recent Vaccine Safety Forum Institute of Medicine workshop, a key conclusion was that lack of trust is a problem (IOM,1997b). Suggestions for improvements in policy included not only increased research and vaccine safeguards, but ranged from allowing philosophical exemptions from mandatory vaccination to making available a more diverse set of well-designed and empirically evaluated vaccine information materials. As argued above, for these materials to be credible, institutional changes may be necessary.

12 Social Trust: Consolidation and Future Advances

George Cvetkovich and Ragnar E Löfstedt

This concluding chapter aims to draw on the issues discussed in the book to suggest the key areas for future research in the trust and risk management field. We have also sought to incorporate our own insights and ideas on what we see to be the most important areas for conceptualization and research.

DEFINITIONS OF SOCIAL TRUST – BEYOND THE BASICS

Dimensions of Social Trust

The progress of normal science is characterized by increasing articulation and specification of basic concepts resulting from the interaction of constructs, process models and empirical observations. There are two directions in which this progress beyond the basic definition will occur for social trust. Both of these are observable in the contemporary social science literature on risk management. One of these directions focuses on the dimensionality of social trust. Does social trust have one dimension or more? If more, what are they and how are they related to each other? Chapters 5 and 8 present efforts along these lines. The other direction focuses on function. How does social trust work? What's it useful for? How did it develop? Examples of this occur in the other contributions in this volume as well as Chapters 5 and 8.

This dual focus and the issues involved in their consideration in the social trust and risk management literature are reminiscent of the divergent directions taken by early theorists of emotion. Wilhem Wundt, the recognized founder of experimental psychology, was concerned with issues of structure. How many basic emotions are there? How do they relate to each other? Is happiness more closely related to elation or to mirth? William James, also a major contributor to the development of psychology as well as pragmatic philosophy, was interested in the functionality of emotions. Indeed, he believed the issue of structure not to be resolvable in a fundamental sense. The important thing to James was to discover why emotions exist and how they facilitate adaptation. Questions of structure are basically issues of conceptual construction. One can slice up the domain 'emotion', or any other domain including social trust, in innumerable ways (cf, Cvetkovich and Earle 1985). It is instructive that the question of the 'basic' structure of emotions has not yet been satisfactorily answered. We should not be optimistic that the structure of trust is amenable to a single solution. This is echoed in Metlay's conclusion to Chapter 8 that the effort to identify a structure of social trust is a 'conceptual quagmire'. James's resolution of structural quandaries was pragmatics. Categories only make sense if they serve the purposes for which they were developed. The implications of this perspective differ from that of Johnson's recommendation in Chapter 5 to avoid theory and to use only purely empirical based searches for structure. The pragmatic perspective also provides a caution for social scientists who would take on the task of identifying the structure of social trust with practical implications for risk management. A categorization that serves well the needs of basic social science research may not serve the purposes of the practising hazard manager. The development of a practical structure seemingly requires the initial identification of the needs of risk managers. This implies that social scientists aspiring to both theoretical and practical goals must give due consideration to balancing the (sometimes) competing needs of each.

Measures and Operational Definitions

Social trust is largely measured through self reports in interviews, focus groups, and questionnaires. Most often, study participants are asked to rate directly how much they trust a particular person or agency. Somewhat less direct techniques such as Q-sorts have also been used (Focht 1997; Frewer, Howard, Hedderley and Shepard 1996). Conceivably a number of alternative behaviour-based measures could be used to the benefit of the field. Measurements other than self reports have the advantage of not inducing a self reflection that could produced biased results. However, they do raise other problems. They require a greater number of assumptions to infer their meaning. To take one admittedly overly simple example: is participation in a public forum an indication of trust (I trust that the efforts I make will be taken seriously and will make a difference) or distrust (I have to take care of representing my views, no one else will)? Conversely, for the same reasons, is failure to participate in a public forum trust or distrust?

Another issue that raises concerns about interpretations is the distinction between trust and distrust. Several commentators have noted the importance of distinguishing distrust as more than just the absence of trust (Luhmann 1988; Earle and Cvetkovich 1995; Bradbury, Branch and Focht, Chapter 9, this volume). Future research might exercise appropriate caution in interpreting behaviour through the use of multiple measures of trust and distrust and the use of contextual information.

The trust evaluations requested in social science research tend to be 'in general' judgements. That is, participants are asked to indicate their trust by making an evaluation without a context (How much do you trust Agency X?). That the measurement of trust should not be based solely on such an abstract, unitary judgement is indicated by the recent experiences of one of us (GC).

Local citizens participating in focus groups on water quality in the Lake Whatcom, Washington, watershed indicated that they generally did not trust the state Department of Energy. It, along with other government agencies, represented special interests not shared by common citizens. A number of examples of how the Department had acted in a seemingly arbitrary and dictatorial way were given. However, many also indicated that their most trusted single source of information about water quality in the watershed was Waterwise, a radio programme funded and produced by the state Department of Ecology. This radio programme was trusted because it provided an open forum for discussion of all perspectives to water quality issues, it provided understandable technical information about water quality, and citizens could have their questions about water quality-related practices answered by calling the programme. While the Department of Ecology was very mistrusted, in general it was a provider of highly trusted information.

This example, in line with the suggestions made by Johnson in Chapter 5 and Frewer et al (1997), suggests that social scientists should make preliminary efforts to explore distinctions in trust based on specific contexts. Assumptions about the validity of unitary, 'in general' judgements may not be justified in all cases.

UNDERSTANDING TRUST

The Functions of Social Trust

The Good of Social Trust – Individual and Group Benefits

Calls for increased trust often assume that this will produce benefits. The application of evolutionary theory concludes that the search for social trust's benefits can begin with the identification of benefits basic to the survival of humans (Bateson 1988; Cosmides and Tooby 1997; Earle 1997). The development of sociality (living in groups) is a major evolutionary adaptation contributing greatly to the continued survival of relatively physically weak individuals. The evolution of a tendency to social trust produced survival advantages for small bands of humans in terms of cohesion and collaboration resulting in collective efficiency. Social trust reduces social transaction costs by circumventing the need for explicit agreements. It thus acts as a 'social lubricant'. The docility reflected in social trust also allows the transcending of the limits of individual rationality by passing on group knowledge through the socialization to each new generation (Caporeal 1997; Caporeal, Dawes, Orbell and van de Kraut 1989; Simon 1990). The benefits suggested by the evolutionary analysis have been documented by the extensive historical cultural analysis of Putnam (1995a, b) and Fukuyama (1996). Societies that were able to develop trust beyond the boundaries of family members and other familiars enjoyed more robust and rapid economic development.

In addition to collective benefits of efficiency, individual benefits can also be identified. Social trust reduces demands on the individual by reducing the cognitive complexity of decisions (Luhmann 1988; Mitzal 1996; Earle and Cvetkovich 1995; Bradbury, Branch and Focht, Chapter 9, this volume).

Relinquishing decision and behavioural control to others relieves the need to understand the technical and other complexities of risks and the various actions that might be needed to mitigate them. Increased feelings of safety also may result from the trade-off of decision and behavioural control for the cognitive and secondary control provided by social trust. These conclusions about individual benefits of social trust are implied by the results of studies that show an inverse relationship between trust and judgements of risk (see Flynn, Slovic, and Mertz 1994; Cvetkovich, Chapter 4, this volume). Those who are more trusting judge a number of environmental hazards as lower in risk than do those who are less trusting. This leads to the expectation that those who are more trusting will be less vigilant about physical risks and experience less stress. Limited evidence from residents around the failed Three Mile Island nuclear plant support this expectation (Baum and Gatchel 1981).

Future social science research is likely to be directed at further identifying the group and individual benefits of social trust. Speculations based on evolutionary theory and the evidence of the limited historical analysis result in a portrait of benefits painted in broad brush strokes. Between the strokes a number of questions remain on the canvas. Prominent among the questions likely to attract future research are those about what specific benefits result from social trust in specific circumstances.

The Bad and the Ugly of Social Trust – Cautions for Risk Management

The above described group benefits of social trust (efficiency, productivity, cohesion, social 'lubrication'), as already noted, are what risk managers and others have in mind when they conclude that more social trust is needed. But the outcomes of social trust are not invariably positive. Sanctioned violence, such as warfare or genocide, happens because those directing the destructive actions are considered to be legitimate authorities. Legitimization of the authority to give orders, including the order to destroy fellow humans, is based on three factors – trust in the one giving the order, a judgement that the order will produce some benevolent effects beyond its immediate destructiveness, and normative support, the judgement that others approve of following the order (Brickman 1974). Other examples of the 'bad' of social trust are prejudice and xenophobia.

The ugly, like the bad, results from social trust being an in-group phenomenon. The ugly results from group members trusting those who are insensitive to the requirements of the environment in which the group operates. This aspect of social trust has been called 'group think' (Janis 1982). With group think, trust in a leader may put into play psychological and social processes that isolate the group. Assured of its specialness and correctness, the group may be led to take ultimately disastrous actions.

Consideration of the bad and the ugly as well as the good of social trust forces a broadening of the perspectives to trust that is taken. The functions of social trust should be considered not only from the narrow perspective of organizational efficiency (the good) but also from the broader perspective of societal functioning (to avoid the bad and the ugly). This broader perspective includes important questions about the quality of risk management decisions and actions (Hammond 1994). From this perspective it seems impossible to convincingly argue that all environmental decisions would be better if there were more social trust. For example, in the US there has been a long history of mistrust of the development of nuclear power (Hohenemser, Kasperson, and Kates 1977) that continues to this day. This has led to the stalemating of efforts to develop a permanent waste storage facility. If there had been more social trust of involved government and industry representatives, this stalemate likely would have been avoided. The question remains: what produces the better environmental outcome, the current stalemate or continued development of nuclear power?

Consideration of the bad and the ugly of social trust raises the question for future research of 'Under what conditions is social trust likely to become a force for undesirable outcomes?' Important questions, discussed later, about how democratic societies can avoid the bad and the ugly, and how important is the good, are also raised.

How are Social Trust Judgements Made?

Those who would offer explanations of how social trust judgements are made are well advised to take seriously the results of studies examining judgements of others. In particular, this research indicates that the factors affecting one's own behaviour are not those that are used commonly to explain the behaviour of others (Wilson 1985). If social trust normally is an automatic cognitive process, as suggested by some observers (eg, Wittgenstein 1968; Earle and Cvetkovich 1995), we should not expect that we can understand how trust judgements are made based only on consciousness of own experiences. Social scientists should be cautious in making inferences in the absence of empirical evidence about what influences judgements of trust. Understandings of social trust would seem not to be derivable solely from exercises of introspection.

Two contributions in this volume present empirical evidence on how trust attribution is made. In Chapter 3, Slovic offers evidence that trust-reducing information has a larger impact on judgements than does trust-inducing information. In Chapter 4, Cvetkovich presents evidence suggesting that this 'asymmetry' of trust may be limited to particular circumstances and also presents evidence that trust judgements may be unconsciously influenced by characteristics of the context in which they are made. Future research might profitably be directed towards contributing to the understanding of the implicit processing of information involved in trust judgements and the implications of the shift to trust judgements using more conscious processes.

Social Trust and Risk Perception

Research conducted by a number of investigators (Slovic et al 1991; Flynn et al 1994; Löfstedt 1996; Frewer et al 1997; Hine, Summers, Prystupa and McKenzie-Richer 1997; Siegrist 1997; Slovic and Cvetkovich, Chapters 3 and 4, this volume; Sjöberg forthcoming) indicates that trust accounts for a significant percentage of the variance in perceptions of risk. That is to say, to a large extent people perceive something to be safe or dangerous because, respectively, they trust or distrust the authorities or regulators or industry.

These findings have been challenged by Sjöberg in Chapter 7. In a study of Swedish and Spanish public perceptions toward policy-makers, he shows that trust in the two nations, vastly different in cultural and historical context, can explain no more than 10 per cent of the variance. He concludes that the variable of trust may be less important than risk researchers have come to believe and it is a popular research area with little explanatory power. He concludes that further studies are needed to explain how much variance in risk perception trust can actually explain. Similarly Drottz-Sjöberg (1996) concludes that trust is overrated. It is concluded that what are considered to be physical variables such as the physical threat of exposure is a more important factor and should receive greater recognition in risk perception research. In her study, the public perception of the risk regarding radiation in Sweden and former CIS countries has much more to do with the threat of exposure to the risk (eg Swedish hunters' fear of eating contaminated moose meat as a result of the Chernobyl accident) than whether the sources that provided the information (in this case the Swedish government) can be trusted.

The measures used in the Sjöberg and Drottz-Sjöberg research tap 'in general' trust. More context-specific measures, as suggested earlier, might yield a higher correlation between trust and risk perception. Swedish hunters may distrust the Swedish government in general, but they may, nevertheless, trust the government's information about the radiation dangers of eating moose meat. This possibility is similar to that described earlier in which Washington state citizens generally mistrusted the state's Department of Ecology. Nevertheless, they trusted as a credible source of information a radio programme sponsored and produced by the agency. Indeed, in the case of the Swedish hunters, information that the radiation danger is high might be especially credible if the source is believed normally to underestimate radiation risks. Future research should explore the possibility (and its attendant complexities) that sources that are generally distrusted may still be judged as credible sources of information (cf Jungermann, Pfister and Fisher 1992).

Further study is needed then on the relationship of trust and risk perception. An additional line that this future research might take is to investigate how understandings of social systems relate both to trust and risk perception (cf Johnson 1997). Recent indications in the US, for example, are that many people trusted the Federal Food and Drug Administration (FDA) because of a lack of understanding of the agency's actual functioning. Many US citizens were surprised that the health risks of the combination pill Fen-phen (fenfluramine and phentermine) were discovered only after the pill was in use by 21 million dieters. There was an apparent assumption that the FDA would have made efforts to assure the safety of this combination pill. While the FDA evaluates single drugs, it is not mandated to evaluate the risks produced by using drugs in combination. An erroneous belief about the FDA's function led to trust in the safety of the diet pill and perhaps to a degree of mistrust following the news about Fen-phen.

Civic Engagement and Public Participation

Bradbury et al (Chapter 9) and Kasperson et al (Chapter 2) and others have discussed the importance of an active civic society in increasing trust and reducing potential conflicts. This strand of argument has its origins in two different schools of thought, that of civic engagement and that of public participation. The notion of civic engagement is based on the work of Robert Putnam (1993; 1995a, b). The importance of civic society has also been elaborated by Fukuyama (1996) in his book *Trust: The Social Virtues and the Creation of Prosperity*. The importance of public participation has been indicated in the work of among others Fischhoff (1995), Freudenberg (1996a, b), Irwin (1995), the National Research Council of the US (1996), Renn et al (1995), Slovic (1987) and Wynne (1992, 1996). Both schools draw the conclusion that civic engagement either directly (participating in the policy making process) or indirectly (by being active in civic society) increases the level of trust in society. While there is much to support these arguments, they need to be further tested. For example, can there be high trust societies without high civic engagement? Putnam says that the answer has to be no. Yet critics of Putnam in the US point out that decreased membership in some civic societies such as the Boy Scouts, the Parents-Teachers Association and bowling clubs should actually be applauded as they are either antiquated institutions or are institutions that are motivated by mistrust (eg the PTA) (Pollitt 1996). One possible explanation is that it depends upon how one defines civic engagement. Swedish researchers have shown that although membership of trade unions and other civic societies has declined, people's social lives are more active than ever (Petersson 1994) and hence the importance of friendship should be included in any discussion on civic engagement.

Another key question is whether greater public participation will always lead to a 'thicker' democracy? For example, Switzerland is seen by many as a positive example of public participation as the Swiss operate by putting forward policies via popular referendum. However, voting participation in Switzerland is the lowest in Europe and even lower than that in the US (Wolff et al 1992). Voting turnout in the US is amongst the lowest in the western world. Hence, what needs to be done is further examination of what makes up civic engagement: eg what type of society are we talking about and does membership in an organized society (eg the PTA) increase or decrease social trust? Additionally, it is important to further examine what types of public participation mechanisms should be advocated. Public referenda are widely used in Switzerland and the US. Has this form of public participation actually led to a decrease in voter turnout?

Some who have argued for greater public participation have also made specific suggestions as to the conditions under which this participation should occur beyond that of participation in existing organizations. Future conceptualization and research is likely to continue efforts in evaluating these proposals. Habermas (1989) and Renn et al (1995) have perhaps been most explicit in making recommendations for specific conditions of participation. It is suggested that a level playing field be established in which all participants, both the technical experts and the general public, have the same level of technical and scientific knowledge. There are several considerations that make the pragmatic application of this proposal less desirable that it sounds in abstract principle. A major problem is that the proposal presumes the superiority of technical/scientific knowledge over the local, lay knowledge of citizens (Wynne 1992). This may have the effect of inducing mistrust of authorities. Another problem is that efforts along these lines that have been attempted (for example in Sweden and The Netherlands with regard to nuclear energy) show that it is difficult and expensive to raise the technical and scientific knowledge of the general public. A considerable amount of resources is needed to support the effort to increase the public's knowledge. Making this effort even more difficult is that many citizens are not interested in knowing about, or unable to understand, issues at a great level of technical specificity. Efforts to circumvent the costs and problems of broad education by educating only selected citizens run other risks (Renn et al 1995). The process by which citizens are selected (for example random selection) and the implementation of decisions by the resultant few trained citizens raise concern that democratic system checks and balances may be superseded (Kasperson et al, Chapter 2, this volume).

Is Trust Necessary For Managing Hazards?

Leiss (1995) has offered a resounding answer of 'No' to this title question. According to his perspective, not only is trust unnecessary, but better resolutions of risk controversies actually occur if involved parties distrust each other. Parties to risk controversies have good reasons for distrust because they have different, often competing self interests. Historical experience shows that in their efforts to prevail, parties may conceal information or distort it to fit their needs. Such distortion, according to Leiss, should be understood as being equivalent to bluffing in the card game of poker. It is an acceptable means to a desired end. These strategic contests of interest groups lead to better resolutions of risk controversies because they help sort out the uncertainties of risk assessment according to particular interests. Trust between the interest groups would short circuit this process because it would eliminate the tension between interest groups that is produced by what is characterized as sensible utility-maximizing strategic behaviour. Trust might induce the immediate wholehearted acceptance of the risk-adverse claims of environmental groups. (Leiss uses as one example Greenpeace's exaggerated claims about the associations of organochlorines and human ill health.) Or trust might induce the immediate wholehearted acceptance of the risk-promoting claims of dominant industries. (Leiss uses as examples industry efforts to minimize or actually cover up health effects on workers of asbestos, benzidine and beta-naphthylamine.) Without trust, a more moderate course among the competing exaggerated claims may be navigated.

This 'down and dirty' approach to risk controversies, as Leiss calls it, raises some important troubling issues for future social science conceptualization and research. At minimum it shakes the foundation of the existing broad faith in social trust as a positive force for better resolutions of risk controversies. It is also interesting because it seems to overlook some issues that recent work has found to be important. The down and dirty approach does not state who it is that actually conducts society's navigation among the claims of competing interest groups. Clearly this role is not left to the special interest stakeholder groups who are battling out their wars of exaggeration. The anonymity of this key actor is curious. Obviously there is a force (albeit anonymous) that is at operation here.

> Bluff and other forms of dissimulation ought to be expected and can be tolerated so long as there are effective procedural safeguards against such practices as concealing relevant information (or failing to disclose it promptly), on the one hand, or excessively alarming the public about not fully confirmed scientific research findings, on the other. These safeguards consist essentially in finding ways to put pressures on all stakeholders to be accountable for their actions and viewpoints in some common public forum. (Leiss 1995)

In other words, just as with the game of poker, the 'game' of risk controversies can only be played if there is trust that the rules are being followed. Unlike the usual case with poker players, with risk controversies we can not trust that the 'players', special interest stakeholder groups, necessarily will do this voluntarily. In this case trust is placed in those who assure that the rules are being followed. We do not know the exact identity of these 'referees', but we can imagine that it is probably government in one form or another. In the end, Leiss seems to be saying that trust is necessary for the management of risks. What the down and dirty approach fails to recognize is a distinction between trust regarding particular actions, including the provision of information, and confidence in the operation of a system. As the research by Bradbury, Branch and Focht (Chapter 9) shows, trust concerning particular actions may not be necessary or even possible in some cases. System trust does seem to be necessary for participation in discourses attempting to address risk controversies. But the specifics of these issues as they apply to a variety of cases are still unclear. What is the exact nature of system trust? Is what constitutes the system the same for all risk controversies? What characteristics of systems produce trust? The social science literature on social justice may well contain some leads for beginning answers these questions (see Chapter 5). The translation of insights from this literature, which mostly examines legal systems to risk controversies, awaits further work.

Is *Dis*trust Functional?

Barber (1983), like Leiss, also considers the possibility that there may be benefits to distrust. While Leiss' view is that of the war of all stakeholder groups against all other stakeholder groups, Barber's perspective is that of the individual citizen. In his book, *The Logic and Limits of Trust*, Barber argues that a certain level of distrust in a society is healthy, as in the long-term as it leads to better policy-making (Barber 1983). Kasperson et al (Chapter 2) argue that today in most countries the balance between the general public and elites is badly skewed and 'rational social distrust holds in check the growing power of economic elites and technical expertise'. They believe that a certain amount of social distrust provides a control mechanism that enables a democratic society to function. Hence, a mixture of social trust and distrust within a given society provides a form of checks and balances for keeping central authority in step.

However, it is unclear whether any amount of distrust is truly positive. High levels of distrust in these authorities in the US have, over the last 50 years, resulted in huge increases in the levels of litigation. This has channelled large amounts of public and private money into the hands of lawyers rather than being directed towards actually reducing risks. In the case of the EPA Super Fund, more than 80 per cent of the expenditure has been used for fighting various legal actions (Breyer 1993). A recent example, again from the US, suggests that distrust does create a climate that makes legislative and other positive actions difficult. In his State of the Union message of February 4, 1997, President Clinton announced an American Heritage Rivers initiative that would help communities clean up local rivers. The initiative would make certain that existing federal programmes of money and expertise would be available to communities whose local river was designated as having heritage status. The programme was voluntary. No additional legislation, appropriations or regulations were required. Water and property rights were protected. It would seem that no one could object to the initiative. But, as reported in *US News and World* this was not to be so:

> Then a curious thing happened. Conservative members of Congress, mostly from rural areas of the West, joined with property rights activists, public land 'wise use' advocates, and media commentators to condemn American Heritage Rivers as a massive conspiracy to extend federal, and perhaps foreign, control over the nation's 3.5 million miles of rivers and streams, over watersheds, even over private river front property. (Sachell, 1997)

The recent creation of a 1.7 million-acre park in Utah without Congressional approval, widely viewed in the West as a federal land grab, fuelled some of the Heritage Rivers distrust. So did the feeling that 'heritage rivers' sounds suspiciously like 'United Nations Heritage Sites'. There are some who believe that the federal administration is aiding a United Nations take-over of the US. In response to this outcry a number of federal representatives have joined to support legislation preventing federal agencies from participating, thus killing the plan.

The key question arises of whether encouraging distrust in society will lead to greater effective public participation in policy making, particularly in countries other than the US. In other words, is distrust beneficial in a society where public trust in policy makers/industry has been built up over time?

For example, Sweden's environmental policy is strongly supported by the public. It was formulated in a process involving environment ministers, advisors and researchers who have gained the public's trust over time through the passing of competent and farsighted environmental regulations.

The role that distrust can play in different societies, with varying degrees of alienation of the public from policy makers, therefore appears to warrant further study. The above considerations also indicate that in this effort future work would do well to keep clear the distinction between distrust and lack of trust (Luhmann 1988; Wynne 1996; Bradbury et al, Chapter 9, this volume). It could be argued that a lack of trust in a democratic society is a good thing, distrust is not. Assume that system trust, as described above, exists to the extent that allows an appropriate discourse of risk controversies to occur and business, government and industry to operate. Within this context an enlightened skepticism (lack of trust and distrust) about particular conclusions and suggested actions would seem to be a good thing. It has been suggested that science provides one existing successful model of this condition (Earle and Cvetkovich 1995). Individual scientists are trusted by their colleagues to operate according to the values of science. There is trust in the system of science. Distrust of an individual scientist occurs only if there is an indication of violation of science's salient values such as evidence of plagiarism or falsification of data. However, a scientist does not trust another scientist when it comes to theorizing or interpreting empirical findings. These are met with enlightened skepticism. To what extent can enlightened skepticism be expected in democratic societies instead of distrust, which is after all cognitively simpler? Also, what institutionalized ways of operating in the absence of trust should be created (see Chapter 2)?

The Role of Leadership?

There are three ways that a leader may attempt to develop and use trust. These can be called normal trust, trust based on changing value constructions, and trust resulting from leading efforts to change value constructions.

Normal Trust

The first of these is called *normal* trust because it reflects the usual way in which the trust of leaders operates. In this case the leader's way of talking and acting are judged by the members to reflect a sharing of group values. We earlier discussed the potential for the bad and the ugly, as well as the good, of this kind of trust. Extreme cases of attempts to discover the group's values and consciously shape one's talking and acting to fit them are sometimes referred to as leadership 'by following the public polls'. While unattractive sounding, this 'leadership by following', to a greater or lesser extent, is probably a persistent part of the way politicians and other risk managers operate in modern societies.[1] Polls, focus groups, town meetings, and other sources will continue to be used by politicians and others involved in risk controversies to discover exiting positions and values. Most politicians are not as candid about this process as was a recent report, *Language of the Twenty-first Century*, circulated to members of the Republican Party in the US Congress. As Gates (1997) reports, the book provides remarkable detail about the language and themes that successful candidates should employ.

1. Those who have directly participated in the establishment of democratic systems have often been aware of the dangers of leadership based on normal trust. The founders of the United States of America, James Madison especially, tended to follow the pessimistic philosophy of Thomas Hobbes which placed 'security ahead of liberty in a system of enlightened despotism' (Kaplan, 1997; p. 56). The astute 19th Century observer of American democracy, Alexis de Tocqueville, warned that totalitarian despotism is to be particularly feared because democracy's populist concern for equality engenders obsessions with self-security and interests.

The successful Republican candidate knows how to 'speak in terms of people, ideas, and vision', rather than dollars and cents, facts and figures. The successful Republican candidate knows the importance of 'listening to women and adopting a new language and a more friendly style'. When the subject is education, the candidate must say things like 'Education is about the future' and 'I don't want one child to fall through the cracks'; even when it is not, the candidate must learn to say, 'It's about the children.' (Gates, 1997)

Similar advice about speaking to the concerns of one's audience has been given to those who communicate to the public about risk controversies (Sandman 1993). Gates notes, however, that the *Language of the Twenty-first Century* report does not assume that the public is infinitely malleable: '. . . all this advice comes with a stunning caveat: "You must not say what you do not believe."' (Gates 1997)

Is normal trust primarily a force for the maintenance of the status quo?[2] This would seem to be so, given that its main outcome may be the continuation of the political power of the leader rather than change in the group's thinking about risk controversies. However, this may not be entirely true. A possibility that should be investigated by future research is that by establishing trust through reflecting existing salient values, a leader might find it easier to take bold ventures on at least some issues. That is, subsequent actions may be viewed through the lens of the established characterization of being trustworthy. Group members may not agree with the specific action or policy but may be willing to give the leader the benefit of the doubt. One historical example of this is the re-establishment during the 1970s of diplomatic, trade and other relationships between China and the US. Reaction in the US to the first step in this reconciliation was perhaps as positive as it was because it was taken by President Richard Nixon, who was trusted for his hard stand against communism. Domestic American reaction at that time might not have been as positive if a president perceived to be more conciliatory towards communism had announced that he would visit China to restart formal relationships between the two countries.

Trust Based on Changing Value Constructions

Efforts to induce trust in this way involve developing value constructions that change the saliency of values. Values that lead to acceptance of actions and policies are made more salient. Values that lead to making actions and policies less attractive are made less salient. The point of the value construction is a reflexive acceptance of the leader's actions or policy by inducing trust. By changing value saliency, the leader may bring about an inclusion of previously divergent sets of values. In this sense, trust based on changing value constructions might be considered to be truly leadership. Unlike normal trust, in which the leader is following accepted views, in this case the leader is 'out front'

---

2. The mistake often made by politicians and others is that the assessed position of the public is primary and immutable. There is considerable evidence that the public's position on issues, particularly complex or new issues, is highly labile. The acceptance of the normal trust approach ignores this. Approaches 2 and 3 are based on an assumption of lability.

attempting to get the group to understand risk controversies in new ways. In Chapter 10, Gowda describes the case of a Native American leader whose efforts may fit this description. Another example of this trust/leader relationship is the current efforts of US President Clinton's administration regarding global climate change. Early in 1997 administration officials cautioned at international meetings that the American public was not ready to accept actions to reduce greenhouse gases or take other measures aimed at reducing possible human contributions to climate change. Planned administration actions since that time have been modest and have been criticized as such by other nations. Nevertheless, there has been a major effort to engender among the American public recognition of the risks of global climate change and support for actions to mitigate it. A large part of this effort has been to construct the issue in ways designed to change the saliency of values automatically associated with it. This effort has include emphasizing in news conferences and public announcements that the threat of global change is immediate, it's happening now, and that it will have negative effects on health, property, safety and economic welfare. The construction attempts to transcend concerns for economic growth (market pricing values) and concerns about the environmental threats and the fairness of solutions (equity matching values) (see Chapter 1).

How effective are such efforts and what conditions determine their acceptability? A major drawback to their use by risk managers is that they often require extensive resources and a fair amount of creativity. They also involve a fair amount of risk. These are all important questions that future social science work might profitably investigate.

Trust Resulting From Leading Efforts to Change Value Constructions

This third approach to managing trust requires the leader to engage group members in a collective effort to construct values that will guide the resolution of risk controversies. It requires other group members as well as the leader to operate in a conscious, rational mode. It is therefore unlike the first two approaches in which group members can operate in an automatic reflexive mode. This approach then runs against the difficulty of requiring a strong commitment and motivation from group members and places a demand of cognitive complexity on those who participate. Issues and questions raised in the earlier discussion on public participation also apply here.

The Role of Regulation?

Regulation is a dominant approach to risk management in most democratic societies. In Chapter 6, Löfstedt and Horlick-Jones consider the question of why, similar to many other regulatory agencies, the Environment Agency in the UK places such high significance on gaining the trust of industry and the public. This seems to be due to a preference for a consensual style of governing which it is thought provides flexibility and reduces the costs of regulation. This, of course, is another instantiation of the good of social trust, discussed earlier. Trust produces efficient regulation.

One might with interesting consequences examine the relationship of trust and regulation in the reverse order. This less conventional perspective asks if regulation has an effect on trust. In one sense regulation implies that those who are being regulated can not be trusted to do the right thing. If they could be, there would not be a need for the regulation. Thus the lack of trust by regulators of the public (expressed through the existence of regulation) may breed distrust of the regulators by the public. To what extent is distrust bred by the mere effort to regulate? This also suggests that there might be in some cases a potential, perhaps irresolvable, conflict between regulation and trust.

Another interesting reversal of conventional causal links occurs when we consider efforts of regulatory agencies to operate without using direct regulatory sanctions. An agency may wish for various reasons to change behaviours having an effect on environmental risks without placing statutory restrictions against the behaviours. To be effective, statutory regulations require policing compliance and administering sanctions to violators. These are costly operations and in some cases impossible to carry out. How could a regulatory agency monitor the household and recreational behaviour of the thousands of residents in a watershed to ensure that the hundreds of activities that might reduce water quality did not occur? It is an impossible task, particularly if there is concern about not violating what are considered basic rights that individuals have in democracies. The alternative is to induce the residents to begin policing themselves. This was the dilemma facing the organizers of efforts to improve water quality in the Lake Whatcom, Washington, watershed, mentioned earlier. The focus groups initiating this indicated that the regulatory officials had to begin thinking of the link of citizens' trust, producing effective regulation in a different way. Citizens in the focus groups made it clear that the planned educational campaign would not be successful unless the regulatory officials first trusted the citizens. A positive campaign based on the assumption that citizens already felt stewardship responsibilities to water quality was suggested. The citizens were also clear in indicating that they wanted the campaign to focus on what they could do positively to improve water quality rather than dwell on what they were doing wrong.

To many regulators the ideas that regulation might adversely affect trust and that they should trust the public may seem alien. Managers might well take a lesson from the operation of trust in interpersonal relationships, which illustrates both possibilities. Trust of one partner usually does not occur in the absence of trust by the other. Jealousy, for example, is a lack of trust that if continued in excess can destroy a relationship. Efforts that are judged to over-regulate the relationship are also potentially detrimental. Spouses may make pre-nuptial agreements for the distribution of property outside of the existing legal system should a marriage break up. There are successful pre-nuptial contracts. But many who have done this come to believe that the very making of the contract indicated an initial mistrust and that this was detrimental to the marriage. A female lawyer who creates pre-nuptial agreements for her clients explained why she did not have one for her recent marriage in this way: 'I know this sounds stupid, but if I didn't have confidence in him I wouldn't have married him.' (Salamon 1997).

Future conceptualization and research on trust should also consider how efforts to regulate risk related behaviour relate to social norms. In Chapter 11, Bostrum considers the problem of non-compliance to infectious disease inoculation programmes confronting public health officials. Most people follow the health officials' recommendations to get inoculations for themselves and their families. That is, most comply to the norm of inoculation. In the US a fairly high proportion of the public, for religious and other reasons, hold to norms contrary to compliance. As Bostrum indicates, the options open to health officials include: a) forced compliance (which likely would reduce trust by both those holding to anti-inoculation norms and others), b) efforts to induce enough trust to shift people from these minority norms to the dominant inoculation norm (a very difficult, perhaps impossible task), and c) deciding that the lack of compliance will not affect overall public health (an option that likely does not negatively affect the trust of the risk managers).

CONCLUSION

Our attempt in this last chapter is not to provide a 'shopping list' of topics for researchers or those who fund research. Rather we have attempted to develop points that will provoke debate on what conceptual development and research needs to be done on different issues. We think it appropriate to end our review of these issues by making one general observation concerning the contributions of social science to understandings of trust and the management of risks. It is our belief that social science can make important and significant contributions to the democratic management of risks. But this will only happen if we recognize and firmly keep in balance two orientations. On one side of our scale we must place the practical considerations of those who do the actual management of risk. If we lose sight of the risk managers' practical concerns and questions we run the risk of developing a social science of trust that is only academic and irrelevant. Such a social science may be intellectually fulfilling to its practitioners but useless to others. On the other side of our scale we must place our concerns for basic questions about trust beyond those that are of immediate concern within particular management contexts. Some practitioners may see no relevance to questions about the definition of trust or the social psychology of trust attributions, to name two examples. And in many cases there may be no immediate application of emerging ideas. However, if we do not make efforts to sort these basic questions out, we run the risk of offering overly simple and ultimately non-productive suggestions of how to manage risks. Not everyone will agree on how this balance should be made. Each social science researcher will probably feel most comfortable with a different balance. What is important to the development of the social science of trust is the effort of keeping the scales balanced.

References

INTRODUCTION

Ayers, R (1998) *Turning Point: An End to the Growth Paradigm* London: Earthscan

Breyer, S (1993) *Breaking the Vicious Circle: Toward Effective Risk Regulation*, Cambridge, MA: Harvard University Press

Earle, T C and Cvetkovich, G T (1995) *Social Trust: Toward a Cosmopolitan Society*, Westport, Connecticut: Praeger

Earle, T C and Cvetkovich, G T (1997) Culture, cosmopolitanism, and risk management, *Risk Analysis* 17, 1, pp 55–65

Etzioni, A (1996) *The New Golden Rule: Community and Morality in a Democratic Society*, London: Profile Books

Fischhoff, B (1995) Risk perception and communication unplugged: Twenty years of process, *Risk Analysis* 15, pp 137–145

Flynn, J, Slovic, P, and Mertz, CK (1994) Gender, race, and perception of environmental health risks, *Risk Analysis*, 14, 6, pp 1101–1108

Gable, R, Burkhardt, R L and Winter, P (1997) *Assessing Community Impressions of a Fee Pilot Project: Final Report*, US National Forest Service

Gallup Polling Organization (1993) Confidence in institutions. In *Gallup Political and Economic Index*, 390 (February) pp 39–40

Giddens, A (1990) *Consequences of Modernity*, Cambridge: Polity Press

Giddens, A (1991) *Modernity and Self-Identity: Self and Society in the Late Modern Age*, Cambridge: Polity Press

Golding, D and Krueger, J R (1997) The price of liberty: What level of public trust ensures eternal vigilance? Unpublished paper, Clark University, Worcester, MA

Hine, D W, Summers, C, Prystupa, M, and McKenzie-Richer, A (1997) Public opinion to a proposed nuclear waste repository in Canada: An investigation of cultural and economic effects, *Risk Analysis*, 17, 3, pp 293–302

Holmberg, S and Weibull, L (Eds) (1997) *Ett Missnojt?* Göthenburg, Sweden: SOM Institute, University of Göthenburg

Johnson, B (1996) *Grounding Trust-related Definitions in Empirical Research*. Presentation at the 2nd Bellingham International Social Trust Conference, Bellingham, WA: Western Washington University

Lipset, S M and Schneider, W (1983) *The Confidence Gap: Business, Labor, and Government in the Public Mind*, New York: Macmillan

Lipset, S M and Schneider, W (1987) *The Confidence Gap: Business, Labor, and Government in the Public Mind* (updated), New York: Macmillan

Luhmann, N (1988) Familiarity, confidence, trust: In D Gambetta (Ed) *Trust: Making and Breaking Cooperative Relations*, London: Basil Blackwell pp 94–107

Macnaughten, P, Grove-White, R, Jacobs, M and Wynne, B (1995) *Public Perceptions and Sustainability in Lancashire*, Lancaster: Lancaster University

Misztal, B A (1996) *Trust in Modern Societies: The Search for the Bases of Social Order*, Cambridge: Polity Press

Nye, et al (1997) *Why Don't People Trust Government?* Cambridge MA: Harvard University Press

Peters, R G, Covello, V T and McCallum, D B (1997) The determinants of trust and credibility in environmental risk communication: An empirical study, *Risk Analysis*, 17, 1, pp 43–54

Petersson, O (1994) Where have all the members gone? *Svenska Dagbladet*, 17 September

Pew Research Center for the People and the Press (1998) *Deconstructing Distrust: How Americans View Government*, http://www.people-press.org/trustrpt.html

Renn, O and Levine, D (1991) Credibility and trust in risk communication. In RE Kasperson and PJM Stallen (Eds) *Communicating Risks to the Public: International Perspectives*, Dordrecht, Holland: Kluwer, pp 175–218

Rosa, E (1997) *Reexamining Trends in Public Confidence in America's Major Institutions: Evidence from National Polls by Harris, Gallup and the National Opinion Research Center*. Presented at the Second Bellingham International Social Trust Conference, Bellingham, Washington

Sandman, P M (1993) *Responding to Community Outrage: Strategies for Effective Risk Communication*, Fairfax, VA: American Industrial Hygiene Association Press

Wynne, B (1996) May the sheep safely graze? In S Lash, B Szerszynski, and B Wynne (Eds) *Risk Environment, and Modernity: Towards a New Ecology*, London: Sage

CHAPTER 1

Arad, S and Carnevale, P J (1994) Partisanship effects in judgments of fairness and trust in third parties in the Palestinian-Israeli conflict, *Journal of Conflict Resolution*, 38, pp 423–451

Clary, E G, Snyder, M, Ridge, R D, Miene, P K, and Haugen, J A (1994) Matching messages to motives in persuasion: A functional approach to promoting volunteerism, *Journal of Applied Social Psychology*, 24, 1, pp 129–1149

Cvetkovich, G and Earle, T C (1992) Social Trust and Value Similarity: New Interpretations of Risk Communication in Hazard Management. Paper presented at the Annual Meeting of the Society for Risk Analysis, San Diego, California

Dake, K (1992) Myths of nature, *Journal of Social Issues*, 48, pp 21–37

Dake, K and Wildavsky, A (1990) Theories of risk perception: Who fears what and why? *Daedalus*, 119, 4, pp 41–60

Douglas, M and Wildavsky, A (1982) *Risk and Culture*, Berkeley: University of California Press.

Earle, T C (1997) *Social Trust in Context: Biology, Culture and Public Policy*, Unpublished manuscript, Western Washington University, Bellingham

Earle, T C and Cvetkovich, G (1994a) La confiance sociale. In G. Heriard Dubreuil (Ed), *La Fonction Sociale de la Confiance: Action Collective et Délégation de Responsabilité Face au Risque*, Paris: Groupe Epistémologie des Cindyniques, pp 39–50

Earle, T E and Cvetkovich, G (1994b) Creeping environmental phenomena: Social construction and social trust. In M H Glantz (Ed), *Creeping Environmental Phenomena and Societal Responses to Them*, Boulder, Colorado: National Center for Atmospheric Research, pp 33–38

Earle, T C and Cvetkovich, G (1994c) Risk communication: The social construction of meaning and trust. In N Sahlin and B Brehmer (Eds), *Future Risks and Risk Management*, Amsterdam: Kluwer

Earle, T C and Cvetkovich, G (1995) *Social Trust: Toward a Cosmopolitan Society*, Westport, CT: Praeger

Earle, T C and Cvetkovich, G (1997) Culture, cosmopolitanism and risk management, *Risk Analysis*, 17, pp 55–65

Fiske, A P (1991a) *Structures of Social Life: The Four Elementary Forms of Human Relations*, New York: The Free Press

Fiske, A P (1991b) The cultural relativity of selfish individualism: anthropological evidence that humans are inherently sociable. In M S Clark (Ed), *Prosocial Behavior*, Newbury Park, CA: Sage Publications, pp 176–213

Fiske, A P (1992). The elementary forms of sociality: Framework for a unified theory of social relations, *Psychological Review*, 99, pp 689–723

Jessor, R and Hammond, K R (1957) Construct validity and the Taylor Anxiety Scale, *Psychological Bulletin*, 54, pp 161–170

Judd, C M, Jessor, R and Donovan, J E (1986) Structural equation models and personality research, *Journal of Personality*, 54, pp149–158

Rayner, S (1992) Cultural theory and risk analysis. In S Krimsky and D Golding (Eds), *Social Theories of Risk*, Westport, CT: Praeger, pp 83–115

Thompson, M, Ellis, R, and Wildavsky, *A Cultural Theory*, Boulder, CO: Westview Press

CHAPTER 2

Almond, G A and Verba, S (1963) *The Civic Culture: Political Attitudes and Democracy in Five Nations*, Princeton, New Jersey: Princeton University Press

Almond, G A and Verba, S (Eds) (1980) *The Civic Culture Revisited*, Boston: Little, Brown and Company

Banfield, E (1958) *The Moral Basis of a Backward Society*, Chicago: Free Press

Barber, B R (1984) *Strong Democracy: Participatory Politics for a New Age*, Berkeley: University of California Press

Breyer, S (1993) *Breaking the Vicious Circle: Toward Effective Risk Regulation*, Cambridge, Mass: Harvard University Press

Buchanan, J and Tullock, G (1962) *The Calculus of Consent: Logical Foundations of Constitutional Democracy*, Ann Arbor: University of Michigan Press.

Carnevale, D G (1995) *Trustworthy Government: Leadership and Management Strategies for Building Trust and High Performance*, San Francisco: Jossey-Bass

Covello, V T and Allen, F W (1988) Seven cardinal rules of risk communication [folded sheet], Washington: US Environmental Protection Agency

Dasgupta, P (1988) Trust as a commodity. In Gambetta, D (Ed), *Trust: Making and Breaking Cooperative Relations*, Oxford: Basil Blackwell, pp 49–72

Earle, T C and Cvetkovich, G T (1995) *Social Trust: Toward a Cosmopolitan Society*, Westport, Conn: Praeger

Easton, D (1965) *A Systems Analysis of Political Life*, New York: Wiley

Etzioni, A (1990) *The Moral Dimension: Toward a New Economics*, London: Collier Macmillan

Hibbing, J R and Theiss-Morse, E (1995) *Congress as Public Enemy: Public Attitudes Toward American Political Institutions*, Cambridge: Cambridge University Press

Inglehart, R (1988) The renaissance of political culture, *American Political Science Review*, 82, December, pp 1203–1230

Inglehart, R (1990) *Culture Shift in Advanced Industrial Countries*, Princeton, NJ: Princeton University Press

Inglehart, R (1997) *Modernization and Postmodernization: Cultural, Economic, and Political Change in 43 Societies*, Princeton, NJ: Princeton University Press

Inglehart, R, Nevitte, N and Basañez, M (1997) *The North American Trajectory: Cultural, Economic, and Political Ties among the United States*, Canada, and Mexico, New York: Aldine de Gruyter

Kasperson, R E, Golding, D and Tuler, S (1992) Social distrust as a factor in siting hazardous facilities and communicating risks, *Journal of Social Issues*, 48, 4, pp 161–187

Kates, R W (1985) Success, strain, and surprise, *Issues in Science and Technology*, 11, 1, Fall, pp 46–58

Koller, M (1988) Risk as a determinant of trust, *Basic and Applied Social Psychology*, 9, pp 265–276

Lewis, J D and Weigert, A (1985) Trust as a social reality, *Social Forces*, 63, 4, pp 967–985

Lipset, S M and Schneider, W (1983) *The Confidence Gap: Business, Labor, and Government in the Public Mind*, New York: Macmillan

Lipset, S M and Schneider, W (1987) *The Confidence Gap: Business, Labor, and Government in the Public Mind* (New Edition), New York: Macmillan

Luhmann, N (1979) *Trust and Power: Two Works by Niklas Luhmann*, Chichester: John Wiley and Sons

Luhmann, N (1993) *Risk: A Sociological Theory*, New York: Aldine de Gruyter

NRC (National Research Council) (1983) *Risk Assessment in the Federal Government: Managing the Process*, Washington, DC: National Academy Press

Ostrom, E (1990) *Governing the Commons: The Evolution of Institutions for Collective Action*, New York: John Wiley

Pennock, J R (1979) *Democratic Political Theory*, Princeton, NJ: Princeton University Press

Putnam, R D (1993) *Making Democracy Work: Civic Traditions in Modern Italy*, Princeton, NJ:Princeton University Press

Putnam, R D (1995a) Bowling alone: America's declining social capital, *Journal of Democracy*, 6, 1, pp 65–78

Putnam, R D (1995b) Tuning in, tuning out: The strange disappearance of social capital in America, *PS: Political Science and Politics*, December, pp 664–683

Putnam, R D (1996) The strange disappearance of civic America, *The American Prospect*, 24, Winter, pp 34–48

Rosa, E A and Clark, D L (1999) 'Historical routes to technological gridlock: Nuclear terminology as prototypical vehicle, *Research in Social Problems and Public Policy*, 7, (forthcoming)

Ruckelshaus, W (1996) Trust in government: A prescription for restoration, The Webb Lecture to the National Academy of Public Administration, November 15

Stern, P C and Fineberg, H V (Eds) (1996) *Understanding Risk: Informing Decisions in a Democratic Society*, Washington: National Academy Press

Tocqueville, A de (1969) *Democracy in America*, tr. J.P. Mayer, tr. George Lawrence, (2 vols. in 1), Garden City, NY: Anchor Books

Williams, B (1988) Formal structures and social reality. In Gambetta, D (Ed), *Trust: Making and Breaking Cooperative Relations*, Oxford: Basil Blackwell, pp 3–13

Williams, B A and Matheny, A R (1995) *Democracy, Dialogue, and Environmental Disputes: The Contested Languages of Social Regulation*, New Haven, Conn: Yale University Press

Yankelovich, D (1991) *Coming to Public Judgment: Making Democracy Work in a Complex Society*, Syracuse: Syracuse University Press

Zimmer, T A (1979) The impact of Watergate on the public's trust in people and confidence in the mass media, *Social Science Quarterly*, 59, 4, pp 743–51

CHAPTER 3

Batt, T (1992) Nevada claims victory in Yucca deal, *Las Vegas Review-Journal*, July 23, pp1A, 3A

Bella, D A (1987) Engineering and erosion of trust, *Journal of Professional Issues in Engineering*, 113, pp117–129

Bella, D A, Mosher, C D and Calvo, S N (1988a) Establishing trust: Nuclear waste disposal, *Journal of Professional Issues in Engineering*, 114, pp 40–50

Bella, D A, Mosher, C D and Calvo, S N (1988b) Technocracy and trust: Nuclear waste controversy, *Journal of Professional Issues in Engineering*, 114, 1,pp 27–39

Bord, R J (1988) The low-level radioactive waste crisis: Is more citizen participation the answer? In M A Burns (Ed), *Low-level Radioactive Waste Regulation: Science, Politics, and Fear*, Chelsea, MI: Lewis, pp 193–213

Bord, R J and O'Connor, R E (1990) Risk communication, knowledge, and attitudes: Explaining reactions to a technology perceived as risky, *Risk Analysis*, 10, pp 499–506

Campbell, J L (1988) *Collapse of an Industry: Nuclear Power and the Contradictions of US policy*, Ithaca, New York: Cornell University Press

Covello, V T, Sandman, P M and Slovic, P (1988) *Risk Communication, Risk Statistics, and Risk Comparisons: A Manual for Plant Managers,* Washington, DC: Chemical Manufacturers' Association

Cvetkovich, G, and Earle, T C (1992) Social Trust and Value Similarity: New Interpretations of Risk Communication in Hazard Management. Paper presented at the 1992 annual meeting of the Society for Risk Analysis, San Diego, CA

Efron, E (1984) *The Apocalyptics*, New York: Simon and Schuster

English, M R (1992) *Siting Low-Level Radioactive Waste Disposal Facilities: The Public Policy Dilemma*, New York: Quorum

Fessendon-Raden, J, Fitchen, J M and Heath, J S (1987) Providing risk information in communities: Factors influencing what is heard and accepted. *Science, Technology, and Human Values*, 12, pp 94–101

Fiorino, D (1989) Technical and democratic values in risk analysis, *Risk Analysis*, 9, pp 293–299

Flynn, J, Burns, W, Mertz, C K and Slovic, P (1992) Trust as a determinant of opposition to a high-level radioactive waste repository: Analysis of a structural model, *Risk Analysis*, 12, 3, pp 417–429

Flynn, J, Kasperson, R, Kunreuther, H and Slovic, P (1992) Time to rethink nuclear waste storage, *Issues in Science and Technology*, 8, 4, pp 42–48

Flynn, J and Slovic, P (1993) Nuclear wastes and public trust, *Forum for Applied Research and Public Policy*, 8, pp 92–100

Freudenburg, W (1991) *Risk and Recreancy: Weber, The Division of Labor, and the Rationality of Risk Perceptions* (Unpublished manuscript, Department of Rural Sociology, University of Wisconsin, Madison)

Graham, J D, Green, L C and Roberts, M J (1988) *In Search of Safety: Chemicals and Cancer Risk*, Cambridge, MA: Harvard

Jacob, G (1990) *Site Unseen: The Politics of Siting a Nuclear Waste Repository*, Pittsburgh: University of Pittsburgh

Jasanoff, S (1986) *Risk Management and Political Culture*, New York: Russell Sage Foundation

Jasper, J M (1990) *Nuclear Politics: Energy and the State in the United States, Sweden, and France*, Princeton, NJ: Princeton University Press

Jenkins-Smith, H C (1992) *Culture, Trust, Ideology and Perceptions of the Risks of Nuclear Wastes: A Causal Analysis*. Paper prepared for the annual meeting of the Society for Risk Analysis, December 6–9, San Diego, CA

Johnson, B B (1992) *Trust in Theory: Many Questions, Few Answers.* Paper presented at the 1992 annual meeting of the Society for Risk Analysis, San Diego, CA

Kasperson, R, Golding, D and Tuler, S (1992) Social distrust as a factor in siting hazardous facilities and communicating risks, *Journal of Social Issues*, 48, 4, pp 161–187

Koren, G and Klein, N (1991) Bias against negative studies in newspaper reports of medical research, *Journal of the American Medical Association*, 266, pp 1824–1826

Kraus, N, Malmfors, T and Slovic, P (1992) Intuitive toxicology: Expert and lay judgments of chemical risks, *Risk Analysis*, 12, pp 215–232

Kunreuther, H, Fitzgerald, K and Aarts, T D (1993) Siting noxious facilities: A test of the facility siting credo, *Risk Analysis*, 13, 3, pp 301–318

Laird, F N (1989) The decline of deference: The political context of risk communication, *Risk Analysis*, 9, pp 543–550

Leroy, D H and Nadler, T S (1993) Negotiate way out of siting dilemmas, *Forum for Applied Research and Public Policy*, 8, 1, Spring, pp 102–107

Levine, S (1984) Probabilistic risk assessment: Identifying the real risks of nuclear power, *Technology Review*, 87, 2, pp 40–44

Lichtenberg, J, and MacLean, D (1992). Is good news no news? The Geneva Papers on Risk and Insurance, 17, pp 362–365

MacGregor, D, Slovic, P and Morgan, M G (1992) *Perception of Risks from Electromagnetic Fields: A Psychometric Evaluation of a Risk-Communication Approach* (Report No. 92–6). Eugene, OR: Decision Research

McCallum, D B, Hammond, S L, Morris, L A and Covello, V T (1990). *Public Knowledge and Perceptions of Chemical Risks in Six Communities* (Report No. 230-01-90-074). Washington, DC: US Environmental Protection Agency

Mitchell, J V (1992) Perception of risk and credibility at toxic sites, *Risk Analysis*, 12, pp 19–26

Morgan, M G, Slovic, P, Nair, I, Geisler, D, MacGregor, D, Fischhoff, B, Lincoln, D and Florig, K (1985) Powerline frequency electric and magnetic fields: A pilot study of risk perception, *Risk Analysis*, 5, pp 139–149

Morone, J F and Woodhouse, E J (1989) *The Demise of Nuclear Energy? Lessons for a Democratic Control of Technology*, New Haven: Yale University

Mushkatel, A H and Pijawka, K D (1992) *Institutional Trust, Information, and Risk Perceptions: Report of Findings of the Las Vegas Metropolitan Area Survey, June 29–July 1, 1992* (NWPO-SE-055-92). Carson City, NV: Nevada Nuclear Waste Project Office

National Research Council (NRC) (1989) *Improving Risk Communication*, Washington, DC: National Academy Press

Nelkin, D and Pollak, M (1979) Public participation in technological decisions: Reality or grand illusion? *Technology Review*, August/September, pp 55–64

Pijawka, K D and Mushkatel, A H (1991/92) Public opposition to the siting of the high-level nuclear waste repository: The importance of trust, *Policy Studies Review*, 10, 4, pp 180–194

Rayner, S and Cantor, R (1987) How fair is safe enough? The cultural approach to societal technology choice, *Risk Analysis*, 7, pp 3–9

Renn, O and Levine, D (1991) Credibility and trust in risk communication. In RE Kasperson and P J M Stallen (Eds), *Communicating Risks to the Public*. Dordrecht: Kluwer Academic, pp 175–218

Rothbart, J and Park, B (1986) On the confirmability and disconfirmability of trait concepts, *Journal of Personality and Social Psychology*, 50, pp 131–142

Ruckelshaus, W D (1983) Science, risk, and public policy, *Science*, 221, pp 1026–1028

Ruckelshaus, W D (1984) Risk in a free society, *Risk Analysis*, 4, pp 157–162

Slovic, P (1987) Perception of risk, *Science*, 236, pp 280–285

Slovic, P (1990) Perception of risk from radiation. In WK Sinclair (Ed), *Proceedings of the Twenty-fifth Annual Meeting of the National Council on Radiation Protection and Measurements. Vol 11: Radiation Protection Today: The NCRP at Sixty Years* (Vol. 11, pp. 73–97) Bethesda, MD: NCRP

Slovic, P, Flynn, J and Layman, M (1991) Perceived risk, trust, and the politics of nuclear waste, *Science*, 254, pp 1603–1607

Slovic, P, Flynn, J, Johnson, S and Mertz, C K (1993) *The Dynamics of Trust in Situations of Risk* (Report No. 93-2). Eugene, OR: Decision Research

Starr, C (1985) Risk management, assessment, and acceptability, *Risk Analysis*, 5, pp 97–102

US Department of Energy (1992) *Draft Final Report of the Secretary of Energy Advisory Board Task Force on Radioactive Waste Management.* Washington, DC

US Nuclear Regulatory Commission (USNRC) (1983) *Safety Goals for Nuclear Power Plant Operation* (USNRC Report NUREG-0880). Washington, DC

Wall Street Journal (1989) How a PR firm executed the Alar scare, October 3, pp A1, A3

CHAPTER 4

Bruner, J S (1958) Social psychology and perception. In E E Macoby, T M Newcomb, and E L Hartley (Eds) *Readings in Social Psychology* (3rd edition) New York: Holt, Rinehart, & Winston

Bruner, J S (1986) *Actual Minds, Possible Worlds*. Cambridge: Harvard University Press

Cvetkovich, G T, Winter, P and Earle, T C (1995) Everybody is Talking About It: Public Participation in Forest Management. Presentation at the 1995 American Psychological Association, August 11–14, New York City

Earle, T C and Cvetkovich, G (1995) *Social Trust: Toward a Cosmopolitan Society*. Westport, CT: Praeger

Earle, T C and Cvetkovich, G T (1997) Culture, cosmopolitanism, and risk management, *Risk Analysis*, 17, 1, pp 55–65

Frewer, J, Howard, C, Hedderley, D and Shepherd, R (1996) What determines trust in information about food-related risks? Underlying psychological constructs, *Risk Analysis*, 16, 4, pp 473–486

Flynn, J, Slovic, P and Mertz, C K (1994) Gender, race, and perception of environmental health risks, *Risk Analysis*, 14, 6, pp 1101–1108

Greenwald, A G and Banaji, M R (1995) Implicit social cognition: Attitudes, self-esteem, and stereotypes, *Psychological Bulletin*, 102, 1, pp 4–27

Jones, E E and Davis, K E (1965) From acts to dispositions: The attribution process in person perception. In L Berkowitz (Ed), *Advances in Experimental Social Psychology*, Vol 2, New York: Academic Press

Jungermann, H, Pfister, H and Fischer, K (1996) Credibility, information preferences, and information, *Risk Analysis*, 16, 2, pp 251–261

Kintsch, W (1988) The role of knowledge in discourse comprehension: A construction-integration model, *Psychological Review*, 95, p 168–182

Miles, J (1996) *God: A Biography*, New York: Vintage Books

Parsons, T (1970) Research with human subjects and the 'professional complex.' In P A Freund (Ed) *Experimentation with Human Subjects*, New York: George Braziller

Read, S (1987) Constructing causal scenarios: A knowledge structure approach to causal reasoning. *Journal of Personality and Social Psychology*, 52, 2, pp 288–302

Slovic, P (1995) The construction of preferences, *American Psychologist*, 50, 5, pp 364–371

Thorpe, Y and Higgins, T (1993) The what, when, and how of dispositional inferences: New Answers and new questions, *Personality and Social Psychology Bulletin*, 19, 5, pp 493–500

CHAPTER 5

Bord, R J and O'Connor, R E (1992) Determinants of risk perceptions of a hazardous waste site, *Risk Analysis*, 12, 3, pp 411–416

Bostrom, A, Fischhoff, B and Morgan M G (1992) Characterizing mental models of hazardous processes: A methodology and an application to radon, *Journal of Social Issues*, 48, 4, pp 85–100

Craig, S C (1993) *The Malevolent Leaders: Popular Discontent in America*, Boulder: Westview Press

Earle, T C and Cvetkovich, G T (1995) *Social Trust: Toward a Cosmopolitan Society*, Westport, Connecticut: Praeger

Frewer, L J, Howard, C, Hedderley, D and Shepherd, R (1996) What determines trust in information about food-related risks? Underlying psychological constructs, *Risk Analysis*, 16, 4, pp 473–486

Hibbing, J R and Theiss-Morse, E (1995) *Congress as Public Enemy: Public Attitudes Toward American Political Institutions*, New York: Cambridge University Press

Johnson, B B (1999) Exploring dimensionality in the origins of hazard-related trust, *Journal of Risk Research*

Luhmann, N (1988) Familiarity, confidence, trust: Problems and alternatives, in D. Gambetta (Ed) *Trust: Making and Breaking Cooperative Relations*, London: Basil Blackwell, pp 94–107

Metlay, D (1996) *Institutional Trustworthiness: The Secretary of Energy Advisory Board Report on Radioactive Waste Management*. Paper presented at the Bellingham International Conference on Social Trust in Risk Management, Bellingham, Washington

Renn, O and Levine, D (1991) Credibility and trust in risk communication, in R E Kasperson and P J M Stallen (Eds) *Communicating Risks to the Public: International Perspectives*. Dordrecht, Holland: Kluwer, pp 175–218

Slovic, P (1993) Perceived risk, trust, and democracy, *Risk Analysis*, 13, 6, pp 675–682

Slovic, P (1997) Trust, emotion, sex, politics, and science: Surveying the risk-assessment battlefield, in M H Bazerman, D M Messick, A E Tenbrunsel and K A Wade-Benzoni (Eds) *Environment, Ethics, and Behavior: The Psychology of Environmental Valuation and Degradation*, San Francisco: New Lexington Press, pp 277–313

Slovic, P, Fischhoff, B and Lichtenstein, S (1980) Facts and fears: Understanding perceived risk, in R C Schwing and W A Albers, Jr (Eds) *Societal Risk Assessment: How Safe Is Safe Enough?* New York: Plenum, pp 181–213

Weatherford, M S (1992) Measuring political legitimacy, *American Political Science Review*, 86, 1, pp 149–166

Webler, T (1995) Right discourse in citizen participation: An evaluative yardstick, in O Renn, T Webler and P Wiedemann (Eds) *Fairness and Competence in Citizen Participation: Evaluating Models for Environmental Discourse*, Dordrecht, The Netherlands: Kluwer, pp 35–86

CHAPTER 6

Ashby, E and Anderson, M (1981) *The Politics of Clean Air*, Oxford: Clarendon Press

Baker, K (1993) *The Turbulent Years*, London: Faber and Faber

Balen, M (1992) *Kenneth Clarke*, London: Fourth Estate

Beck, U (1992) *Risk Society*, London: Sage

Beck, U (1995) *Ecological Politics in an Age of Risk*, Cambridge: Polity

Beck, U, Giddens, A and Lash, S (1994) *Reflexive Modernisation: Politics, Tradition and Aesthetics in the Modern Social Order*, Cambridge: Polity

Boehmer-Christiansen, S and Skea, J (1991) *Acid Politics*, London: Belhaven

Bord, R and O'Connor, R (1992) Determinants of risk perception of a hazardous waste site, *Risk Analysis*, 12, pp 41–46

Breyer, S (1993) *Breaking the Vicious Circle: Toward Effective Risk Regulation*, Cambridge MA: Harvard University Press

Butler, D G, Adonis, A and Travers, T (1994) *Failure in British Government*, Oxford: Oxford University Press

Chess, C, Salomone K et al (1995) Results of a national symposium on risk communication: Next steps for Government agencies, *Risk Analysis*, 15, pp 115–125

Christie, I (1994) Britain's sustainable development strategy: Environmental quality and policy change, *Policy Studies*, 15, pp 4–20

Crickhowell, Lord (1995) Britain – the clean man of Europe – Giving a lead for the European Union to follow. Speech available from the Environment Agency, Bristol

Department of Environment (1990) *This Common Inheritance*, London: HMSO

Department of Environment (1991) *Improving Environmental Quality: The Government's Proposals for a New Independent Environment Agency*, London: Department of Environment

Department of Environment (1994) *Sustainable Development: The UK Strategy*, London: HMSO

Department of Environment (1995) *Guide to Risk Assessment and Risk Management for Environmental Protection*, London: HMSO

De Ramsey, Lord (1995) The Gardner Environmental Law Lecture. Speech available from the Environment Agency, Bristol

Drucker, H and Dunleavy, P et al (Eds) (1986) *Developments in British Politics 2*, Basingstoke: Macmillan

Dunleavy, P and Rhodes, R A W (1986) Government beyond Whitehall, in Drucker, H and Dunleavy, P et al, *Developments in British Politics 2*, Basingstoke: Macmillan, pp 107–143

Environment Agency (1996a) Agency must make a lasting difference, *Environment Action*, 1, pp 1

Environment Agency (1996) Popular support to boost agency, *Environment Action*, 1, pp 3

Ferguson, J (1995) An ever-greener profile for waste regulation as it joins the Environment Agency, *Environmental Law*, 16, pp 1–3

Foster, C D and Plowden, F J (1996) *The State under Stress*, Buckingham: Open University Press

Gallagher, E (1996) A rugged path between wasteland and greenfield, The Monday Interview, *The Independent*, 18th March

Giddens, A (1990) *The Consequences of Modernity*, Cambridge: Polity

Grove-White, R (1995) Environment and society: Some reflections, *Environmental Politics*, 4, pp 65–275

Grubb, M (1990) *Energy Policies and the Greenhouse Effect: Volume 1: Policy Appraisal*, Dartmouth, Aldershot UK

Habermas, J (1976) *Legitimation Crisis*, London: Heinemann

Hawkins, K (1984) *Environment and Enforcement*, Oxford: Oxford University Press

Hennessy, P (1989) *Whitehall*, London: Secker & Warburg

Hill, J and Jordan A (1993) The greening of government: Lessons from the White Paper process, *ECOS*, 14, 3/4, pp 3–9

Hood, C (1991) A public management for all seasons? *Public Administration*, 69, Spring, pp 3–19

Horlick-Jones, T (in press) 'Blame, responsibility and the symbolic politics of disasters', *Journal of Risk Research*

Horlick-Jones, T and De Marchi, B (1995) The crisis of scientific expertise in fin de siecle Europe. In T Horlick-Jones and B De Marchi (Eds) *Scientific Expertise in Europe Special Issue of Science and Public Policy*, 22, pp 139–145

Horlick-Jones, T, Pidgeon, N, De Marchi, B and Prades Lopez, A (1996) Recent developments in major accident hazard regulation in the European Union, in *Proceedings of the Society for Risk Analysis-Europe 1996 Annual Conference*, Guildford: University of Surrey Centre for Environmental Strategy

House of Commons Environment Select Committee (1989) *Session 1988–89 Second Report Toxic Waste*, HC Paper 22. London: HMSO

House of Commons (1992) *The Government's Proposals for an Environment Agency*, Session 1991–92 London: House of Commons

Hutton, W (1995) *The State We're In – 2nd Edition*, London: Vintage

Hutton, W (1996) Investing in social capital can help to counter the spate of evil, *Guardian*, 18 March, pp 14

ILGRA (Interdepartmental Liaison Group on Risk Assessment) (1996) *Use of Risk Assessment Within Government Departments*, London: Health and Safety Executive

The Independent (1996) High risk half-truths, 24th March, pp 20

Jacques, M (1988) Why Thatcher turned green, *Sunday Times*, 2nd October pp B3

Jasanoff, S (1986) *Risk Management and Political Culture*, New York: Russell Sage Foundation

Jasanoff, S (1987) Cultural aspects of risk assessment in Britain and the United States, in BB Johnson and VT Covello (Eds) *The Social and Cultural Construction of Risk*, Leiden: D.Reidel Publishing Company, pp 359–397

Jenkins, S (1995) *Accountable to None: the Tory Nationalization of Britain*, London: Hamish Hamilton

Jewell, T and Steele, J (1996) UK regulatory reform and the pursuit of sustainable development: The Environment Act 1995, *Journal of Environmental Law*, 8, pp 281–300

Kasperson, R E, Golding, D and Tuler, S (1992) Siting hazardous facilities and communicating risks under conditions of high social distrust, *Journal of Social Issues*, 48, pp 161–187

Kunreuther, H and Slovic P (1996) Science, values and risk, *The Annals of the American Academy of Political and Social Science*, 545, pp 116–125

Lascelles, D (1996) New agency established today, *Financial Times*, 1 April, pp 6

Lawson, N (1992) *The View from No.11*, London: Baltham Press

Löfstedt, R (1993) *Dilemma of Swedish Energy Policy*, Aldershot: Avebury

Löfstedt, R E and Renn, O (1997) The Brent Spar controversy: An example of risk communication gone wrong, *Risk Analysis*, 17, pp 131–136

Macnaghten, P and Scott, J (1994) Changing world views of students, *ECOS*, 15, 2, pp 2–7

Macnaghten, P et al. (1995) *Public Perceptions and Sustainability in Lancashire*, Preston: Lancashire City Council

Marr, A (1995) *Ruling Britannia: The Failure and Future of British Democracy*, London: Michael Joseph

Marris, C, Langford, I and O'Riordan, T (1996) *Integrating Sociological and Psychological Approaches to Public Perceptions of Environmental Risks: Detailed Results from a Questionnaire Survey*, Norwich: CSERGE

McCormick, J (1991) *British Politics and the Environment*, London: Earthscan

National Motorways Action Committee (1975) *A Case Against the M16 Motorway*, London: Friends of the Earth

North, R D (1996) Ballot box not the tree tops, *Observer*, 21 January, pp C4

O'Riordan, T (1985) Approaches to regulation, in H Otway and M Peltu (Eds) *Regulating Industrial Risks*, London: Butterworth, pp 20–39

O'Riordan, T and Jordan, A (1995) British environmental politics in the 1990s *Environmental Politics*, 4, pp 237–246

Osborne, D and Gaebler, T (1992) *Reinventing Government*, Reading, Mass: Addison-Wesley

Peters, G (1993) Managing the hollow state. In J Elliasen and KA Kooiman (Eds) *Managing Public Organisations*, London: Sage

Power, M (1994) *The Audit Explosion*, London: Demos

Rappaport, R A (1996) Risk and the human environment, *Annals of the American Academy of Political and Social Science*, 545, pp 64–74

Reiss, A J Jr (1985) Compliance without coercion, *University of Michigan Law Review*, 4, pp 813–819

Renn, O (1995) Style of using scientific expertise: a comparative framework, *Science and Public Policy*, 22, pp 147–156

Renn, O, Webler, T and Wiedemann, P (1995) *Fairness and Competence in Citizen Participation*, Dordrecht, Kluwer

Rhodes, R (1994) The hollowing out of the state: The changing nature of public service in Britain, *Political Quarterly*, 65, pp 138–151

Rimmington, J D (1993) *Coping with Technological Risk: a 21st Century Problem*, London: The Royal Academy of Engineering

Robinson, A (1995) Risk management and emergency planning: Prevention, containment and communication in the chemical industry, paper presented at the *IBC Conference on Preventing and Managing Emergencies*, 27th September

Royal Commission on Environmental Pollution (1988) *Twelfth Report: Best Practicable Environmental Option*. CM310, London: HMSO

Schoon, N (1996) Fears for role of new Environment Agency, *Independent*, 1 April, pp 7

Slater, D (1996) The future role of risk assessment and risk management in environmental regulations, in *Proceedings of the Society for Risk Analysis-Europe 1996 Annual Conference*, Guildford: University of Surrey Centre for Environmental Strategy

SCPR (Social and Community Planning Research) (1995) *British Social Attitudes 1995–96*, Aldershot, Dartmouth

SCPR (Social and Community Planning Research) (1997) *British Social Attitudes: The End of Conservative Values? 14th Report*, Aldershot: Ashgate Publishing

Slovic, P (1993) Perceived risk, trust and democracy, *Risk Analysis*, 13, pp 675–681

Stern, P and Fineberg H V (1996) *Understanding Risk: Informing Decisions in a Democratic Society*, Washington: National Academy of Sciences

US Department of Energy (1993) *Earning Public Trust and Confidence: Requisites for Managing Radioactive Waste. Final Report of the Secretary of Energy Advisory Board Task Force on Radioactive Waste Management*. Washington DC.

Widdicombe, D (1986) *The Conduct of Local Authority Business, Cmnd.9797*, London: London

Willetts, D (1996) *Blair's Gurus: An Examination of Labour's Rhetoric*, London: Centre for Policy Studies

Woolf, G (1994) Slater fights back, *The Chemical Engineer*, 17 March, pp 38

Worcester, R (1995) Assessing public opinion on the environment: The predictable shock of Brent Spar, Paper to the *Environmental Protection 1995 Conference National Society for Clean Air and Environmental Protection*, 23–26th October, Scarborough

CHAPTER 7

Biel, A and Dahlstrand, U (1995) Risk perception and the location for a repository of spent nuclear fuel. *Scandinavian Journal of Psychology*, 36, pp 25–36

Bord, R J and O'Connor, R E (1990) Risk comunication, knowledge, and attitudes: Explaining reactions to a technology perceived as risky, *Risk Analysis*, 10, pp 499–506

Bord, R J and O'Connor, R E (1992) Determinants of risk perceptions of a hazardous waste site, *Risk Analysis*, 12, pp 411–416

Dake, K (1990) *Technology on trial: Orienting dispositions toward environmental and health hazards*. PhD thesis, University of California, Berkeley

Douglas, M and Wildavsky, A (1982) *Risk and Culture*, Berkeley, CA: University of California Press

Drottz-Sjöberg, B-M (1991) *Perception of Risk. Studies of Risk Attitudes, Perceptions and Definitions*, Stockholm: Stockholm School of Economics, Center for Risk Research.

Earle, T C and Cvetkovich, G (1994) Risk communication: The societal construction of meaning and trust. In B Brehmer and NE Sahlin (Eds), *Future Risks and Risk Management*, Amsterdam: Kluwer, pp 141–182.

Earle, T C and Cvetkovich, G T (1995). *Social Trust: Toward a Cosmopolitan Society*. Westport, CT: Praeger

Fischhoff, B, Slovic, P, Lichtenstein, S, Read, S and Combs, B (1978) How safe is safe enough? A psychometric study of attitudes towards technological risks and benefits, *Policy Sciences*, 9, pp 127–152

Flynn, J, Burns, W, Mertz, C K and Slovic, P (1992) Trust as a determinant of opposition to a high-level radioactive waste repository: Analysis of a structural model, *Risk Analysis*, 12, pp 417–429

Freudenburg, W R (1993) Risk and reactancy: Weber, the division of labor, and the rationality of risk perceptions, *Social Forces*, 71, pp 909–932

Frewer, L J, Howard, C, Hedderley, D and Shepherd, R (1996) What determines trust in information about food-related risk? *Risk Analysis*, 16, pp 473–486

Frewer, L J, Shepherd, R and Howard, C (1994) *What Factors Determine Trust in Information about Technological Hazards?* Paper presented at The Society for Risk Analysis Annual Meeting, Baltimore, MD

Frewer, L J, Shepherd, R and Sparks, P (1993) Validation of cultural bias in the context of risk and trust perceptions associated with food-related hazards, *British Psychological Society Abstracts*, 2, pp 42

Hallman, W K and Wandersman, A H (1995) Present risk, future risk or no risk? Measuring and predicting perceptions of health risks of a hazardous waste landfill, *Risk – Health, Safety & Environment*, 6, pp 261–280

Kasperson, R E, Golding, D and Tuler, S (1992) Social distrust as a factor in siting hazardous facilities and communicating risks, *Journal of Social Issues*, 48, pp 161–187

Marris, C, Langford, I and O'Riordan, T (1996) *Integrating Sociological and Psychological Approaches to Public Perceptions of Environmental Risks: Detailed Results from a Questionnaire Study* (CSERGE Working Paper No. GEC 96-07). Norwich: University of East Anglia, Centre for Social and Economic Research into the Global Environment

Pijawka, K D and Mushkatel, A H (1991/92) Public opposition to the siting of the high-level nuclear waste repository: The importance of trust, *Policy Studies Review*, 10, pp 180–194

Poumadère, M (1995) Enjeux de la communication publique des risques pour la santé et l'environnement, *European Review of Applied Psychology*, 45, pp 7–15

Renn, O and Levine, D (1991) Credibility and trust in risk communication. In RE Kasperson and PJM Stallen (Eds), *Communicating Risks to the Public*. Dordrecht: Kluwer, pp 175–218

Sandman, P M (1993) *Responding to Community Outrage: Strategies for Effective Risk Communication*. Fairfax, Va.: American Industrial Hygiene Association

Sjöberg, L (1991) *Risk Perception by Experts and the Public* (Rhizikon: Risk Research Report No. 4). Stockholm: Stockholm School of Economics, Center for Risk Research

Sjöberg, L (1994) *Perceived Risk vs Demand for Risk Reduction* (RHIZIKON: Risk Research Report No. 18). Center for Risk Research, Stockholm School of Economics

Sjöberg, L (1996) A discussion of the limitations of the psychometric and Cultural Theory approaches to risk perception, *Radiation Protection Dosimetry*, 68, pp 219–225

Sjöberg, L (1996) *Risk Perceptions by Politicians and the Public* (RHIZIKON: Risk Research Reports No 23). Stockholm: Stockholm School of Economics, Center for Risk Research

Sjöberg, L (1997) Explaining risk perception: An empirical and quantitative evaluation of cultural theory, *Risk Decision and Policy*, 2, pp 113–130

Sjöberg, L (In press) World views, political attitudes and risk perception, *Risk – Health, Safety and Environment*, 8

Sjöberg, L and Drottz-Sjöberg, B-M (1994) *Risk Perception of Nuclear Waste: Experts and the Public* (RHIZIKON: Risk Research Report No 16). Center for Risk Research, Stockholm School of Economics

Slovic, P (1993) Perceived risk, trust, and democracy, *Risk Analysis*, 13, pp 675–682

Slovic, P, Flynn, J H and Layman, M (1991). Perceived risk, trust, and the politics of nuclear waste, *Science*, 254, pp 1603–1607

Slovic, P, Layman, M and Flynn, J (1991) Risk perception, trust, and nuclear waste: Lessons from Yucca Mountain, *Environment*, 33, pp 6–11, 28–30

Wildavsky, A and Dake, K (1990) Theories of risk perception: Who fears what and why? *Daedalus*, 119, 4, pp 41–60

CHAPTER 8

Barber, B (1983) *The Logic and Limits of Trust*, New Brunswick, NJ: Rutgers University Press

Bromley, P and Cummings L L (1993) Organizations with trust: Theory and measurement, *Working Paper*, University of Minnesota

Butler, J K (1991) Toward understanding and measuring conditions of trust: Evolution of a conditions of trust inventory, *Journal of Management*, 3, pp 643–663

Department of Energy (DOE) (1994) *Fueling a competitive economy: Strategic plan*, Washington, DC: Department of Energy

Douglas, M and Wildavsky A (1982) *Risk and Culture: An Essay on the Selection of Technological and Environmental Dangers*, Berkeley, CA: University of California Press

Earle, T C and Cvetkovich G (1995) *Social Trust: Toward a Cosmopolitan Society*, Westport, CT: Praeger

Earle, T C and Cvetkovich G (1997) Culture, cosmopolitanism, and risk management, *Risk Analysis*, 17, pp 55–65

Flynn, J, Burns, J, Mertz, C K and Slovic P (1993) Trust as a determinant of opposition to a high-level radioactive waste repository: Analysis of a structural model, *Risk Analysis*, 12, pp 417–429

Fromer, A, Jenkins-Smith, J, Silva, C and Gastil J (1995) *Understanding Public Reaction to the Foreign Spent Nuclear Fuel Return Program: 1994–1995*, Albuquerque, NM: University of New Mexico Institute for Public Policy

Gabarro, J (1996) *The Dynamics of Taking Charge*, Cambridge, MA: Harvard Business School Press

Harmon, H (1967) *Modern Factor Analysis*, Chicago, IL: University of Chicago Press

Inglehart, R (1990) *Cultural Shifts in Advanced Society*, Princeton, NJ: Princeton University Press

Kirkpatrick, S and Locke, E (1991) Leadership: Do traits matter? *Academy of Management Executive*, 5, pp 48–60

Kmenta, J (1971) *Elements of Econometrics*, New York: Macmillan

Lewicki, R J and Bunker, B (1996) Developing and maintaining trust in work relationships, in RM Kramer and T R Tyler (Eds) *Trust in Organizations: Frontiers of Theory and Research*, Thousand Oaks, CA: Sage

March, J and Olsen, J (1989) *Rediscovering Institutions: The Organizational Basis of Politics*, New York: Free Press

McGregor, D (1967) *The Professional Manager*, New York: McGraw-Hill

Meyer, D, Weick, K and Kramer, R M (1996) Swift trust and temporary groups, in R M Kramer and T R Tyler, (Eds) *Trust in Organizations: Frontiers of Theory and Research*, Thousand Oaks, CA: Sage

Mishra, A (1996) Organizational responses to crisis: The centrality of trust, in RM Kramer and TR Tyler (Eds) *Trust in Organizations: Frontiers of Theory and Research*, Thousand Oaks, CA: Sage

Mushkatel, A, Pijawka, K D, Jones, P and Ibitayo, N (1992) Governmental trust and risk perceptions related to the high-level nuclear waste repository, Nevada Nuclear Waste Project Office, NWPO-SE-052-92

Ouchi, W G (1981) *Theory Z: How American Business Can Meet the Japanese Challenge*, Reading MA: Addison-Wesley

Peters, R G, Covello, V T and McCallum, D B (1997) The determinants of trust and credibility in environmental risk communication: An empirical study, *Risk Analysis*, 17, pp 43–54

Putnam, R (1993) *Making Democracy Work*, Princeton, NJ: Princeton University Press

Renn, O and Levine, D (1991) Credibility and trust in risk communications, in R E Kasperson and P J M Stallen (Eds), *Communicating Risks to the Public*, Netherlands: Kluwer Academic Publishers

Sako, M (1992) *Prices, Quality, and Trust: Inter-firm Relations in Britain and Japan*, New York: Cambridge University Press

Secretary of Energy Advisory Board (SEAB) (1993) Earning public trust and confidence: Requisites for managing radioactive waste, Washington, DC: US Department of Energy.

Slovic, P (1993) Perceived risk, trust, and democracy, *Risk Analysis*, 13, pp 675–682

Zucker, L G (1996) Production of trust: Institutional sources of economic structure, 1840–1920, *Research in Organizational Behavior*, 8, pp 53–111

CHAPTER 9

Arendt, H (1968) What is authority? In *Between Past and future: Eight Exercises in Political Thought*. New York: Viking Press

Barber, B (1983) *The Logic and Limits of Trust*. New Brunswick, NJ: Rutgers University Press

Bradbury, J A, Branch, K M, Heerwagen, J H and Liebow, E (1994) *Community Viewpoints of the Chemical Stockpile Disposal Program*. Report prepared by Battelle, Pacific Northwest National Laboratory, Washington, DC

Bradbury, J A (1994) Risk communication in environmental programs. *Risk Analysis*, 14, 3, pp 357–36

Covello, V T (1992) Trust and credibility in risk communication. *Health and Environment Digest*, 6, 1, pp 1–3

Earle, T C and Cvetkovich, G T (1995) *Social Trust: Toward a Cosmopolitan Society*. Westport, CT: Praeger Press

Giddens, A (1990) *The Consequence of Modernity*. Oxford, UK: Polity Press

Habermas, J (1973) *Theory and Practice*. New York: Beacon Press

Hollander, EP (1958) Conformity, status and idiosyncrasy credit, *Psychological Review*, 65, pp 117–127

Focht, W (1995) A synoptic process theory of legitimized environmental decision making and communication. Presented at the annual meeting of the Society for Risk Analysis, Honolulu, Hawaii

Focht, W (1996) Uncertainty, controversy, and distrust: Why risk-based decision making has limited utility as a decision rule. Presented at the First International Conference on Social Trust in Risk Management, Bellingham, WA

French, J R P and Raven, B (1959) The bases of social power. In D Cartwright (Ed) *Studies in Social Power*, Ann Arbor, MI: Institute for Social Research

Funtowicz, S O and Ravetz, J R (1985) Three types of risk assessment: A methodological analysis. In V T Covello, J L Mumpower, P J M Stallen and V R Uppuluri (Eds) *Environmental Impact Assessment, Technology Assessment, and Risk Analysis*, New York: Springer-Verlag

Kasperson, R E (1986) Six propositions on public participation and their relevance for risk communication, *Risk Analysis*, 6 3 pp 275–281

Kasperson, R E, Golding, D and Tuler, S (1992) Social distrust as a factor in siting hazardous facilities and communicating risks, *Journal of Social Issues*, 48, pp 161–187

Kramer, R M and Tyler, T R (1996) *Trust in Organizations: Frontiers of Theory and Research*. Thousand Oaks, CA: Sage

Lind, E A and Tyler, T R (1988) *The Social Psychology of Justice*. New York: Plenum Press

Luhmann, N (1979) *Trust and Power*. Translated from the German 1973 and 1975 editions. Chichester: Wiley

Luhmann, N (1988) Familiarity, confidence, trust: Problems and alternatives. In D Gambetta (Ed) *Trust: Making and Breaking Cooperative Relations*, Oxford, UK: Basil Blackwell

Lewis, J D and Weigert, A (1985) Trust as a social reality, *Social Forces*, 63, pp 967–85

Misztal, B A (1996) *Trust in Modern Societies*, Cambridge, MA: Polity Press

Peters, R G, Covello, V T and McCallum D B (1997) The determinants of trust and credibility in environmental risk communication: An empirical study, *Risk Analysis*, 17, 1 pp 43–54

Putnam, R (1993) *Making Democracy Work*. Princeton, NJ: Princeton University Press

Renn, O and Levine, D (1991) Credibility and trust in risk communication: An empirical study. In R E Kasperson and P M Stallen (Eds) *Communicating Risks to the Public: International Perspectives*. Boston: Kluwer Academic Publishers, pp 175–218

Renn, O, Webler, T and Wiedemann P (Eds) (1995) *Fairness and Competence in Citizen Participation: Evaluating Models for Environmental Discourse*. Dordrecht: Kluwer Academic Publishers

Webler, T (1995) Right discourse in citizen participation: An evaluation yardstick. In O Renn, T Webler and P Wiedemann (Eds), *Fairness and Competence in Citizen Participation: Evaluating Models for Environmental Discourse*. Dordrecht: Kluwer Academic Publishers

Wynne, B (1996) May the sheep safely graze? In S Lash, B Szersyznyski and B Wynne (Eds) *Risk, Environment & Modernity: Towards a New Ecology*. London: Sage

CHAPTER 10

Anderson, T (1995) *Sovereign Nations or Reservations?*, San Francisco: Pacific Research Institute for Public Policy

Cornell, S and Kalt, J (1992) Reloading the dice: Improving the chances of economic development on American Indian reservations, in S Cornell and J Kalt (Eds) *What Can Tribes Do? Strategies and Institutions in American Indian Economic Development*, Los Angeles: University of California Press

Black Elk, W and Lyons, W (1990) *Black Elk: The Sacred Ways of a Lakota*, San Francisco: Harper and Row

Border, H and Weiss, C (1994) Tribe signs pact for temporary nuclear waste dump, *Las Vegas Review-Journal*, Las Vegas, July 10

Dake, K (1992) Myths of nature: Culture and the social construction of risk, *Journal of Social Issues*, 48, pp 21–37

Earle, T and Cvetkovich, G (1995) *Social Trust: Toward A Cosmopolitan Society*, Westport, CT: Praeger

Flynn, J, Burns, W, Mertz, C, and Slovic, P (1992) Trust as a determinant of opposition to a high-level radioactive waste repository: Analysis of a structural model, *Risk Analysis*, 12, pp 417–429

Foster, M (1996) *The Mvskoke*, Working Paper, Department of Anthropology, Norman, OK: University of Oklahoma

Gowda, R and Easterling, D (1996) *Voluntary Siting: Lessons from the MRS Process in Native America*, Working Paper, Science and Public Policy Program, Norman, OK: University of Oklahoma

Jorgensen, J (1984) Land is cultural, so is a commodity: The locus of differences among Indians, cowboys, sod-busters, and environmentalists, *Journal of Ethnic Studies*, 12, pp 1–21

Kasperson, R, Golding, D, and Tuler, S (1992) Siting hazardous facilities and communicating risks under conditions of high social distrust, *Journal of Social Issues*, 48, pp 161–187

Momaday, S (1976) Native American attitudes to the environment, in W Capps (Ed) *Seeing With a Native Eye: Essays on Native American Religion*, New York: Harper and Row

Native North American Almanac (1994) Gale Research, Detroit

Nuclear Review (1995) A conversation with Miller Hudson, *The Nuclear Review*, August, pp 20–28

Pildes, R and Sunstein, C (1995) Reinventing the regulatory state, *University of Chicago Law Review*, 65, pp 1–129

Rayner, S (1992) Cultural theories of risk, in S Krimsky and D Golding (Eds) *Social Theories of Risk*, Westport, CT: Praeger

Satchell, M (1996) Dances with nuclear waste, *US News and World Report*, 8 January 1996, pp 29–30

Schneider, K (1993) A longtime pillar of the government now aids those hurt by its bombs, *New York Times*, June 9

Slovic, P (1993) Perceived risk, trust, and democracy, *Risk Analysis*, 13, pp 675–682

Slovic, P (1992) Perception of risk: Reflections on the psychometric paradigm, in S Krimsky and D Golding (Eds) *Social Theories of Risk*, Westport, CT: Praeger

Slovic, P, Fischhoff, B and Lichtenstein, S (1979) Rating the risks, *Environment*, 21, pp 14–20, 36–9

Stoffle, R and Evans, M (1990) Holistic conservation and cultural triage: American Indian perspectives on cultural resources, *Human Organization*, 49, pp 91–99

Strickland, R (1992) Native Americans, in the *Oxford Companion on the United States Supreme Court*, Oxford University Press, New York

Vaughan, E (1995) The significance of socioeconomic and ethnic diversity for the risk communication process, *Risk Analysis*, 15, pp 169–180

Vaughan, E and Seifert, M (1992) Variability in the framing of risk issues, *Journal of Social Issues*, 48, pp 119–135

Wildavsky, A and Dake, K (1990) Theories of risk perception: Who fears what and why?, *Daedalus*, 119, pp 41–60

CHAPTER 11

Asch, D, Baron, J, Hershey, J C, Kunreuther, H, Meszaros, J, Ritov, I and Spranca, M (1994) Omission bias and pertussis vaccine. *Medical Decision Making*, 14, 2, pp 118–123

Askew, G L, Finelli, L, Lutz, J, DeGraaf, J, Siegel, B and Spitalny K (1995) Beliefs and practices regarding childhood vaccination among urban pediatric providers in New Jersey. *Pediatrics*, 96, 5, pp 889–892

Atkinson, W, Gantt, J, Mayfield, M and Furphy L (1995) *Epidemiology and Prevention of Vaccine-Preventable Diseases*. Centers for Disease Control, Department of Health & Human Services, Public Health Service

Baron, J (1995) Blind justice: fairness to groups and the do-no-harm principle. *Journal of Behavioral Decision Making*, 8, pp 71–83

Binkin, N J, Salmaso, S. Tozzi, A E (1992) Epidemiology of pertussis in a developed country with low vaccination coverage: the Italian experience. *Pediatric Infectious Disease Journal*, 11, pp 653–661

Bostrom, A (1997) Vaccine risk communication: lessons from risk perception, decision making and environmental risk communication research. *RISK: Health, Safety and Environment*, 8, 2, pp 173–200

Campbell, J R, Szilagyi, P G Rodewald, L E Winter, N L Humiston, S G and Roghmann, K J (1995) Intent to immunize among pediatric and family medicine residents. *Archives of Pediatric and Adolescent Medicine*, 148, pp 926-929 Published erratum appears in *Arch Pediatr Adolesc Med*, 149, 1, pp 60

Centers for Disease Control and Prevention (CDC) (1994) *State Immunization Requirements 1993–94*. US Department of Health & Human Services, Public Health Service, Centers for Disease Control and Prevention, National Immunization Program

Centers for Disease Control and Prevention (1996) *6 Common Misconceptions about Vaccination and How to Respond to Them*. Author (National Immunization Program, US Department of Health and Human Services, Public Health Service), Atlanta, GA.

Centers for Disease Control and Prevention (1997) Pertussis Vaccinations: Use of Acellular Pertussis Vaccines Among Infants and Young Children – Recommendations of the Advisory Committee on Immunization Practices (ACIP) Morbidity and Mortality Weekly Reports, Recommendations and Reports 46 (RR-7) March 28, 1997, pp 1–25 Atlanta, GA: CDC

Earle, T C and Cvetkovich, G T (1995) *Social Trust: Toward a Cosmopolitan Society*. Westport, CT: Praeger

Fedson, D S (1994) Special communication: adult immunization: Summary of the National Vaccine Advisory Committee Report, *Journal of the American Medical Association*, 272, 14, pp 1133–1137

Fiebach, N H and Viscoli, C M (1991) Patient acceptance of influenza vaccination, *American Journal of Medicine*, 91, pp 393–400

Fitzgerald, T M and Glotzer, D E (1995) Vaccine Information Pamphlets: More information than parents want? *Pediatrics*, 95, 3, pp 331–334

Gangerosa, E J, Phillips, L M, Wolfe, C R, and Chen, R T (1996) An historical analysis of the impact of the antivaccine movements on the control of pertussis. Draft manuscript, Atlanta GA:Centers for Disease Control

Ganguly, R and Webster, T B (1995) Influenza vaccination in the elderly. *Journal of Investigational Allergology and Clinical Immunology*, 5, pp 73–77

Hardin, G (1968) The tragedy of the commons, *Science*, 162, pp 1243–1248

Harding, C M and Bolden, K J (1983) Whooping cough vaccination: A worrying decision for parents. *The Practitioner*, 227, pp 283–287

Hatcher, P (1993) Comments and Recommendations by Penny Hatcher, MSN, MPH, August 11, 1993, LAN#32874. Summary of a 2 1/2 week survey during July and August, 1993, of on-call phone inquiries, National Immunization Program, Centers for Disease Control, Atlanta, GA

Hershey, J C, Asch, D A, Thumasathit, T, Meszaros, J and Waters VV (1994) The roles of altruism, free riding, and bandwagoning in vaccination decisions. *Organizational Behavior and Human Decision Processes*, 59, pp 177–187

Hinman, A R and Orenstein W A (1994) Public health considerations in S A Plotkin and E A Mortimer, Jr (Eds), Vaccines, 2nd edition, W.B. Saunders Co., Philadelphia, pp 903–932

Institute of Medicine (1997a) *Vaccine Safety Forum: Summaries of Two Workshops*. Vaccine Safety Forum, Board on Health Promotion and Disease Prevention. National Academy Press, Washington DC

Institute of Medicine (1997b) *Risk Communication and Vaccination: Workshop Summary*. Vaccine Safety Forum, Board on Health Promotion and Disease Prevention. National Academy Press, Washington DC

National Institute of Allergy and Infectious Diseases, US National Institutes of Health (1995) *The Jordan Report: Accelerated Development of Vaccines, 1995*. Published annually by the Division of Microbiology and Infectious Diseases, US National Institute of Allergies and Infectious Diseases. Bethesda, Maryland, USA

Jungermann, H, Schütz, H and Thüring, M (1988) Mental models in risk assessment: informing people about drugs, *Risk Analysis*, 8, pp 147–155

Kunreuther, H, Slovic, P and MacGregor, D (1996) Risk perception and trust: challenges for facility siting, *RISK: Health, Safety & Environment*, 7, 2, pp 109–118

Leventhal, H, Diefenbach, M, Leventhal, E A (1992) Illness cognition: using common sense to understand treatment adherence and affect cognition interactions. *Cognitive Therapy and Research*, 16, 2, pp 143–163

Loewenson, P R, White, K E, Osterholm, M T and MacDonald, K L (1994) Physician attitudes and practices regarding universal infant vaccination against hepatitis B infection in Minnesota: implications for public health policy. *Pediatric Infectious Disease Journal*, 13, pp 373–378

McCallum, D B, Hammond, S L and Covello, V T (1991) Communicating about environmental risks: how the public uses and perceives information sources. *Health Education Quarterly*, 18, 3 pp 349–361

Merz, J F, Fischhoff, B, Mazur, D J and Fischbeck, P S (1993) A decision-analytic approach to developing standards of disclosure for medical informed consent, *Journal of Products & Toxics Liability*, 15, pp 191–215

Meszaros, J R, Asch, D A, Baron, J, Hershey, J C, Kunreuther, H and Schwartz-Buzaglo, J (1996) Cognitive processes and the decisions of some parents to forgo pertussis vaccination for their children. *Journal of Clinical Epidemiology*, 49, 6, pp 697–703

Napoli, M (1996) The chickenpox vaccine. *Mothering Magazine*, 79, Summer, pp 56–61

Parkman, P D and Hardegree, M C, Regulation and testing of vaccines in SA Plotkin and EA Mortimer, Jr (Eds), *Vaccines*, 2nd edition, W.B. Saunders Co: Philadelphia, pp 889–901

Pilgrim, D and Rogers, A (1995) Mass childhood immunization: Some ethical doubts for primary health care workers. *Nursing Ethics*, 2, 1, pp 63–70

Renn O (1998) The role of risk perception for risk management. *Reliability Engineering and System Safety*, 59, pp 49–62

Ritov, I and Baron, J (1994) Reference points and omission bias. *Organizational Behavior and Human Decision Processes*, 59, pp 475–498

Ritov, I and Baron, J (1995) Outcome knowledge, regret, and omission bias. *Organizational Behavior and Human Decision Processes*, 64, 2, pp 119–127

Salsberry, P J, Nickel, J T and Mitch, R (1995) Missed opportunities to immunize preschoolers. *Applied Nursing Research*, 8, pp 56–60

Swales, JD (1992) The Leicester anti-vaccination movement. *Lancet*, 340, pp 1019–1021

Task Force on Safer Childhood Vaccines, Advisory Commission on Childhood Vaccines, Division of Microbiology and Infectious Diseases, National Institute of Allergy and Infectious Disease, Washington DC. Final Draft Report, presented September 13, 1995

Trauth, J M, Mattison, D R, Nutini, J F, Zimmerman, R K and Musa, D (1996) *A Mental Models Approach to Parental Decision Making regarding Childhood Immunizations*. Graduate School of Public Health, School of Medicine, and University Center for Social and Urban Research, University of Pittsburgh. Paper presented at the National Immunization Conference, Washington DC, April

Watson, B (1996) interview in *Mothering Magazine*, No 79, Summer, p 31

Woodin, K A, Rodewald, L E, Humiston, S G, Carges, M S, Schaffer, S J and Szilagyi PG (1995) Physician and parent opinions. Are children becoming pincushions from immunizations? *Archives of Pediatrics and Adolescent Medicine*, 149, pp 845–849

Chapter 12

Bateson, P (1988) The biological evolution of cooperation and trust. In D Gambetta (Ed.) *Trust: Making and Breaking Cooperative Relations*. Oxford: Basil Blackwell

Baum, A and Gatchel, R J (1981) Cognitive determinants of responses to uncontrollable events: Development of reactance and learned helplessness. *Journal of Personality and Social Psychology*, 40, pp 1078–1089

Barber, B (1983) *The Logic and Limits of Trust*. New Brunswick, NJ: Rutgers University Press

Bickman, L (1974) The social power of a uniform. *Journal of Applied Social Psychology*, 4, 1, pp 47–61

Breyer, S (1993) *Breaking the Vicious Circle: Toward Effective Risk Regulation*. Cambridge, MA: Harvard University Press

Caporeal, L R (1997) The evolution of truly social cognition: The core configurations model. *Personality and Social Review*, 1, 4, pp 276–298

Caporeal, L R, Dawes, R M, Orbell, J M and van de Kraut, A J C (1989) Selfishness examined: Cooperation in the absence of egotistic incentives. *Behavioural and Brain Science*, 12, pp 683–739

Cosmides, L and Tooby, J (1997) *Evolutionary Psychology: A Primer*. Manuscript published on the Web site of the Center for Evolutionary Psychology, University of California, Santa Barbara

Cvetkovich, G and Earle, T C (1985) Classifying hazardous events, *Journal of Environmental Psychology*, 5, pp 5–35

Drotz-Sjoberg, B (1996) Exposure to risk and trust in information: Implications for risk and social trust. Paper presented to the Second Bellingham International Conference on Social Trust July 14–16 1996, Bellingham, Washington

Earle, T C (1997) *Social Trust in Context: Biology, Culture and Public Policy*, Unpublished manuscript. Department of Psychology, Western Washington University

Earle, T C (1998) *Social Trust: Outline of a New Understanding*, Unpublished manuscript. Department of Psychology, Western Washington University

Earle, T C and Cvetkovich, G T (1995) *Social Trust: Toward a Cosmopolitan Society*, Westport, CT: Praeger

Earle, T C and Cvetkovich, G T (1997) Culture, cosmopolitanism, and risk management. *Risk Analysis*, 17, 1, pp 55–65

Fischhoff, B (1996) Public values in risk research. *The Annals of the American Academy of Political and Social Science*, 545, pp 75–84

Flynn, J, Slovic, P and Mertz, C K (1994) Gender, race, and perception of environmental health risks, *Risk Analysis*, 14, 6, pp 1101–1108

Freudenberg, (1996a) Risky thinking: Irrational fears about risk and society. *The annals of the American Academy of Political and Social Science*, 545, pp 44–53

Freudenberg, (1996b) Strange chemistry: Environmental risk conflicts in a world of science, values, and blind spots, in C R Cothern (Ed). *Handbook of Environmental Risk Decision Making*. Boca Raton, Fl: CRC Press

Frewer, L J, Howard, C, Hedderley, D and Shepard, R (1996) What determines trust in information about food-related risks? *Risk Analysis*, 16, 4, pp 473–486

Focht, W (1997) *Qualities of Social Trust of Public Environmental Policy: Comparison of Oklahoman and Venezulean Stakeholders*. Presented at the Second Bellingham International Social Trust Conference, Bellingham, Washington

Fukuyama, F (1996) *Trust: The Social Virtues and the Creation of Prosperity*, New York: Free Press

Gates, H L, Jr, (1997) The next President: Dole 2000. *New Yorker*, Oct. 20 and 27, pp 288–236

Habermas, J (1989) *On Society and Politics: A Reader*. Edited by S. Seidman. Boston: Beacon Press

Hammond, K (1994) *Human Judgement and Social Policy: Irreducible Uncertainty, Inevitable Error, Unavoidable Injustice*, New York: Oxford University Press

Hine, D W, Summers, C, Prystupa, M and McKenzie-Richer, A (1997) Public opinion to a proposed nuclear waste repository in Canada: An investigation of cultural and economic effects. *Risk Analysis*, 17, 3, pp 293–302

Hohenemser, C, Kasperson, R and Kates, R (1977) The distrust of nuclear power, *Science* 196, pp 25–34

Irwin, A (1995) *Citizen Science: A Study of People, Expertise and Sustainable Development*, London: Routledge

Janis, I (1982) Counteracting the adverse effects of concurrence seeking in policy making groups: Theory and research perspectives, in H Brandstatter, J H Davis, and G Stocker-Kreichgauer (Eds) *Group Decision Making*, New York: Academic Press

Johnson, B B (1997) *Trust Judgements in Complex Hazard Management Systems: The Potential Role of Concepts of 'The System'*. Presented at the Second Bellingham International Social Trust Conference, Bellingham, Washington

Jungermann, H, Pfister, H and Fisher, K (1992) Credibility, information preferences, and information interests, *Risk Analysis*, 16, 2, pp 251–261

Kaplan, R D (1997) Was democracy just a moment? *The Atlantic Monthly*, 280, 6, pp 55–80

Leiss, W (1995) 'Down and dirty': The use and abuse of public trust in risk communication. *Risk Analysis*, 15, 6, pp 685–692

Löfstedt, R (1996). Risk communication: The Barsebä nuclear plant case. *Energy Policy*, 24, 8, pp 689–696

Luhmann, N (1979) *Trust and Power*, Chichester: John Wiley and Sons

Luhmann, N (1988) Familiarity, confidence, trust, in D Gambetta (Ed) *Trust: Making and Breaking Cooperative Relations*, London: Basil Blackwell, pp 94–107

Misztal, B A (1996) *Trust in Modern Societies: The Search for the Bases of Social Order*. Cambridge, UK: Polity Press

National Research Council (1996) *Understanding Risk: Informing Decisions in a Democratic Society*. National Academy Press

Petersson, O (1994) Where have all the members gone? *Svenska Dagbladet*, 17 September

Pollitt, K (1996) For whom the ball rolls, *The Nation*, 15 April

Putnam, R D (1993) *Making Democracy Work: Civic Traditions in Modern Italy*, Princeton: Princeton University Press

Putnam, RD (1995a) Bowling alone: America's declining social capital, *Journal of Democracy*, 6, 1, pp 65–78

Putnam, RD (1995b) Tuning in, tuning out: The strange disappearance of social capital in America, *PS: Political Science and Politics*, pp 664–683

Renn, O, Webler, T and Widemann, P (Eds)(1995) *Fairness and Competence in Citizen Participation*, Dordrecht: Kluwer

Satchell, M (1997) A UN 'plot' on US rivers, *US News and World Report*, October 27, pp 42

Salamon, J (1997) Popping the pre-nup question, *New Yorker*, Aug 25 and Sept 1, pp 70–89

Siegrist, M (1997) *A Causal Model Explaining the Perception and Acceptance of Gene Technology*, Unpublished paper, University of Zürich

Seligman, A B (1933) *The Problem of Trust*, Princeton: Princeton University Press

Simon, H A (1990) A mechanism for social selection and successful altruism. *Science*, 250, pp 1665–1668

Sjöberg, L (1997) Explaining risk perception: an empirical evaluation of cultural theory. *Risk, Decision and Policy*, 2, 2, pp 113–130

Sjöberg, L (1996) A discussion of the limitations of the psychometric and cultural theory approaches to risk perception, *Radiation Protection Dosimetry*, 68, p 219

Slovic, P, (1987) Risk perception, *Science*, 236, pp 280–285

Wilson, T D (1985) Strangers to ourselves: The origins and accuracy of beliefs about one's own mental states, in J H Harvey and G Weary (Eds) *Attribution in Contemporary Psychology*, New York: Academic Press

Wittgenstein, L (1968) *Philosophical Investigations*, translated by GEM Anscombe. Oxford, UK: Basil Blackwell

Wolff, M, Rutten, P and Bayers III, A F (1992) *Where We Stand*, New York: Bantam

Wynne, B (1992) Sheep farming after Chernobyl: A case study in communicating scientific information, in BV Lewenstein (Ed) *When Science Meets the Public*, Washington, DC: American Association for the Advancement of Science, pp 43–67

Wynne, B (1996) May the sheep safely graze? in S Lash, B Szerszynski and B Wynne (Eds) *Risk Environment, and Modernity: Towards a New Ecology*, London: Sage

Index

AAP *see* American Academy of
    Pediatrics
accessibility, trust attribution 59
Advisory Committee on Immunization
    Practices (ACIP) 145, 146, 147–8
affective dimensions, social trust
    119–20
ageing effects 31–2
Almond, G A 27
American Academy of Pediatrics
    (AAP) 145, 146, 147–8
Arad, S 11
Arendt, H 120
Askew, G L 146
asymmetry principle 46, 49, 59
attribution of trust 53–61
authority 156
Authority Ranking 15–20

bad news, salience 50
Banaji, M R 55
Banfield, E 31
Barber, B 2, 28, 108, 109, 120, 161
Beck, Ulrich 75
behavioural dimensions, social trust 120
behavioural trust 37
Bellingham International Social Trust
    Conference (BIST) xiii-xiv 3–4
benefits, social trust x 155–6
biases 129, 149–50
Bible 57–8
Biologics Control Act 1902 142, 148
BIST *see* Bellingham International
    Social Trust Conference
Blair, Tony 80
Bord, R 75, 90
Bostrom, Ann 8, 140–52, 166–7
Bradbury, Judith A 8, 117–27, 159, 161
Branch, Kristi M 8, 117–27, 161
'brave reciprocity' 31, 37
Breyer, Stephen 6, 22, 39, 83
Buchanan, J 25
building trust 129–30

Bush, George 34, 54
Butler, J K 108

Campbell, J L 51
caring approach, basis of social trust
    102, 105–7, 109, 141, 147
Carnevale, P J 11
CBA *see* cost-benefit analysis
Center for Disease Control (CDC)
    141–4, 147, 150, 151
centralization 78–9, 87
chicken pox 144, 147–8
childhood diseases, vaccine risks 141,
    142–52
China 164
Chino, Wendell 136, 137, 138
choice, freedom of 65–6
civic engagement 29–32, 159–60
civil society 29–32
Clary, E G 11
Clift, Roland xiii
Clinton, Bill 54, 68, 110, 162, 165
cognitive complexity 9, 121, 123
cognitive processes
    trust as 118, 119
    trust attribution 56–9, 60
cognitive trust 37
collaboration 121
Communal Sharing 15–20
communication
    democratic theory 27–9, 44–5
    problems 1–2
    risk policy issues 123–4, 126–7
    vaccination risks 140, 150–2
communities xi–xii
competence
    basis of social trust x–xi 7, 9, 10, 20,
        129
    Environment Agency 83–4
    health care risks 141, 146–7
    institutional trust 101, 102, 105,
        106–7
    perceived 89–99

risk mitigation 99
  trust attribution 60
complexity, reduction through trust 9,
    121, 123
concern, institutional trust 102, 109
confidence 44, 100–16
  see also public confidence
consensual approach 76–7, 141, 147
consequence severity 94–5
Conservative Party 77–81, 86
consistency 101
constitutional designs 25
context effects 56–7, 59, 60
cooperation 123, 130
Cornell, S 137
corporations, trust in 90, 91–3, 98
correspondent inference 54, 55
cosmopolitanism 21, 28, 110, 130–1,
    134, 137–8
cost-benefit analysis (CBA) 88
Covello, V T 119, 120
creation of social trust 36–7, 45–9,
    58–9, 129–30
credibility
  basis of social trust 129
  Environment Agency 82–4, 86, 87
  institutional trust 102, 105, 106–7
Crickhowell, Lord 85, 86, 87
CT *see* Cultural Theory
cultural norms 131
cultural pluralism 10
cultural singularity 10
Cultural Theory (CT) 11–12, 15, 26–7,
    90, 93, 98, 130
cultural variation 9, 21
cultural-values hypothesis 9–21
culture, political 27
Cvetkovich, Fran xiv
Cvetkovich, George 127, 151, 153–67
  attribution of social trust 53–61
  cosmopolitanism 28, 110–12, 130–1,
    134, 137–8
  cultural-values hypothesis 9–21, 28,
    110–12, 121
  definitions of social trust 122
  distrust 119
  public dialogue 123
  public participation 124–5

Dake, Karl 10–11, 90, 92–3, 130, 136

Dawes Act 1887 133–4
De Ramsey, Lord 74, 82–5, 87
decision-making 148–50
definitions of social trust xi–xii 4–5,
    118–20, 122, 129–30, 153–5
democracy, perceived risk 50–2
democratic theory 8, 22–41
  civic engagement 29–32
  civil society 29–32
  cultural approaches 26–7
  dialogic models 27–9
  economic development 25–6
  institutional designs 25
  justificatory 24–5
  operational 25
Department of Energy (DOE) 7–8, 44,
    100, 102–8, 110–18, 123, 125–6
Department of Energy Public Trust
    and Confidence (DOEPTC)
    104–8, 111–13
dependency 122
destruction of social trust *see* erosion of
    social trust
dialogic models, democracy 27–9
Diana, Princess of Wales 1
diphtheria 142, 143
diphtheria-tetanus-pertussis (DTP)
    vaccine 145, 146
disease, vaccines 140–52, 166–7
disillusionment 6–7
distrust 1–2, 122, 127
  attribution 53, 60–1
  democratic theory 22, 38–9, 40, 41
  functionality 38–9, 161–3
  governments 2–3, 5–7, 22, 38–9,
    74–6, 81, 86, 158, 161–3
  hazard management systems 68–9
  Native Americans 135, 136–7
  nuclear technology 157, 158
  perceived risk 43, 45–50, 51
  rationalist hypothesis 9
  trust continuum 130
  trust distinction 119, 154
do-no-harm bias 150
doctors, public trust 148–50
DOE *see* Department of Energy
DOEPTC *see* Department of Energy
    Public Trust and Confidence
Douglas, M 10, 110, 111
'down and dirty' approach 160–1

Drottz-Sjöberg, B 158
DTP (diphtheria-tetanus-pertussis)
   vaccine 145, 146

Earle, Timothy C
   cosmopolitanism 28, 110–12, 130–1,
      134, 137–8
   cultural-values hypothesis 9–21, 28,
      110–12, 121
   definitions of social trust 122
   distrust 119
   public dialogue 123
   public participation 124–5
Earle, Timothy C xiii 54–5, 127, 151
Easton, David 27
economic constraints 77–8, 79
economic development 25–6
Edmonston-Zagreb (EZ) measles
   vaccine 144
Egalitarianism 11–13, 111, 130
Elich, Peter xiii
emergence of social trust 36–7
  see also creation of social trust
emotional trust 37
emotions 153–4
Environment Agency 73–88, 165
environmental injustice 131
environmental regulation, UK 73–88
environmental risk 2
   BIST xiii
   cultural-values hypothesis 13–20
   democratic theory 22–3, 25
   perception 90–3, 128–9, 131, 134–7
environmentalism 76, 80–1
Equality Matching 15–20
equity 129
erosion of social trust 2, 5–7, 58–9
   cultural-values hypothesis 9
   democratic theory 36–8, 45–9
   governments 74–6
   Native Americans 136–7
   secrecy 86
   trust-decreasing events 59, 130
   vaccinations 140–1
   see also distrust
ethics, third generation 23
Etzioni, A 6, 28
Evans, M 134
events
   negative 46–50, 130

order effects 57–9
evolutionary theory 155
experimental design
   cultural-values hypothesis 11–21
   risk perception 90–6
   salient values similarity theory 55–9
expertise 2, 59–60, 109, 122, 146–7
explicit reasoning 54–5
EZ measles vaccine 144

fairness 102, 105, 106–7, 119
FDA *see* Food and Drug
   Administration
Fen-phen 158
fiduciary responsibility 7, 67, 120
Fiske, Alan Paige 10, 15–16, 17
Flynn, J 57, 130
Focht, Will 8, 117–27, 161
Food and Drug Administration (FDA)
   147–8, 158
four elementary forms of sociality
   15–16
France 50–1, 89
free market 80
French model 50–1
Frewer, L J 60, 61, 70, 155
Fromer, A 102
Fukuyama, F 155, 159
functions of social trust 9, 120–2, 155–7
Funtowicz, S O 123, 125

Gabarro, J 102
Gallagher, Ed 74, 84, 87
Gallup polls 35–6
Garrett, J T 132
Gates 163–4
gender differences, trust attribution 57
general social survey (GSS) 31
generational trends 31–2
Giddens, Anthony 75, 120
Golding, Dominic 6, 8, 22–41, 120, 130
government
   democratic theory 22–3, 25, 28–9,
      32–6, 38–41
   environmental regulation 73–88
   hazard management systems 64–5
   nuclear technologies 44, 50–1
   perceived risk 44, 50–1, 89–99
   public confidence 32–6, 44
   public distrust 2–3, 5–7, 22, 38–9,

74–6, 81, 86, 158, 161–3
vaccination programs 148–9
Gowda, M V Rajeev 7, 8, 128–39, 165
green vote 76, 80–1
Greenwald, A G 55
'group think' 156
groups
    benefits of social trust 155, 156
    cultural-values hypothesis 21
    membership 31–2
    pressure groups 76, 82, 84
    special interest 50, 160–1
GSS *see* general social survey
Gummer, John 78

Habermas, J 123, 126, 159
haemophilus influenza (Hib) 144
Hallman, W K 90
Hardin, G 150
Harris polls 5, 32, 34–5
hazard management systems (HMS)
    62–72
    constraints 67–9
    methods for studying 69–72
hazard managers 8, 64, 67–8, 69–70, 72
health care
    risk perception 166–7
    vaccines 140–52
health risks
    democratic theory 25
    perception 128, 129, 131–2, 133,
        136, 137
Hedderley, D 60
hepatitis B 144
Her Majesty's Inspectorate of
    Pollution (HMIP) 73, 84, 85, 88
heuristics 129
Hib *see* haemophilus influenza
Hibbing, J R 33
Hierarchical culture 11–13
Higgins, T 60–1
HMIP *see* Her Majesty's Inspectorate
    of Pollution
HMS *see* hazard management systems
holistic approaches, health care 132
honesty 90, 91–3, 98, 102, 109
Hood, C 78
Horlick-Jones, Tom xiii 8, 73–88, 165
Howard, C 60
Hutton, W 80

IHS *see* Indian Health Service
immunizations *see* vaccines
implicit reasoning 54–5, 60
Indian Health Service (IHS) 137
individualists 11–13, 130
individuals
    benefits of social trust 155–6
    cultural-values hypothesis 11–12,
        15–16, 21
industry, perceived risk 2–3, 89–99
influenza 142
Inglehart, R 28
Institutes of Medicine (IOM) 140, 141
institutional designs 25
institutions
    democratic theory 25, 29, 32–6, 37,
        39–41
    public confidence 32–6, 100–16
Integrated Pollution Control (IPC) 74
integrity 102, 105, 106–7
interpersonal relationships 37
interpersonal trust 37, 120–1, 127, 129,
    146
interviews 115–16
IOM *see* Institutes of Medicine
IPC *see* Integrated Pollution Control
Italy 29, 31

Jackson, Andrew 133
Jacob, Gerald 52
James, William 153–4
Jasper, J M 51
Jefferson, Thomas 51
Jewell, T 79
Johnson, B B 8, 62–72, 141, 154, 155
judgements of trust 3
    cultural values 10, 13, 15, 18–21
    hazard management systems 62–72
    processes 157
    reliability 154–5
    riskiness 122
    see also attribution, trust
justificatory democratic theory 24–5

Kalt, J 137
Kasperson, Jeanne X 8, 22–41
Kasperson, Roger E xiii 6, 8, 22–41,
    119–20, 130, 159, 161
Kastenholtz 119
Kates, R W 23

Kelly, Laura xiv
Key, V O 39
Kirkpatrick, S 102
Klein, N 50
knowledge 60, 109, 159–60
Koren, G 50
Kramer, R M 119, 120

Labour Party 80
land ownership, Native Americans 133–4
language 27–8, 123
Laws, Rufina Marie 135, 138
Lawson, Nigel 80
leadership 8, 163–5
Leiss, W 2, 160–1
Levine, D 102, 119
Lewis, J D 118, 119
licensure dates, vaccinations 145
Lincoln, Abraham 45, 46
Linear Structural Relationships (LISREL) 27
Lipset, S M 5, 6, 32, 34, 38
LISREL *see* Linear Structural Relationships
list approach, trust judgements 70
local government 78
Locke, E 102
Löfstedt, Ragnar 8, 73–88, 153–67
Luhmann, N 28–9, 37, 65, 66, 118, 119, 121–2

McCallum, D B 119, 120
McClure, Alexander 45
McGregor, D 101
McKechnie 122
macro-level trust 120–1
Market Pricing 15–20
Matheny, A R 27–8
measles 143, 144
measures of social trust 154
media 50, 84–6, 87
medical technology 43
meningitis 144
Mertz, C K 57
Mescalero Apache 129, 135–6, 138
messages, cultural-values hypothesis 11, 12–13, 16–17
Metlay, Daniel 7–8, 100–16, 154
micro-level trust 120–1

Miles, J 57–8
minority groups 131
Mishra, A 108
mistrust *see* distrust
Misztal, B A 120, 121, 123
mitigation, risk 93–6, 98–9
modernity 74–6
modernization 25–6
Monitored Retrievable Storage (MRS) facility 134–6, 137
Mothering Magazine 141
motivation 11, 89–99
MRS facility *see* Monitored Retrievable Storage facility
mumps 143
Mushkatel, A H 90, 101, 108
Mvskoke tribe 128, 131–2, 136, 137

National Academic of Sciences 44
National Childhood Vaccine Injury Compensation Act (NCVIA) 1986 148, 150
National Institute of Health (NIH) 147, 148
National Opinion Research Center (NORC) polls 5, 31, 32, 34–5
National Research Council (NRC) 22–3
National Rivers Authority (NRA) 73, 83, 84–5, 88
Native Americans 128–9, 131–9
NCVIA *see* National Childhood Vaccine Injury Compensation Act 1986
negative events 46–50, 130
NGOs *see* non-governmental organizations
NIH *see* National Institute of Health
Nixon, Richard 164
non-governmental organizations (NGOs) 76, 82, 87
NORC *see* National Opinion Research Center
'normal trust' 163–4
norms
    cultural 131
    of reciprocity 30–1, 37
NRA *see* National Rivers Authority
NRC *see* National Research Council
nuclear technologies 13–14, 125

distrust 128–9, 134–7, 138, 157, 158
  institutional trust 102–3
  perceived risk 43–5, 46–9, 50–2, 90,
    97–8
Nuclear Waste Negotiator 134–5, 137

O'Connor, R 75, 90
Official Secrets legislation, UK 76–7
O'Leary, Hazel 103, 110–11, 112, 113
omission bias 149–50
openness
  basis of social trust x–xi
  Environment Agency 85–6
  institutional trust 101, 105, 106–7,
    109
operational democratic theory 25
opinion polls 5, 24, 32–6, 38, 40, 103
optimism 38
order effects, trust attribution 57–9
O'Riordan, T 76–7
Ostrom, Elinor 25
Ouchi, W G 101
'outrage' (risk perception) 89

parents, vaccination risks 146
Park, B 46
Parson, Talcott 59–60
Patten, Chris 80
Pauker, Stephen 149
Pennock, J R 24–5
Pentreath, Jan 82, 83, 85, 86
perceived competence 89–99
perceived risk 3, 42–52, 68, 89–99, 129,
    150–1, 157–8
perception
  general honesty 90, 91–3, 98
  social harmony 90, 91–3, 98
Persian Gulf 54
personal characteristics, trust
    attribution 61
personal relationships, trust building
    127
pertussis 143, 145, 147
Peters, R G 109, 119, 120
Pijawka, K D 90
Pildes, R 129
pincushion effect 142
pluralistic social trust 21, 130–1
pneumonia 142
policy culture 27

policy development 112–14, 123–7
  public participation 162
  vaccinations 145–8, 151–2
poliomyelitis 143, 147
political
  community 37, 40
  culture 27
  institutions 37
  regimes 37, 40
politicians, trust in 90, 91–3, 98
pollution, UK controls 73–4
positive events, trust formation 46–9
power 24–5, 114
pre-nuptial contracts 166
preferences 58
pressure groups 76, 82, 84
privatization 79
process culture 27
psychometric theories 129, 130, 136–7
public
  confidence 32–6, 44
  discourse 27–9
  knowledge 159–60
  participation 117–27, 159–60, 162
  perceived risk 42–52
  relations 87
  see also distrust
Putnam, Robert 25, 29–32, 37, 38, 121,
    155, 159

quasi-government agencies (QGAs)
    78
quasi-non-governmental agencies
    (QUANGOS) 78
questionnaires 11–14, 18, 91, 114

racial issues, trust attribution 57
rationalist hypothesis 9, 10, 20, 21
Ravetz, J R 123, 125
Rayner, S 10
Read, S 57
reasoning 54–5, 60
reciprocity 30–1, 37
regulation 73–88, 165–7
relationships 118, 120–1, 127
reliability 101, 105, 106–7
Renn, O 102, 119, 125, 126, 159
responsibility 67
  basis of social trust 7, 9, 10, 20, 120
  risk mitigation 99

Risk Assessment in the Federal Government (NRC) 23
Rothbart, J 46
Royal Society for the Protection of Birds (RSPB) 84
rubella 144
Ruckelshaus, William 22, 38, 44

Sac and Fox Nation 129, 135, 136, 137
Sako, M 102
salient values similarity theory 7–8, 9–21, 55–7, 59, 61
Sandman, P M 89
scepticism 38
Schneider, W 5, 6, 32, 34, 38
SEAB 125, 127
secrecy 76–7, 85–6, 87
Seifert, M 131
SESRC *see* Social and Economic Sciences Research Center
Shepherd, R 60
Site-Specific Advisory Boards (SSAB) 125–6
situational factors, trust attribution 60–1
Sjöberg, Lennart 89–99, 158
skepticism, enlightened 163
Slater, David 74, 82, 83–5
Slovic, Paul xiii 8, 36, 42–52, 57–9, 75, 102, 113, 157
smallpox 141, 142
social capital 30–1, 41
social cognition, trust attribution 56–9, 60
Social and Economic Sciences Research Center (SESRC) 114, 116
social functions, trust 120–2
social harmony 90, 91–3, 98
social knowledge 60
social networks 30–1, 32, 37, 38
social relationships 37, 118, 120–1
Soviet Union (former) 68–9
Spain 158
special interest groups 50, 160–1
see also pressure groups
SSAB *see* Site-Specific Advisory Boards
Starr, C 43
Steele, J 79
Stewart, Potter 101

Stoffle, R 134
Sunstein, C 129
survey experiment 11
surveys
    institutional trust 103–4, 115–16
    public confidence 24, 32–6, 38, 40
Sweden 6–7, 87, 89, 91, 158, 162
Swedish Environmental Protection Agency 87
Switzerland 159
systems
    culture 27
    hazard management 62–72
    trust 8, 37, 75, 120–1, 162–3

technical expertise 2, 59–60, 122
technology
    change 74–5
    hazardous 43–52, 122, 123, 125
    see also nuclear technologies
television 32
tetanus 142, 143, 145
Thatcher, Margaret 78, 80
Theiss-Morse, E 33
thick trust 31
thin trust 31
Thomas, Clarence 34
Thompson, M 10
Thorpe, Y 60–1
Tocqueville, Alexis de 29, 133
tolerance, risk 97–9
transformative involvement strategies 125
trust values 13, 14–15, 18–19, 21
trust-decreasing events 46–50, 58–9
trust-increasing events 46–9, 58–9
Tuler, S 120, 130
Tullock, G 25
Tyler, T R 119, 120

uncertainty, trust 121–2
Understanding Risk (NRC) 22–3
United Kingdom 1, 6–7
    environmental regulation 73–88, 165
    structural changes 77–9
    water quality 68
United States 1, 3, 157
    civic engagement 159
    democratic theory 22–3, 24, 31–6, 38–9, 41

environmental regulation 74
governmental distrust 5–7, 119, 157, 162
hazard management systems 62–3, 65, 68
institutional confidence 100–16
Native Americans 128–39
normal trust 163–4
perceived risk 42, 44, 50–1, 89
trust attribution 60
vaccinations 140–1, 142–52, 167
water quality 62–3, 68, 166

Vaccine Adverse Reporting System (VAERS) 148
Vaccine Information Statements (VIS) 150
vaccines 140–52, 166–7
VAERS *see* Vaccine Adverse Reporting System
values
    conflict 131–4
    consensual 141, 147
    constructions 164–5
    cultural-values hypothesis 9–21
    Native Americans 131–4, 135
    salient values similarity theory 7–8, 9–21, 55–7, 59, 61

similarity 120–1, 130–1
    cultural-values hypothesis 9–11, 13, 15, 21
    institutional trust 110–12
    trust attribution 54, 55–7, 59, 61
varicella 144, 147–8
Vaughan, E 131
Verba, S 27
Vietnam war 38, 39
violence, sanctioned 156
VIS *see* Vaccine Information Statements

Wandersman, A H 90
warfare 38, 39, 54, 155, 156
water quality 62–5, 67–8, 70, 71, 85, 166
Watkins, James D 102–3, 110
Webler, T 119, 125, 126
Weigert, A 118, 119
Welsh 122
whooping cough *see* pertussis
Wiedemann 125, 126
Wildavsky, A 10, 11, 110, 111, 130, 136
Williams, B A 27–8
Wundt, William 153
Wynne, B 122, 125

Yankelovich, D 39